# THE TRIANGLE
# INDIA-NEPAL-CHINA

# THE TRIANGLE
# INDIA-NEPAL-CHINA
## A Study of Treaty Relations

S. C. BHATT

GYAN PUBLISHING HOUSE

New Delhi 110 002

The Triangle India-Nepal-China: A Study of Treaty Relations

ISBN: 81-212-0523-9



Reprinted in 2012 in India by
Gyan Publishing House
23, Main Ansari Road, Daryaganj,
New Delhi - 110002
Phone : 23282060, 23261060
Fax : (011) 23285914
E-mail : books@gyanbooks.com
Website: gyanbooks.com

*Printed at*: G. Print Process, Delhi

# CONTENTS

## APPENDICES 233

***(Treaties, Agreements and Some other Documents)***

# PREFACE

There is no apparent dearth of documentation on the relations between India and her neighbours, like Nepal and China, but the wealth of critical writings on the theme cannot be said to be matchingly abundant in recent years. This book seeks to look at the problem in the context of the treaty relations between India and Nepal on the one hand and India and China on the other as well as those between Nepal and China. In shaping Nepal's ties with India, the relations between Kathmandu and Beijing have always played a key role, almost to the point of determining the nature of ties. While exploring the relationship with both, the book is an effort at probing this unique triangle.

Nepal is the focus of the book, although the much larger format of India-China relations is also dealt with, both as an independent subject and in its linkage with the triangular theme. The relevant treaties and agreements are reproduced in the appendices along with the SAARC (South Asian Association for Regional Cooperation) Charter, although the book does not deal with SAARC at all.

Notwithstanding India's desire and effort to befriend the neighbours there have been serious difficulties. Obstructions and impediments have been encountered and, at best, it has been a mixed experience. Nepal and, to an extent, China also have been typical examples of this process. Mistakes have been committed in forging this relationship both by the Indian political leaders as well as by the diplomats which have been examined as objectively as possible. No sympathy is, however, to be shown to the elements who often attack their own country to prove their objectivity and gain the sympathy of others. If 'my country, right or wrong' is not right, 'another country, right or wrong' is really reprehensible.

It is a pleasant duty to express my thanks to the librarian and staff of the Research and Reference Division library in Delhi's Shastri Bhavan for making a number of books, including reference works, available to me for this study. I had full access to their excellent facilities for studies of current affairs. The library of the Historical Division of the Ministry of External Affairs was also helpful. While affording me this facility, the Ministry avoided giving any other help and did not even respond to my request for detailed information. I am grateful to friends in Kathmandu and Delhi for their help by way of books, articles and notes on the subject.

S. C. BHATT

# 1

# TREATIES AND AGREEMENTS

# 1

# INTERNATIONAL TREATIES

From ancient times nation states have been entering into written agreements or treaties with one another to govern their relations and what they undertake to do in a specified area like regulation of boundaries, bringing to an end a short or prolonged war, prevention of piracy, fishing rights, trade and transit, defensive or offensive alliance, assisting another state in putting down an internal rebellion, or just proclaiming eternal peace and friendship with one another and the like. Any written instrument signed by two or more countries to regulate their relations can go under this the generic name of treaty. The treaty has the same force which a contract has between two or more individuals or a law enacted by a national legislature.

A large number of names exist in the world of diplomacy for the simple word treaty—agreement, charter, covenant, convention, protocol, joint declaration or just declaration, pact, concordat, agreed minutes, exchange of letters, memorandum of agreement and so on although naunces and shades of meaning differentiate some of them. Thus when India and Pakistan reached an agreement at Simla (now called Shimla) in July 1972, with the two heads of governments, Indira Gandhi, Prime Minister of India, and Zulfikar Ali Bhutto, President of Pakistan, putting their signatures to the document, it was just called an agreement but it has all the attributes of a treaty. Bilateralism in Indo-Pak relations is the essence of the agreement and is guaranteed by it. Pakistan's efforts to extricate itself from it have not succeeded.

**Kautilya's Arthashastra** (321-296 B.C.), which is a standard work on the art and technique of government, statecraft, diplomacy and war, deals, in Book VII, with peace treaties called *Sandhis* —war and neutrality. There are much older examples of treaties like the 3100 B.C. treaty fixing the boundary between the cities of Lagash and Umma. In 1271 B.C., King Rameses II of Egypt and King Hattushilish of the Hittites entered into a treaty guaranteeing eternal peace between each other, providing a defensive and offensive alliance as well as extradition of criminals and going to each other's aid in case of internal rebellion. The ancient city states of Greece contracted a number of treaties with one another covering besides peace and friendship such other activities as trade and commerce, piracy, fugitives and fugitive slaves. Thus Athens and Sparta entered into a thirty-year treaty in 447-446 B.C. which also provided for the settlement of disputes by arbitration.

Hostages were exchanged if the treaty was contracted by equals after a war and if one party was weak it sent hostages to the other. In India too, the victorious king would take hostages and sometimes the crown prince or any other member of the defeated king's family would be kept as a hostage as a guarantee for keeping the peace.

All sovereign states have full treaty rights meaning they can enter into treaties with other states. But the Vatican City, the Seat of the Pope, head of the Roman Catholics worldwide, has treaty making powers and so have a number of international organisations. The United Nations has a treaty with the United States about the location of its headquarters in New York which governs the rights of delegates to the various UN bodies. This is different from the multilateral treaties between more than two states and between a number of states and an international organisation which is dealt with a little later in this chapter.

A treaty would usually consist of a preamble, the dispositive clauses and the so-called final clauses. The preamble may contain a statement of the broad objectives, the names of the high contracting parties, the representatives or plenipotentiaries authorised to conduct negotiations for and to enter into a treaty, the credentials of such representatives being found in order and so on. The dispositive articles are the real essence of the treaty as they contain the rights and obligations of each other and these have precedence over the general statements of intentions. The final part refers to the signatories to the treaty, the ratification and enforcement of the treaty, which is an important part of it, its language (which would be treated as authentic text) and related matters.

**Ratification Procedure**

As we said just now, a treaty must be generally ratified before it comes into effect. While some treaties come into effect at once and need no ratification, the signatories being authorised to enter into that kind of instant treaty, most other international agreements provide for their ratification by virtue of which they come into effect. Usually the government, meaning the cabinet or the head of state is the ratifying authority but in some countries the national legislature alone has the ratification powers, for example, the Senate in the United States. In India, there is no hard and fast rule on ratification and the Indian Constitution, which is rightly admired for its elaborateness, among other things, has no provision for either treaty making powers or ratification. (Just as the Constitution has failed to provide for powers to determine the stationing of Indian armed forces in foreign countries, no authority being specified for sending troops out of India; yet they have been regularly going abroad.)

In the absence of any specific provision, the practice in India is to ratify a treaty by the cabinet or President on the advice of the cabinet, or by Parliament if the government feels that it would be prudent to get the national legislature committed. Thus the Simla accord was approved by Parliament before it was ratified by India. And so was the agreement on the WTO (World Trade Organisation).

There were quaint practices in ancient times to complete the formality of ratification. Oath was the most common form of ratification and the Romans would appear in public and secure acceptance of a treaty by public acclaim. Both the Romans and Greeks followed an elaborate procedure for making treaties which the diplomats today would love to follow if only they were permitted to do so. There would be preliminary proceedings through hearlds followed by negotiations by plenipotentiaries and special embassies. The universal practice of granting a semblace of equality of rights to both sides came into vogue much later.

Ratification of a treaty is a ticklish matter and there is the classic example of the American President, Woodrow Wilson (1913-21), being denied ratification by the US Senate of the Versailles treaty, specially the clauses providing for the setting of the League of Nations, on which Wilson had set his heart. Under Article II, Section 2 of the US Constitution, the President can enter into a treaty with the consent and advice of the Senate. Of course, under certain circumstances strong

Presidents have used their discretionary powers and not submitted their decisions in international relations even for an *ex-post facto* approval by the Senate. President Franklin Delano Roosevelt, elected President for four succeeding (1932-44), transferred some destroyers of the US Navy to Britain when the Second World War had started and was in progress. He also accorded recognition to the Soviet Union without waiting for Senate to underwrite his actions.

President Wilson failed to get a two-thirds majority in the US Senate in 1920 and his country went back into isolation for some time. Only in the Second World War and in the post-war period from 1945 onwards the Americans began their world domination and emerged as the universal policeman ordering everyone about and telling them what they should and should not do. Wilson who was often described as an impractical idealist was well known for his fourteen principles and his dictum that covenants (between nations) must be open and openly arrived at. This was, in fact, his first principle. The League of Nations was specially his brainchild but he failed to realise that imperialist Britain and France, who were only interested in sharing the spoils of the war they had fought with Germany, looked upon it as an instrument to perpetuate their rule over vast areas of Asia and Africa.

Wilson bitterly fought his principal foe, Senator Henry Cabot Lodge, who got the treaty defeated in the Senate, and called him and his ilk as "Bolsheviks", a term of abuse in the US which even now fears and despises Communists. He called his opponents "absolutely ignorant" and "absolute, contemptible quitters."In 1919, in order to win public support for his policy and beat down the Republican opposition, Wilson travelled 8,000 miles (more than 13,000 km) delivering 34 major addresses, granting innumerable media interviews, participating in scores of parades, and making dozens of rear-platform talks. The people cheered him but despite winning their approval he could not get the US Congress to endorse his appeal for a referendum on the treaty. He died a sick and heart-broken man and the League became a playground of the imperialist forces which, in no small measure, contributed to the growth of Nazism in Germany and Fascism in Italy. The seeds of the Second World War were thus sown.

Wilson was made a cat's paw by both the French leaders, Georges Clemenceau and David Lloyd George of Britain. Economist John Maynard Keynes, who resigned his position as a technical adviser to the British delegation following the signing of the Versailles Treaty, called him "that blind and deaf Don Quixote". No wonder Clemenceau said exultantly, when Wilson was leaving Europe for the United States, "I feel as though I were losing one of the best friends I ever had." Among Wilson's own staff, William C. Bullit, who later became the first US Ambassador to the Soviet Union, resigned in protest against the imperfect treaty.[1]

**Multilateral Treaties:** When more than two nations enter into a treaty for a common cause it is called a multilateral treaty, although most treaties are bilateral in nature. (There are besides treaties between international organisations and member nations.) The era of multilateral treaties began with the treaty of Westphalia in Europe in 1648 which set the tone for treaties seeking to lay down an international order. The Congress of Vienna (1815) and the Treaty of Versailles (1919) are other examples of multilateral treaties. The Vienna Congress created a framework for European politics and although the League of Nations, created by the Versailles Treaty, failed because of the greed of the two principal imperialist powers, the ILO (International Labour Organisation) has endured. This is mainly because it has sought to serve the working classes of all nations and laid down over 100 ILO conventions to protect them and ensure better conditions of work for others.

The International Telegraphic Union came into being in 1865 and the UPU (Universal Postal Union) in 1874 by virtue of similar multilateral treaties and they succeeded because it suited nations to regulate the growing telegraph and postal traffic in the world. The Inter-governmental Maritime Union came into being later and all these agencies became specialised UN agencies when this organisation was created by member nations which had fought the Second World War together.

The United Nations Charter is an outstanding example of a multilateral treaty providing for an international framework for political and non-political cooperation. The UN itself has generated several conventions like the one on Genocide in 1948 prohibiting the destruction of minority groups. The Charter also provides for multilateral action, called sanctions, to be enforced by the Security Council or the General Assembly.

Negotiations and reciprocal benefits are the strongest practical sanctions for enforcing a treaty. The contracting parties have to realise that having entered into a treaty they cannot get out of its obligations easily even if they find them irksome and inconvenient. Often, the parties to a treaty, or one of the contracting parties has discovered that the treaty is not working to its advantage. Both may have contracted it in circumstances when it was inevitable for them to do so but these circumstances may change, or so they may feel or the regime which entered into the treaty may be overthrown. They cannot, however, easily denounce the treaty or forswear its obligations. The period of validity of the treaty may come to their help sometimes. Most international agreements provide for a time limit although some peace treaties and treaties of friendship are of an eternal nature. But barring such covenants, which pledge the two sides to friendship in perpetuity, other treaties lay down a specified period for which the agreement is valid for 20 years, or less or more. There is also a clause for renewal of the agreement and sometimes the nations may find it convenient to extend the treaty by another set of 15 or 25 years even if the extension is not built in. But the side waiting to denounce a treaty may also find the validity clause convenient to end the relationship.

## REFERENCE

1. *The President as World Leader,* Sidney Warren, J.B. Lippincott Company, Philadelphia and New York.

# 2

# APPLICATIONS AND LIMITATIONS

In the preceding chapter we examined briefly how some nations try to extricate themselves from treaty obligations when they find these irksome and obstructing their freedom of action. Bangladesh entered into a 25-year treaty of peace and friendship with its neighbour India in March 1972 at a time when the relations between the two countries were excellent at the governmental level. At the popular level too they were still good although the euphoria of the war of liberation fought only four months earlier against Pakistan was almost over. All the same the victor of the war, Mrs Indira Gandhi, was received with acclaim when she visited Dhaka to sign the treaty with the popular leader, Sheikh Mujibur Rahman. She had worked ceaselessly for a year to prepare India and the world for the denouement and put the liberation plan into action. She signed the treaty with Mujib, as he was popularly known. She was given a memorable welcome at a public rally in the capital city when a record crowd attended the ceremony.

On the day following the signing of the treaty, Mrs Gandhi described it in the Lok Sabha (lower house of Parliament) in New Delhi as a document embodying the will of the two governments "to pursue common policies in matters of interest to both countries." The treaty was welcomed in similar terms in Dhaka too. But before the 25-year period could expire it had lost much of the gloss and was treated as a scrap of paper by Bangladesh. Prime Minister Begum Khaleda Zia said the treaty would not be renewed (in 1997 when the 25-year period expires) and the Bangladesh Foreign Secretary, Farooq Sobhan, told foreign journalists in Dhaka that the treaty existed *only in name* (emphasis added). Told by a journalist that he had perused the treaty and found nothing wrong in it. Sobhan said, "It has only a significance and has no practical application.[1]"

On two contentious issues, the continued influx of illegal immigrants from Bangladesh into India (estimated by some to be as high as 15 million people) and the presence of Pakistani intelligence agents of the Inter Services Intelligence (ISI), working in that country, Bangladesh could not give a satisfactory clarification to India. This was despite the treaty of peace and friendship. The ULFA (United Liberation Front of Assam) insurgents from Assam in India have found shelter in Bangladesh and so have some Naga rebels, both of whom receive arms and other material help from the Pakistan army's subversion wing, the ISI, operating in Bangladesh. Bangladesh too had its grievances like the Farakka waters distribution but it surely does not betoken friendship, much less peace, if the Dhaka authorities offer the hospitality of their soil to an agency working against India.

Of course, the issue of the illegal immigrants entering India in search of work and food is a little complicated because some of the Indian political parties believing in the theory of votebank are believed to be conniving at it. Among them are the ruling Congress (I) party and the ruling party in the state nearest to Bangladesh, West Bengal, which has linguistic and other affinities with that country. Some of the English media also behave as though the illegal immigrants had a right to be in India and work here. In any case, the Bangladeshi behaviour was in contradiction of the provisions of the treaty and against the sacrifices made by India's gallant armed forces who brought the Pakistani army in the then East Pakistan province under their grip in just 13 days and some 90,000 of them surrendered[1].

The war in 1971 could not have been won without the active help of the people of Bangladesh, certainly not so swiftly, and the enthusiastic participation of many men who had earlier been enlisted in the Pakistan army but deserted it to join the forces of liberation. The fact, however, remains that the victory could not have been won against the forces of repression represented by the army of occupation from West Pakistan but for the presence of the Indian army for which Pakistan still seeks revenge. But Bangladesh has long since stopped giving India credit for the liberation. It could not, however, denounce the treaty of friendship with India for practical and pragmatic reasons and nor give up its obligations under the treaty for fear of international repercussions.

**Scrap of Paper**

A treaty may be treated as a scrap of paper without inviting much media attention but its formal denunciation would surely raise a minor or major storm. This only shows that you can play fast and loose with a treaty or openly flout it but not formally denounce it and get out of your obligations in an open manner. There is something sacrosanct about the institution. It is like a religious shrine to which you may do only occasional obeisance and look the other way when its surroundings or even premises are used for bootlegging, gambling or worse, as long as the religious character is maintained for form's sake at least.

As the Indo-Nepal treaty of friendship of July 1950 is one of the principal themes of this book, we refrain from taking it up as an example at this stage. But let us take another treaty, the Simla (now called Shimla) agreement between India and Pakistan. This agreement was also signed in July, which seems to be a fateful month for some crucial treaties of India, July 1972 in this case. Any deal between India and Pakistan is destined to run into difficulties almost from the word go and this was no exception, although the Indus waters treaty has endured for over thirty years. The present Prime Minister of Pakistan, Ms. Benazir Bhutto, daughter of the slain Zulfikar Ali Bhutto, was herself in Simla during the talks, though not as a delegate. The treaty came in the wake of the Bangladesh war in which Pakistan lost badly. Its main feature is the bilateral commitment of the two sides which endured for some time at least. Under it, the two countries

> "... are resolved to settle their differences by peaceful means through bilateral negotiations or any other peaceful means mutually agreed upon between them." (Clause 1 (ii) of the Simla treaty)

This commitment to bilateral negotiations, as opposed to access to the United Nations, pressure through Pakistan's extra-territorial benefactors like the United States, which has provided unlimited arms and other aid to Pakistan, the Organisation of Islamic Countries or any other source which suits Pakistan for the time being, has proved irksome to Pakistan.

Islamabad has often behaved as though the Simla treaty did not exist, although it is wrong because this is the basis on which the formalities of ending the 1971 war were completed and Pakistan could take back 90,000 war prisoners and also regain some lost territory in the western sector. India has always maintained that the Kashmir dispute, and any other problem between the two countries, must be settled by bilateral negotiations as envisaged in the Simla agreement. Some Pakophiles in India try to play this country against Pakistan because they expect the red carpet to be rolled out when they visit it (by invitation, of course,) and interviews are arranged for them but made to look as though everything was by accident. Then they would say India has "forgotten" the Simla treaty. How could she when the whole international battle revolves around the bilateralism enshrined in the Simla accord? But when the other side treats it as a "forgotten treaty", or one about which it would like to forget, India could not organise celebrations with the usual quota of experts being invited to write or speak.

The question whether the Pakistan President, who signed the treaty for his country, also committed himself to the acceptance of the ceasefire line in Kashmir, also called the line of control, as a permanent border between the two countries, is not worth pursuing. According to a scribe[2], "He (Bhutto) might have made the promise to fool India's Prime Minister, as the Pakistani journal (*Politics and Business*) wrote the other day." A strange admission to make and record, with obvious glee, that India's Prime Minister was fooled by Bhutto, who was killed after his successor, Gen. Zia, who ousted him from power by force staged a murder prosecution. If the head of state and government of a country indulges in such crude perfidies and there are admirers to applaud him even in death, where will international diplomacy come to? The choice of the expression 'fooled' shows to what level writing can descend and quoting such an offensive remark can go.

The main point of this chapter, that some nations find solemn treaties, solemnly arrived at, irksome and they would like to treat them as scraps of paper to extricate themselves from its obligations is fully illustrated by the manner in which Islamabad has tried to ignore and forget its commitments under the Simla agreement. A good case is made to look a bad one, almost a gone case, when the Indian government unnecessarily appears to be weak and tolerates some in the Indian media and the foreigners who take their cue from these men.

The media have, of course, their duty to perform but so also has the government.

This malady of treaty obligations being given the gobye is, however, fairly old. Even Jawaharlal Nehru did little when others tried to take their treaty obligations lightly. He was India's Prime Minister for seventeen long years during which he always handled the foreign portfolio. The five principles of peaceful coexistence, *Panchsheel*, were enunciated for the first time in the world, in India's treaty on trade and intercourse between India and Tibet, with China in April 1954[3]. Both India and China agreed to abide by these principles, of which non-aggression, was one. Yet, even before the ink was dry on the treaty, China was known to be infiltrating into Indian territory, was then involved in cartographic aggression leading finally to open aggression in 1962.

In this context, what an American scholar of Nepal has to say is relevant. Commenting on the tendency of several Nepali writers to speak adversely of India for not signing a treaty with Nepal incorporating the five principles of peaceful coexistence. He said:

> "Many Nepali commentators have noted that China was willing to sign a 'peaceful coexistence' treaty with Nepal but India has never done so, and have drawn some obvious but probably wrong conclusions from this. The fact that China's 'peaceful coexistence' treaty with India in no way deterred the Chinese from attacking India in the fall of 1962 has not seemed to reduce the value which many Nepalis attach to such treaties."[4]

The relations between India and China are much better now but that does not take away from the fact that a solemn treaty was trampled upon by one of the signatories. The Chinese, of course, always attach great importance to the five principles and lose no opportunity to make a formal commitment to them. Here we have a peculiar phenomenon—treaties are often violated by one or both signatories and the obligations are ignored when it suits a party which has acquired for itself a position of strength but some nations are not able to get out of the obligations. What is clear is that treaties do not necessarily determine the relationship between nations and the flouting occurs by the side which feels strong enough to do so with impunity. The aggrived party has no choice but to acknowledge the realities on the ground and swallow its pride, unless there is a provision for arbitration by the International Court of Justice or some other party.

Yet many nations believe in formalising their relations with others, particularly nations in their neighbourhood, by mutual accords called treaties or agreements. An enormous number of treaties are entered into by countries in the world from time to time. While some like agreements on air services or cultural pacts serve their purpose as expected, there are political treaties of friendship and peace which are often treated as a scrap of paper or a treaty only in name.

In this somewhat complicated situation, there are also some shining examples of cooperation and real friendship. Such treaties often play a crucial role in a given situation and influence the course of action by the affected parties. In August 1971, India and the Soviet Union entered into a 20-year treaty of friendship. The crucial clause was about the two countries consulting each other in the event of a war or threat of war. The treaty played a vital role in the 1971 Bangladesh liberation war which was fought between India and Pakistan just four months after it was signed. In the war, the Soviet Union supplied India with much needed arms and ammunition and in the UN Security Council it exercised its veto power in India's favour. What is more, the existence of the treaty prevented the Americans from intervening on the side of Pakistan and the Chinese were made to offer only words of sympathy of which there was no dearth. Both knew that their intervention on the side of Islamabad would draw the Soviet Union directly into the war. This was a powerful deterrent. The United States had even sent its Seventh Fleet to the Bay of Bengal but it stopped short of actual war. It was no doubt, a shameful betrayal on Washington's part of the cause of the people of Bangladesh who were fighting for their liberation but the Americans are always on the side of the dictators, not of the suffering people.

Undoubtedly, there was a strong feeling of sympathy for the Bangladeshis and for the ten million refugees who had entered India fleeing from the terror of the jackboots of the Pakistani army. President Nixon, who was then in the Whitehouse before he was driven out by the American people, had to contend with it. So had the Chinese who are keen observers of the world scene. Much as they valued their friendship with Pakistan they did not like to appear to be entirely on the side of Yahya Khan, the Pakistani dictator. But the Indo-Soviet treaty was a real bulwark for India. American governments have often defied public opinion at home and in the world in the pursuit of their foreign policy goals. The rulers who launched the only known nuclear attacks in history on civilians could be trusted to take a cynical view of human lives which would be lost by their offensive action. But then they had to contend with a real war with the Soviet Union and they were definitely not prepared for it.

The treaty obligations are thus a double-edged weapon. As long as the two contracting parties remain friendly to a reasonable extent and are interested in upholding the provisions of the treaty and in upholding each other's integrity and sovereignty things go well. If, however, one of the parties become lukewarm or hostile to the other difficulties arise for the second party. The treaty is then considered a scrap of paper, as in the case of Bangladesh, or formal tribute is paid without the least desire to abide by it, as in the case of the Chinese. Sometimes, the first party may not find it convenient to denounce the treaty although it is no longer honoured. But the aggrived party, like India, has also to have the strength to point out that the treaty is being violated or not honoured. This has been the case with most of the treaties signed by India with neighbours with the exception of the treaty with Bhutan and Burma (now Myanmar).

Before we go on to the only point that remains to be considered, namely the fact that relations could be friendly without a formal treaty being entered into, some factual details about the Indo-Soviet treaty may be presented here. Called the treaty of peace, friendship and cooperation, it was signed in Delhi on August 9, 1971 by Swarn Singh, India's External Affairs Minister, and Andre A Gromyko, Foreign Minister of the Soviet Union, on behalf of their respective countries. The Lok Sabha gave it a massive vote of confidence and approval on the morrow of the signing. It was approved by the Supreme Soviet in Moscow and ratified by both countries the same day. The treaty had actually provided that the ratification could be done within a month of the signatures being put. The documents of ratification were exchanged in Moscow on August 18. Gromyko stayed in Delhi for other talks until August 12.

Article IX is the most important part of the treaty. It says:

> "Each high contracting party undertakes to abstain from providing any assistance to any third country which engages in armed conflict with the other party. In the event of either party being subjected to an attack or a threat thereof the high contracting parties shall immediately enter into mutual consultations in order to remove such threat and to take appropriate effective measures to ensure peace and the security of their countries."

The treaty was valid for a period of twenty years and provided for automatic renewal for five years at the end of the 20-year period unless one of the parties gave a twelve-month notice of termination. But when the twenty-year period was to expire in 1991 the two countries renewed it for another twenty years. After the breakup of the Soviet Union, the Russians who inherited much of the burden of external policies of the USSR have reaffirmed their commitment to the treaty.

But, as we said earlier, nations could find themselves acting in friendship and rushing to each other's help without a formal treaty to bind them together. This is proved by the manner in which India rushed a brigade of paratroopers and other arms aid to the Maldives in the Indian ocean in 1988. Both are, of course, members of the SAARC, South Asian Association for Regional Cooperation, and they have excellent bilateral ties. The Maldives was about to be taken over by a band of rebels and the elected President Abdul Gayoom was about to be overthrown. The rebels had sailed in from Sri Lanka and they were led by a former key politician of the island country. The Maldives is a Muslim country and 'he self-proclaimed champion of Islam, Pakistan, had offered to help, besides being as close physically as India. But Gayoom deliberately chose Indian help. He thus indicated his preference for a country which had the capability for a speedy strike action against the rebels and one which would keep its word to withdraw its troops' when no longer required. Knowing Islamabad's propensity to poke its nose in others' affairs—India's Kashmir and Punjab states and Afghanistan, for example—Gayoom chose to keep this fellow SAARC country at bay. He might have suspected that the Pakistanis, instead of putting down the rebels might even help them in their mission. India's help not only resulted in the rebels being beaten but also in the country being made secure by the time the Indian troops withdrew.[5]

All this happened without any kind of treaty binding India and the Maldives. You do not really need a treaty if your bilateral relations are cordial and based on mutual trust and equality. It may be advisable to formalise the relations with a treaty but it is not absolutely essential. India's relations with Sri Lanka are friendly without a treaty of friendship. In 1987, Rajiv Gandhi as Prime Minister signed a specific agreement with President Jayawardene under which a massive force, called the Indian Peace Keeping Force (IPKF) was sent to the island republic on what finally turned out to be a disastrous mission. Instead of being a bridge between the Srilankan army and the LTTE (Liberation Tigers of Tamil Ilam, or freedom) the force was soon hunting for the Tigers. The LTTE, after the force was withdrawn from Sri Lanka, captured the Jaffna fort from the Srilankan army from which they were evicted by a determined action by the Srilankan army. In a revengeful and cowardly action, the LTTE is believed to have assassinated Rajiv Gandhi on May 21, 1991, at Sriperambudur, near Madras, when he was out of power and was campaigning for his Congress (I) party in the Lok Sabha elections.

## REFERENCES

1. *The Hindustan Times*, Delhi, July 17, 1995.
2. "A Forgotten Treaty", Kuldip Nayar, *Indian Express*, Delhi, July 10, 1995.
3. The treaty was signed on April 29, 1954, in Peking (Now Beijing) by Indian Ambassador, Nedyam Raghavan, and Chinese Vice-Foreign Minister, Chang Han-Fu.
4. Leo E Rose, in *Nepal: An Assertive Monarchy*, Chetna, Delhi.
5. *Asian Recorder*, Vol. XXXIV, 1988.

# 2

# INDIA-NEPAL

"A king who is situated between two powerful kings shall seek protection from the stronger of the two or from one of them on whom he can rely, or he may make peace with both of them on equal terms. Then he may begin to set one of them against the other by telling each that the other is a tyrant causing utter ruin to himself and thus cause dissension between them ... or throwing himself on the protection of any two immediate kings of considerable power.*"

---

* *Kautilya Arthasastra*, Dr. R. Shamasatri, Book VII, Chapter II, sixth edition, Mysore Printing and Publishing House, Mysore.

# 3

# HISTORICAL BACKGROUND

Variously described as a buffer state or a bridge between India and China, the two giants of Asia, or as a small landlocked country in the Himalayan range of mountains, Nepal is bounded by India on three sides; east, south and west and by China on the north. The founder of the present ruling dynasty, now a constitutional monarchy, Prithvi Narayan Shah, who had conquered the Himalayan kingdom in the eighteenth century, described Nepal as a "root between two stones."[1] Prithvi Narayan was the predecessor of many kings before the present King Birendra who is his tenth successor. Except when the Rana Prime Ministers seized power and put the kingship institution in the shade, from 1846 to 1951 when, with India's help, the Rana oligarchy was overthrown and the king once again emerged as the focal point of the polity, the monarch has ruled Nepal. King Tribhuvan was restored as the supreme authority in the Revolution of 1951.

This bridge between south Asia and east Asia has an area of 147, 181 sq.km (56.827 sq. miles), and a population of 19.36 million. It is one of the poorest nations in the world, with a per capita income of US dollars 170 (according to 1981 figures). Nepali is the official language of the country, although Maithili, 11.1 per cent and Bhojpuri, 7.6 per cent, both dialects of Hindi, are spoken by sections of the people, mainly in the Terai (foothills) region of the country, close to the border with the Indian states of Bihar and Uttar Pradesh.

Nepal, of course, has the highest mountain in the world, Mount Everest (29,002 feet) which attracts keen sportspersons and men and women of adventure from all parts of the world. Everest was first climbed in May 1953, by a British expedition but the first to set foot on the world's tallest mountain were two non-British members of that team, a New Zealander, Sir Edmund Hillary, and a Nepali settled in India, the great Tensing Norgay. Since then it has been climbed more than once by Indian expeditions and other national and international expeditions both from the south side, the more favoured and familiar side, and the less known north side by the Chinese. They even once claimed territorial possession of the mountain but later gave it up as part of a strategy to mollify the Nepalis. This and other issues are discussed at greater length in Part III of the book.

The climate, naturally, in the northern parts of the country is extremely cold, almost arctic type weather, with temperatures below the freezing point but warm and sunny in the Kathmandu valley in central Nepal. Kathmandu, the national capital, is 1,337 m (4,386 feet) above the sea level and the temperature varies from 2°C (35°F) in the winter to 30°C (86°F) in the summer months. A deliberate Nepal policy of encouraging foreign tourists, mainly Japanese, west Europeans and Americans, brings in a large number of them to savour of its pleasant climate and historical and religious sites, besides such attractions as gambling, a major draw for a section of them, and other usual tourist features.

Nearly 90 per cent of the people follow the Hindu religion which is a special element in binding the Nepalis to India, the world's largest Hindu nation, although these ties have proved somewhat tenuous as we will see later. Nepal itself is proud of being the only Hindu monarchy in the world. The country, which holds Lumbini, the birthplace of the Buddha, the founder of Buddhism, has 5.3 per cent Buddhists and some 2.7 per cent Muslims in its population.

The unsettled state of the polity in north India in the later part of the eighteenth century and the rise of the British power in India from the nineteenth century compelled Nepal to look more to the north. Not only were wars fought with Tibet in the eighteenth and nineteenth centuries but much trade flowed between Nepal and Tibet those days. Under the 1789 treaty, somewhat shortlived, between Nepal and Tibet, even the right to Tibet's trade with India was vested in the Nepalis. This northward outlook altered substantially with the advent of modern education and many young Nepalis going to India for higher education or accompanying their parents working in India, and thus finding it easy to be educated in the schools, colleges and universities coming up in different parts of India particularly in the United Provinces, now called Uttar Pradesh state, close to the terai region of Nepal. (As we will presently see, there were political reasons too.) Among them was the twentieth century's outstanding Nepali, Bishweshwar Prasad Koirala, who was born in Varanasi in Uttar Pradesh. King Mahendra was another outstanding personality whose somewhat negative role at times diminished his greatness.

B.P. Koirala also took part in India's freedom movement like his father, Krishna Prasad Koirala, often called the Nepali Gandhi, along with his brothers, Matrika Prasad and Girija Prasad, both of whom rose to be the country's Prime Minister.[2] In fact, before the era of going to the United States for university educations dawned (both in India and Nepal) many Nepalis who later rose high in the administration as well as political life of Nepal used to be educated in India. The fact that one can travel to and from India without needing a passport or visa across one of the freest frontiers in the world facilitates this situation. Several of the Nepali young men and women who came to India for education or found themselves there because their parents happened to be in India also enriched the freedom movement against British rule and thereby received their own blooding in politics which later stood them in good stead in their own country. Despite political developments, which at times have taken a crooked course, hearts often beat in unison in India and Nepal.

**Never Away from India**

Nepal was, of course, never away from India and even during the days of the East India Company which made several inroads into Nepal in the traditional British style of the flag, following trade, Nepal wittingly or unwittingly practised the art of balancing its interests between China and (British) India. Although this policy of playing one against the other often did not pay dividends, a finished practitioner of the art, Jang Bahadur Rana, founder of the Rana dynasty which ruled Nepal from 1846 to 1951, easily made himself a darling of the British rulers in India.

Jang Bahadur was an astute, bold and ruthless man who first ousted the Queen, Lakshmi Devi, and then packed off her husband, King Rajendra, to Varanasi in India in exile like the Queen. Then he made their son King Surendra totally dependent on him and obtained a *sanad* from him in 1846 with the help of which he ousted the royalty from power, made himself the Prime Minister and Commander-in-Chief and established his own dynasty. He was even given the *lal* (red) seal of the king and had the full support of the British in India who were emerging as a suzerain power over Nepal. Jang Bahadur Rana earned their eternal gratitude by choosing to collaborate with the British during the greatest challenge they faced to their rule in the nineteenth century, the 1857 revolt by many Indian soldiers of the British army and by some Rajas and Nawabs and finally by the nominal Mughal King of Delhi, Bahadurshah Zafar, wrongly glorified by some Indians. Jang Bahadur did this in the face of strong opposition from his own brothers and other noblemen of Nepal who not only had sympathy with the rebels but also believed that British rule in India was on its last legs. The Emperor of China to whom Nepal had turned in the immediate past for support against the British incursions was in no position to help it because he was subject to greater pressure in the mainland during the opium war which brought China under the western influence. Nepal was, in any case, on China's peripherry, although traditionally China regarded Nepal as a tributary state. Jang Bahadur also became the first prominent Nepali to cross the seas by travelling to Britain, then considered as unpardonable act for a Hindu, whether in Nepal or India.[3]

The Ranas of Nepal became eventually so powerful that they came to be known as Sri Tin Maharaja, ("Sri, Sri, Sri Maharaja") which was the title conferred on Jang Bahadur by King Surendra. Traditionally the King of Nepal is known as "Sri Panch", ("Sri, Sri, Sri, Sri, Sri"), five times the prefix "Shri" or "Sri" for a gentleman or man of honour (wealth or good position), both in India and Nepal. Shri or Sri is the prefix in any Indian language (with its variation, Thiru in Tamil) for every man, woman being referred to as Sushri or Shrimati. There are so many things which Indians and Nepalis have in common.

References have been made to the Terai (plains) region of Nepal close to the populous Indian states of U.P., Bihar and West Bengal, the first two being the most populous states in a country which boasts of or carries the burden of a huge population of 844, 324, 222, according to the 1991 census. This census shows the population of U.P. to be 139,112,287, Bihar 86,374,465 and West Bengal 68,007,965. Because of the availability of land and its general fertility, its trade and industry the Terai region of Nepal is important in many ways to its economy and polity. It is the backbone of Nepal's economy and accounts for 59 per cent of its GDP and generates nearly three-fourth of the country's revenue because of its large trade and the location of industries there. Although the Terai accounts for only 15 per cent of the land area of Nepal and 31 per cent of its population, it is thus of great importance to the nation.

Nepal may be far removed from the heartland of China but it is thus close to the Indian plains and it is mainly dependent on India for its access to the world outside. The Terai population is substantially of Indian origin and much of Nepal's political movement has originated and flourished in the Terai. The Nepali Congress (NC) and later both the NC and the Communists have drawn upon the mainsprings of the Terai for their democratic movements resulting in the overthrow of the archaic Panchayat system and the growth of party democracy that now obtains in Nepal. The Terai is 500 miles (about 830 km) long and on an average 20 miles (about 33 km) wide. At points it is considerably wider and also very narrow at places.[4]

It is through the Terai that much of the smuggling into India of important goods, brought into Nepal in bond through India's Calcutta port, takes place and essential Indian commodities, like fuel, food articles and textiles are smuggled into Nepal to circumvent the quota restrictions as well as customs tariff. Synthetic yarn, sugar (when this commodity is scarce in India), watches, fountain pens, cigarette lighters and electronic goods are among the foreign articles smuggled from Nepal into India. It is customary for Indians travelling to Nepal to purchase some of these goods and carry the goods with them as part of their personal baggage. The Customs authorities raid business establishments and make seizures of goods while they are moved by traders but that is only a fraction of what goes on, the proverbial tip of the iceberg.

When India became independent in August 1947, it had to make its borders secure on all sides and the Himalayan states of Nepal, Bhutan and Sikkim which had been treated with special care by the preceding British rulers came in for special attention. Treaties of friendship were entered into with both Nepal and Bhutan. Sikkim was always treated as above the other princely states. Some 526 in number, which were all merged into India and fully integrated under Sardar Patel's leadership, (Patel was Deputy Prime Minister, Minister of Home, States and Information and Broadcasting and a figure of almost equal status with Nehru in the affairs of the country and the Congress ruling party). Sikkim was assigned a special status and kept in a category of its own. This went on until 1974 when a popular movement, led mainly by the majority Nepali population of the state, with which some Sikkimese and Bhutia indigenous people were associated, campaigned for the merger of the state with India and succeeded, in the face of a feeble intellectual and some English media opposition within India. These media are generally opposed to the government, which is understandable, but they cannot see the difference between the policies and actions of the government and the interests of the nation. They thus often find themselves ranged against national interests.

Bhutan and Nepal have always been treated by free India on a separate footing and while the treaties of friendship formed the basis of relations their independence and sovereignty were not circumscribed, except to a limited extent in the case of Bhutan which is required to be "guided by the advice" of India in external relations. The relevant Article II of the Treaty, entered into by India and Bhutan at Darjeeling, West Bengal, on August 8, 1949 says:

> "The Government of India undertakes to exercise no interference in the internal administration of Bhutan. On its part, the Government of Bhutan agrees to be guided by the advice of the Government of India in regard to its external relations."

The treaty with Nepal, signed on July 31, 1950, nearly a year after the treaty with Bhutan, has no such clause binding Nepal to India's apron strings, although here too Article 2, and more particularly the letters exchanged between the signatories, take care of the security concerns of each contracting party. The relevant article says :

> "The two Governments hereby undertake to inform each other of any serious friction or misunderstanding with any neighbouring state likely to cause any breach in the friendly relations subsisting between the two Governments."[5]

**Indian Help in Abolition of Rana Rule**

What is important is that India helped in the process of the abolition of the Ranas' century-old oligarchy and restoration of the authority of King of Nepal, King Tribhuvan, in 1951. All those who are now critical of the treaty and their supporters in Nepal, and some in India, have to bear this big fact in mind. It is the Rana Prime Minister who had signed the treaty with India and for India to side with the system established in 1846 would not have been inexcusable, the Ranas being more amenable to India. But India made a deliberate choice and also realised that the democratic forces in Nepal were supporting the restoration of the monarchy.

What actually happened after the restoration of the institution of the King is highly interesting. Things went very well during the lifetime of King Tribhuvan who recognised the value of the Indian association and had a succession of Prime Ministers who were friendly towards India. Except for the shortlived democratic experiment in 1959-60, the

King always chosen his PM, both Tribhuvan and Mahendra. This position was maintained until 1990. Cooperation developed in all spheres and the Nepal's Foreign Minister, D.R. Regmi, even denied the charge of India interference by some Nepali politicians. In almost all respects of foreign relations, the Nepalis accepted Indian advice, where such advice was relevant.

But things changed radically and adversely for India, with the death of King Tribhuvan on March 13, 1955 and the emergence of his son, King Mahendra, a person who liked not only to reign but also to rule and who found the Indian connection irksome. His first anti-Indian act was the appointment of Tanka Prasad Acharya as Prime Minister, a politician who did not hide his pro-China leftism in contrast with his anti-Indian attitude. Within just three days of taking over as Prime Minister, Acharya spoke of modifying the special relations with India. No wonder, the Chinese ambassador to India who was concurrently accredited to Nepal also (the position continued for some time and even an understanding of friendship between China and Nepal was signed by this gentleman, Pan Tzu-li, while he was mainly ambassador to India) rushed to Kathmandu and responding to Acharya's declaration of diversifying Nepal's foreign relations offered economic aid to Nepal.

Of course, India was itself normalising its relations with China and signed the 1954 treaty with Peking on trade and intercourse between India and the Tibet region of China. This was bound to encourage elements in Nepal which favoured China at India's cost. But what was China's traditional outlook on Nepal? In December 1939, a brochure by the supreme leader of the Communist movement in that country, which finally captured power in October 1949, the great helmsman Mao Tse-tung (now spelt Mao Zedong) said:

> "In defeating China in war, the imperialists have taken away many Chinese dependent states and a part of her territories. Japan took away Korea, Taiwan and Ryuku islands, the Pescadores, Port Arthur: England seized Burma, Bhutan and Nepal and Hong Kong, France occupied Annam, and even an insignificant country like Portugal took Macao."

Sinophiles may like to note that the references to Nepal and some other countries were omitted in subsequent editions of the brochure as an obvious gimmick to win over Nepal's sympathy and the sympathy of the other nations and allay their fears but could not hide Mao's and China's hegemonistic approach to the small neighbours.[6]

China even laid claim to the world's highest mountain and ridiculed the Nepalis for not even having a name of their own and going along with the British name, Everest being the name of the Surveyor-General of India during whose tenure the mountain was first discovered, by some Indian employees of his department, as claimed by Indian sources. The Chinese announced that they had climbed the mountain from the north side and did not even seek Nepali permission to do so. B.P. Koirala, who signed a China-Nepal boundary agreement in Peking on March 21, 1960, made interesting remarks at a press conference in Kathmandu on April 4, less than a month later, "China had claimed that Mount Everest belonged to her but Nepal had refused to entertain the claim ... There had been some minor border disputes but the claim on Everest was a new one and was made during his recent visit to Peking. Since Mr Koirala had summarily rejected it there was no discussion on it. The extent of the claim was not known. Mr. Koirala said that the Chinese claim might be discussed during Mr Chou En-lai's visit to Kathmandu beginning on April 26.

"He hoped that the claim as also other border disputes would be amicably settled through the machinery devised by the two Premiers in their recent border agreement for the delineation of the 500-mile-long border." He said: "The Chinese said that Everest was a British name and that there was no word for it in Nepalese although the Tibetan name, Chomo Lungma had existed since long. I said the Nepalese name for it was Sagarmatha. The Chinese thought it was of recent origin."[7]

So not only the Chinese laid claim to the mountain but also decided that the Nepali name for it was of recent origin. Such is the attitude of the strong. But when Chou En-lai visited Kathmandu this happened to be the first question raised at his press conference by a Nepali correspondent, on April 28, 1960. Kishore Raman Rana, chief editor of *Kalpana*, a Nepali paper, asked the Chinese Prime Minister, whether he had discussed Sagarmatha (he used this word, obviously deliberately) with Prime Minister Koirala and whether China had laid claim to the mountain.

**The Highest Mountain**

Chou En-lai's reply was conciliatory and appreciated the Nepali point of view on the highest mountain in the world. In his reply the veteran Chinese leader said : "We have never laid any territorial claim to Mount Jolmo Lungma or Sagarmatha ever since the question was raised during the talks in Peking. During the talks in Peking, the two parties just exchanged maps. The delineations of the two countries are different .... At that time, Prime Minister Koirala made the point that Nepal had always regarded the peak as Nepal's. Chairman Mao Tse-tung, when he received Prime Minister Koirala, expressed the view we could follow the Nepali delineation which shows the mountain on the boundary line, that is to say, with the northern half of the peak belonging to China and the southern half of the peak belonging to Nepal. Since Chairman Mao Tse-tung's talk with Prime Minister Koirala, our government has all along maintained this attitude."[8]

The Chinese Prime Minister went on to say that even Indian maps showed the same delineation[9], that is, the mountain on the boundary between Nepal and Tibet, and claimed that Koirala had told him that anyone wanting to climb the peak from the northern side had to take China's permission as those who wished to climb it from the southern side obtained Nepal's permission. In reality, the northern side is not all that popular and after the Chou statement not many international expeditions have been launched from the northern side. Two things are very clear. First, that China had earlier laid claim to the mountain but later found it convenient to associate itself with the Nepali view that the mountain was on the border. Secondly, that this position was formalised in the final settlement of the border under a treaty signed in Peking during King Mahendra's visit to China, on October 5, 1961, by the King himself and by Chairman Liu Shao-Chi, head of the Chinese state. The question of the ownership of the mountain was not pressed by the Nepalis as strongly as had been done by B.P. Koirala, who was dismissed by King Mahendra in what is regarded as a royal coup in December 1960, which marked the end of the Nepali honeymoon with democracy for the next 30 years. (The details of the Nepal-China boundary and other relevant issues have been discussed in greater detail in part III of the book.)

B. P. Koirala died in July 1982 after long periods of harassment by the Nepal government which staged even a treason trial against him (Koirala was acquitted) and kept him under house detention, although he was allowed to go abroad for treatment of his cancer ailment when the Janata government in India put pressure on Kathmandu. The Janata party came to power in Delhi in March 1977 and went out after it lost its majority when Charan Singh and his supporters defected from the party, under an offer of support from the Congress (I), a promise which was kept in the breach. It has always been a sore point with Nepal that from time to time the government in Delhi has been expressing itself strongly on Nepal's affairs on the issue of democracy, specially its restoration, and shown its concern about some of the popular leaders, their health and safety. When Mahendra dismissed the elected Koirala government in December 1960 Nehru, who was Prime Minister in India, criticised it in unequivocal terms. That Nehru had done a similar thing when the Pakistan Army Chief Ayub Khan seized power in Pakistan and put an end to its fragile democracy only two years earlier did not bother the Nepal establishment which had by now assumed a strong anti-Indian slant. The government reaction to Nepal developments has been minimal and confined to special occasions but the Indian press, which enjoys much freedom and strongly believes in exercising it, has more often written on the internal affairs of Nepal which is also resented by the Kathmandu establishment.

After the restoration of the monarchy with India's help in 1951, King Tribhuvan had appointed his own Prime Ministers as a royal prerogative pending the finalisation of a constitution. After his death in 1955, his son, King Mahendra, continued to use his right but in 1959 elections were held to the lower house of Parliament, the Pratinidhi Sabha (House of Representatives). The NC won a majority of seats and B.P. Koirala was appointed Prime Minister. This was only a brief interlude and the King dismissed the government in December 1960, only a year and ten months after it had been in office. Koirala and several of his associates were imprisoned. One day they were ministers and the next day they were in prison. Not only that, but Mahendra promulgated in 1962 a new constitution of partyless democracy with a King-appointed Prime Minister to head it. The system of "Panchayat" democracy was instituted. Panchayat is a hallowed word in India and Nepal, meaning that the village elders or those who have become opinion leaders in the village decide many issues affecting the welfare of the village and its residents. These bodies could also be elected by the vote of the villagers but that a Rashtriya (national) panchayat could also be formed and deliberate on the issues affecting the nation was a Mahendra innovation. Many nations in Asia and Africa, which gave a go-by to the one-man one-vote party-based democracy have created instead, different systems, like a partyless democracy, guided democracy and the military junta-led democracy, as in Indonesia, to give the facade of a democracy to the political and administrative set-up.

Known India-baiters became Prime Ministers one after the other. Mahendra first appointed Dr Tulsi Giri who was in power from 1962 to 1965, Surya Bahadur Thapa from 1965 to 1969, and Kirti Nidhi Bista from 1969 to 1970. King Mahendra became his own Prime Minister from April 1970 to April 1971 after which Kirti Nidhi Bista came back to power from 1970 to 1973. Mahendra died in January 1972 and Birendra, his son, succeeded him and kept up the tradition of Panchayat democracy. He had Nagendra Prasad Rijal as Prime Minister from 1973 to 1975, when Giri came back to power and on his resignation from that high office in September 1977 Bista again became Prime Minister. The people were apparently fed up with this system of musical chairs and the facade of democracy in the name of the Panchayat system and demonstrations were held after which King Birendra ordered a referendum. This eased the situation somewhat but again the succession of Prime Ministers continued.

In June 1981, Surya Bahadur Thapa came back at the helm but in a vote of no confidence in the partyless Rashtriya Panchayat he was ousted from power through the exertions of a former Speaker, Lokendra Bahadur Chand, whom the King now chose to be the new Prime Minister. Thapa wanted to retaliate and bring a no confidence motion against the man who had thrown him out of power but he was persuaded by some leaders not to do so as the Panchayat system would be weakened thereby. Nagendra Bahadur Rijal succeeded Chand but Chand came back to power after the India-baiter, Marich Mansingh Shreshta was sacked following extensive violence in Kathmandu some of it near the royal palace itself. This was the consequence of an anti-Panchayat agitation, launched by the NC and the Communists, called the Movement for Restoration of Democracy. As many as 50 persons were killed in the capital and there were clashes in other towns too.

**End of 30-year Regime**

The thirty-year long regime by nominated Prime Ministers, whose main task appeared to be to make anti-Indian statements from time to time, came to an end and democracy was restored. For thirteen of these years, from 1960 to 1972 the country was under King Mahendra, and from 1973 to 1990 under the present King Birendra. During the period, the two kings had given a kind of toy to the politicians in the form of the Rashtriya Panchayat. The agitation during which there was a day and night curfew for seven days in the capital was terminated after the King put an end to the Panchayat system and formed a new Constitution Recommendation Commission under Justice Bishwanath Upadhyaya of the Supreme Court who later became its Chief Justice and declared the Communist regime's recommendation for dissolution of the Pratinidhi Sabha as invalid in August 1995. Pending elections Krishna Prasad Bhattarai, a senior leader of the NC, was asked to form a coalition government in 1990 consisting of the NC representatives, the Communists, two Independents and two nominees of the King.

Bhattarai held the Foreign Affairs and Defence portfolios himself besides being the head of the government. The Independent members of the government were Devendra Raj Pandey, human rights activist, and a professor, Mathura Prasad Shreshta.

The Constitutional Commission recommended a 205-member lower house, elected every five years and an upper house of 50 members. They along with the King constitute the Sansad or Parliament. The Constitution specifically prohibits the executive from signing any treaty or agreement which is detrimental to the territorial integrity of the country. Elections to the Pratinidhi Sabha were to be held before April 1991 and until then the interim government under Bhattarai was to be in office. Bhattarai and his entourage of ministers and officials visited India in June 1990 at the invitation of the Janata Dal Prime Minister, V.P. Singh. But before that in January Shailendra Kumar Upadhyaya, Foreign Minister in the previous King-fashioned government had visited India and had talks with the External Affairs Minister I.K. Gujral. It was then agreed between the two countries that the 1950 treaty would remain a bedrock of bilateral relations. This was also the view taken when official level talks were held between Shailendra Kumar Singh, India's Foreign Secretary, (the same name as Nepal's Foreign Minister showing the close proximity between the two nations), and his Nepali counterpart, Narendra Bikram Shah, later in February.

During Bhattarai's visit to India many of the issues affecting trade and transit were sorted out and the *status quo ante* prior to April 1981 was restored. The Nepali purchase of anti-aircraft guns from China, in violation of the 1950 treaty, and the trade restrictions imposed by India resulting in acute shortage of essential commodities like petrol and kerosene in Nepal were done away with.[10]

After many years, the two sides again referred to the "unique, friendly and brotherly" relations between India and Nepal, which should be normalised and imparted new dynamism and dimensions and "elevate them to ever-rising levels of cordiality." Both countries also reiterated their adherence to the five principles of co-existence, something which Nepali India-baiters were holding against Delhi as the latter's alleged refusal to commit itself to. The joint communique also said that "Nepal and India will fully respect each other's security concerns... Neither side will allow activities in its territory prejudicial to the security of the other." The two countries also agreed to have prior consultations with a view to reaching mutual agreement on such defence-related matters, which in the view of either country, could pose a threat to its security.

In November 1990, the King promulgated the democratic constitution of Nepal and ended the thirty-year long autocratic rule by his father and himself. The NC and the National Democratic party, led by a former Prime Minister Surya Bahadur Thapa, welcomed the constitution. The Communists, led by Manmohan Adhikari, General Secretary of the Communist Party of Nepal (Marxist) and Madan Bhandari, leader of another faction of the Communists, objected to Hinduism being made the state religion of Nepal and Nepali the sole official language of the country. Surprisingly the same communists encouraged Islamic religious activities when in power and even sought Pakistan's help in developing Nepal's industry. Pakistan only sent more ISI (Inter Services Intelligence) operatives to Nepal and one of them had an open brawl with a boss who had come down from Islamabad. Both the red factions were, of course, in the interim Bhattarai government and Adhikari later became Prime Minister at the head of a minority government after a second spate of elections in 1994. The two factions had merged into a Unified Communist Party of Nepal (Unified Marxist and Leninist) in January 1991.

In the first election, under the new constitution, the Nepali Congress won 110 seats out of 205 and secured the right to form the government. Bhattarai having lost his election to Madan Bhandari in a Kathmandu constituency by 751 votes, Girija Prasad Koirala, younger brother of the late B. P. Koirala became the Prime Minister. Manmohan Adhikari, whose unified CPN, had won the second highest 66 seats fulminated against India, "I warn foreign powers against interfering in the internal affairs of Nepal" and disapproved of the foreign policy of the NC. He said: "We want a true non-aligned foreign policy between India and China." This was a new twist to non-alignment given by the Communists of Nepal because non-alignment does not prevent you from choosing your friends.

The NC once again proved that it had a large measure of popular support among the people of Nepal. Way back in 1959, when Nepal had a brief interlude of democracy, it was this party which had won the first ever democratic elections in Nepal and now after 31 years it again proved the same thing. In this long period, many politicians, without a base of their own, had a free run of the country and indulged in critical and hostile attacks on men like B. P. Koirala and the NC as a party. Koirala was hounded, made to face a treason trial and kept in imprisonment, by politicians dancing to the tune of the King. That in spite of all this they could not humiliate the Nepali Congress party and its leaders was proved by the results of the 1991 elections. Although internal factionalism in the NC resulted in the squandering of the gains, it once again shot back to the helm with Sher Bahadur Deuba as Prime Minister in September 1991.

The G. P. Koirala government resigned following squabbles within the NC party and in the fresh elections held in 1994, the NC emerged as the largest single party but without a majority of its own, paving the way for a minority Manmohan Adhikari government of the UCPN (ML). It also lost its power as it could not face a no-confidence motion but ruled for same time without any mandate until the Supreme Court ruled in August 1995 that the Pratinidhi Sabha dissolved at Adhikari's instance be restored and how a coalition led by Sher Bahadur Deuba of the NC came to power and won a vote of confidence from the lower house is recent history.

Manmohan Adhikari, a veteran of Nepal politics, had launched a campaign to modify the Indo-Nepal treaty of 1950 while in office but he did not specify what changes he wanted. He, however, made it quite patent that he and his party were leaning towards China as against India. Unfortunately for Adhikari and people of his ilk, the relations between India and China have been gradually improving and his party cannot play the old game of balancing India against China and playing one country against another. For the Communists to show their preference for a communist regime in a neighbouring country may be in its eyes the right policy to follow but Nepal's interests may indicate a different course. In other words, Nepal's interests cannot be equated with China's which the Nepali reds have to recognise. The King showed his preference for the Communists by allowing Manmohan Adhikari to remain in power while fresh elections were to be held, the third such exercise in a small country like Nepal in just four years, but the Supreme Court ruled otherwise.

## REFERENCES

1. *Nepal-Strategy for Survival*, Leo E. Rose, Oxford University Press, Bombay.
2. *Koirala Life and Times*, Kiran Mishra, Vishwa Prakashan.
3. Rose's book and several other books on the history and evolution of Nepal give details of the rise of the Ranas and of the role played by the Nepal rulers in the Himalayas in the 18th and 19th centuries.
4. The subject of the Terai has been dealt with in much detail in *Regionalism and National Unity in Nepal*, Frederick H Gaige, Vikas Publishing House, Delhi.

5. See appendices when these two and other relevant treaties have been reproduced.
6. *China-South Asian Relations 1947-1980*, Vol. 2, R. K. Jain, Radiant Publishers, Delhi.
   Nepal, on the other hand, claimed that it had suzerainty over Tibet. B. P. Koirala, when he was Prime Minister, said at a press conference in Kathmandu on August 11, 1959 that "Tibet paid us a tribute and we enjoyed extra-territorial concessions there."
   Historically speaking, we had some suzerainty over Tibet. *China-South Asian Relations*, Vol. 2, (p. 301). Of course, later Nepal swallowed its pride, as India did even earlier, in recognising Tibet as a region of China and withdrawing all extra-territorial claims. Such claims are even otherwise inconsistent with the modern concept of equality of nations but that Tibet should be treated as Chinese territory is different.
7. *Ibid.*, pp. 312-13.
8. *Ibid.*, p. 316.
9. Perhaps the only time China recognised the veracity of Indian border maps. Obviously when it suits you, you can quote the devil.
10. These and other details taken from *Asian Recorder*, Vol. XXXVI, 1990.

# 4

# A TREATY OF DISCORD

As explained in the previous chapter, the Ranas were very friendly with the British in India and had even gone to their help in the 1857 revolt against the British rulers. They now felt nervous at the prospect of the end of British rule in India which had become as clear as daylight by 1946-47. While the Communists in India did not recognize the rise of Indian independence, probably awaiting a signal from Moscow, the Ranas, well entrenched for a century in Nepal, wished that somehow that eventuality would not come to pass and their British benefactors would stay on. That, of course, did not happen and the Ranas had to deal with the new Indian government in New Delhi.

This they did with the same alacrity which they had displayed in their dealings with the British who had not acquired direct control over Nepal but had established a kind of suzerainty over the Himalayan kingdom. The British rulers of India had always treated Nepal (and Bhutan) separately from and a cut or two above the other 526-odd Indian princely states and the Ranas wanted that the New Indian government would extend to them the same treatment, the integrity of Nepal would be protected and the Ranas would continue to rule the kingdom. They even cited the 1923 treaty which the British had signed with them and which the Indian successors to alien rule had to honour. The Indian reply was that a new treaty would be entered into.

The Ranas had two more concerns. They knew that the democratic government in New Delhi would be fully sympathetic to the democratic forces in their own country and with the rise of egalitarianism and the retreat of the colonial forces in Asia, which began with Indian independence, Nepal was bound to be affected too. Secondly, the rulers of Nepal were worried over the developments in neighbouring Tibet where the Chinese Communists were advancing after their victories in the mainland. As we have seen in the earlier chapter, Nepal always regarded Tibet as its sphere of influence until the position was given up after King Mahendra adopted a vigorous anti-India policy and had to make concessions to the Chinese to placate them. The Ranas, in any case, were feeling very uncomfortable with the rise of the Communists in China and desperately needed continued protection against them from the South. As a token of their desire to achieve the maximum collaboration with India they sent a contingent of Nepali army to fight along with the Indian forces in Hyderabad during the police action in September 1948 which resulted in the Nizam suing for peace and the emergence of democracy in the premier Indian princely state.

India and Nepal had reached a Standstill Agreement in 1947 to maintain the status quo in their relations, Nepal recognising the successor status of the Indian government on the one hand and India acknowledging Nepal's integrity on the other. On August 9, 1947 there was also a tripartite agreement among India, Nepal and Britain (India was to emerge as a free country in eight days time and the British recognised that position) for the division of the Gurkha regiments of the former Indian army, four of them going to the British army and six to the army of free India. The Gurkhas have had a glorious record of service, both before India's independence and after, and have been among the most loyal and brave components of India's armed forces. The British ironically used their Gurkhas in Hong Kong, in a feeble gesture of protection of the island territory and the adjoining Kowloon mainland which they have to return to China in 1997. The Rana rulers also agreed, under the tripartite agreement, that the arrangement for the use of the Gurkhas by India would remain in force as long as neither side formally requested its abrogation whereas the agreement with the British was renewable every five years. The Ranas stipulated that the Gurkha troops would not be used against Nepal, other Gurkhas and Hindus in general but no restrictions were placed on their use against a foreign power (like China as they were used in the 1962 conflict between China and India).[1]

The 1947 Standstill Agreement served as a useful stopgap

arrangement but soon talks began between the two countries on a full time treaty to place their relations on a firm footing. Obviously, the Ranas were more concerned to ensure that this step was taken soon enough, although the Indian side could not be said to be reluctant participants either. Having entered into a treaty of perpetual peace and friendship with Bhutan, somewhat similarly placed, in 1949, the stage was set for a similar, but not the same, treaty with Nepal. Both countries are landlocked and have little access to the outside world except through India which enjoine close, good-neighbourly and friendly relations between Bhutan and India and Nepal and India and a closer outlook of identity of interest on each other's security. It is notable that the Nepali Congress leaders, who had become quite vocal and prominent in their country's affairs, made a demand while the treaty was being negotiated that India should look after Nepal's defence and foreign relations.

The main issue which somewhat delayed the conclusion of the treaty of friendship was not the aspect which later became a bone of contention but the Indian insistence that the regime in Nepal be liberalised and the popular leaders be associated with the administration of the country. Nehru appointed in the middle of 1949 Chandreshwar Prasad Narain Singh (C.P.N. Singh), as India's ambassador to Kathmandu and this was a fateful decision. Nehru was greatly impressed with the high social status of an individual, his table manners and his possession of a smart English-speaking spouse, which accounted for his appointment of a number of Rajas, Maharajas and Nawabs as ambassadors or senior diplomats. C. P. N. Singh was a gentleman of an aristocratic background who conducted himself as a 'brown sahib' (he was later on made even a governor) and had several strong points in his favour but also a number of disadvantages about which we will speak in greater detail in the next chapter.

The growing Chinese pressure on Tibet, about which both countries were equally concerned, persuaded them to enter into the treaty without further delay. Accordingly, the treaty of Peace and Friendship was signed in Kathmandu on July 31, 1950, Prime Minister Mohan Shamsher signing it on behalf of Nepal and C. P. N. Singh for India. As provided in the treaty, it came into force at once. Along with it another treaty was also signed on trade and commerce, which was actually a treaty of trade and transit, by both the signatories.

India, frankly speaking, took the same attitude in determining the contents of the treaty as had the British who looked upon Nepal as a bulwark of the country's security from any danger to it from the north.

India acted as a successor state in this respect but, it must be pointed out. India also made significant and material changes by recognising the sovereignty and independence of Nepal. Article 1 clearly states: "There shall be everlasting peace and friendship between the Government of India and the Government of Nepal. The two governments agree mutually to acknowledge and respect the complete sovereignty, territorial integrity and independence of each other."

Although the security elements are important and they have been repeatedly referred to, critically by many Nepalis, what is forgotten is the provision for reciprocal treatment for each other's nationals in industrial and economic development, in residence, ownership of property, participation in trade and commerce, movement and other privileges of a similar nature. This is provided in Articles 6 and 7 of the treaty but Nepal has honoured these commitments often in the breach. Even a foreign observer of the scene, Leo E Rose, an American scholar, had to admit that "although the obligation (of reciprocal rights to citizens) has been fully applied to Nepalis resident in India, who enjoy virtually equal rights with Indian citizens in these respects, the reverse has not been the case of Indians resident in Nepal."[2] Rose's book was first published in India in 1971 but the position in all these respects of owning property, carrying on trade and engaging in other gainful activities has not changed a bit in the following 24 years. Nepalis in India can apply for any job under the Government of India and be selected and appointed if they are qualified on equal terms with Indians but no Indian has been given that privilege in Nepal. They are, on the contrary, subjected to a work permit system at times. If some people can circumvent the rules and carry on business in the name of a Nepali citizen that is a different matter and calls for greater enforcement of its own rules by the Nepal government.

The situation is so irksome for Indians that they can see before their eyes affluent Nepalis holding property in India, like orchards in Himachal Pradesh and houses everywhere, but an Indian cannot own a house in Nepal. Neither can he ply transport or own a truck nor can he run a business but some manage to do it with Nepali partners if they are dealing in third country goods. (Violations of the law, with the connivance of the law enforcing authorities, is common in many countries.) There are other discriminatory actions too. For example, the advance income tax rate for Indians in Nepal is Rs. 50,000 while for the Nepali citizen it is just a tenth of this amount. The airport tax levied on Indians at Kathmandu airport is Rs. 600 if they are travelling to India whereas it is Rs. 500 for a Nepali citizen. At the airport in Delhi, both are treated equally and are charged only Rs. 150 if they are flying to the Nepali capital.

For India this is a familiar scenario all right. Any number of Pakistanis visit India, in the name of culture, and take away with them large amounts of cash earned from their performances. Ghulam Ali, the Ghazal singer, is at the top of this circle, although there is no dearth of Ghazal singers in India. An occasional visit by a Pakistani singer could hardly be objected to but at times one feels as if this gentleman has all along been in India.[3] And what is the experience of noted Indian singers and other artists who could legitimately aspire to perform in Pakistan? The door is closed. Even a top artist like Lata Mangeshkar cannot go across the border and sing, in any large or small city in Pakistan. Pakistani authorities are afraid that not only they would get a phenomenal response from the audiences but also they would put to shame some of the local artists who masquerade as great singers.

The Pakistan government, of course, does not believe in encouraging any exchange in arts or sciences. It has the full backing of artists like Mehdi Hasan who is at the head of Pakistanis wanting to keep Indian singers out of their country although he himself has paid many visits to India and each visit means money. The same thing goes for cinema actors and actresses. Any number of them can get the so-called "work permits"—Zeba Bakhtier, Anita Ayub and others like the faded actor of yesteryear, Mohsin Khan. How many Indian actors and actresses can be seen to be acting in Pakistani films? None. Of course, Indian films and movie music, although much of it is just copied from the west, is immensely popular with the Pakistani audiences who watch them on videos and now in satellite TV programmes beamed from India and other countries. Here again, Pakistan has rejected India's suggestions for a cultural exchange, although the mediamen who frequently manage "professional" trips to Pakistan would still blame India for not doing enough to promote such exchanges.

Coming back to the 1950 treaty between India and Nepal, we have to record that along with the treaty being signed letters were exchanged between the two sides which strengthened the security of the two countries. The treaty lays down that the two governments undertake to inform each other of any serious friction of misunderstanding with a neighbouring state likely to cause any breach in the friendly relations between India and Nepal. This was obviously in relation to China which was considered a source of danger by both sides at that time but which has emerged as a friend of Nepal since the advent of King Mahendra (1956-71). The improvement in the relations between the governments of India and China has also removed some of the friction referred to in the treaty.

The treaty was accompanied by an exchange of letters between the two signatories, the Nepali Prime Minister, Mohan Shamsher Jang Bahadur Rana, and the Indian Ambassador, C. P. N. Singh. The letters spell out the security aspects much more fully and contain commitments not made in the treaty. The very first point in the letters (actually it is only one letter, the other party simply acknowledging it as correctly setting out the understanding) says:

"Nether government shall tolerate any threat to the security of the other by a foreign aggressor. To deal with such a threat the two governments shall consult with each other and devise effective counter-measures."

As we have pointed out, the treaty provision was concerned mainly or wholly, with China without mentioning it by name. The letters also were similarly concerned with the likely threat from Peking but since no name was mentioned here too only a "foreign aggressor" was referred to both countries were bound to go to each other's help in the event of foreign aggression of any kind. Did Nepal rise to the occasion when India was attacked twice by Pakistan, in 1965 and 1971, or when China committed aggression against India in 1962? The answer is a big 'no'. Not even a token gesture of friendship or sympathy was expressed by Nepal during any of these critical periods for India. Bhutan recognised Bangladesh on the morrow of the Indian troops' glorious victory and the surrender of the Pakistani army in the Bangladesh capital, Dhaka, which brought the war in the eastern sector to an end, but Nepal took its own time to grant recognition and did it after a number of other countries had done it and when it was not likely to cause any misunderstanding of the action in Islamabad.

### No Effective Action

In terms of consultations, which are obligatory under the letters exchanged with the treaty, also there has been no effective action. It is true, that Kathmandu was in no position to render any material assistance to India but moral support would have been of great relevance if it had been forthcoming. It is quite evident that Nepal was more concerned about reactions in Pakistan by the act of recognition of Bangladesh (Islamabad itself granted recognition in 1974) than about India's feelings over lack of any support or sympathy. It is well known when peoples all over the world were identifying themselves with the liberation struggle of the Bangladeshis. Nepal, under the two Kings and under the short-lived Communist Government of Manmohan Adhikari, has always been against the treaty and the letters.

Of course, India could have asked Kathmandu to fulfil its obligations under the 1950 treaty and the letters accompanying it, but it never made Nepal honour its commitment. The entire Nepali outlook vis-a-vis India has always been to raise grievances and nurse grouses whether it is the treaty or anything else. India has, of course, not been above putting some pressure on Kathmandu on the trade and transit arrangements which causes immense hardship to the ordinary Nepalis. We will go into this aspect in the next chapter.

There is one more irksome provision of the treaty and the letters from the Nepali point of view. Article 5 of the treaty says: "The Government of Nepal shall be free to import, from or through the territory of India, arms, ammunition and or warlike material and equipment necessary for the security of Nepal...." To this, the letters add more explicit provisions: "Any arms, ammunition or warlike material and equipment necessary for the security of Nepal that the Government of Nepal may import through the territory of India shall be so imported with the assistance of and agreement of the Government of India. The Government of India will take steps for the smooth and expeditions transport of such arms and ammunition through India."

In what way does the treaty or the letters restrict Nepal's freedom of action under the clause? It is commonsense to ensure that the neighbour who uses your territory for such imports does it in a manner which does not adversely affect the security of the country which lends its territory to be so used. Nepal has faced no threat to its security from India all these years and even after it made its peace with China and made some concessions to the latter in regard to the boundary and on the status of Tibet which Nepal had always perceived in the past as its tributary state. Yet Nepal has contracted some arms supplies from China and if this is a friendly action towards India it should say so.

Pakistan imposes all kinds of restrictions on goods imported by Afghanistan through its ports and even on essential supplies from Pakistan needed for the day-to-day existence of the Afghans. In October 1955, Islamabad even searched some aircraft on their way from India to the Central Asian Republics which are all Islamic in terms of population. This attitude of an avowed Islamic state like Pakistan towards its Islamic neighbours, Afghanistan and the Central Asian Republics, is based on its claimed security concern and its privileged position as a country through which the landlocked countries have to requisition their requirements. The point made here is that countries which are rightly or wrongly concerned about their security being affected by the action of their landlocked neighbours have always had recourse to such action, treaty or no treaty. India need not imitate Pakistan but the security concerns have to be understood.

There are several other examples of how Nepal has honoured in the breach its obligations under the Friendship treaty, for example, in respect of equal treatment for Indian citizens in Nepal. Under King Mahendra's Hostile policy towards India, initiated by him after coming to the throne in 1955, an order was issued by the Nepali government in October 1957 to the effect that school teachers in Nepal must be Nepali citizens. This order, of course, applied to all non-Nepalis but since almost all the non-Nepali teachers were Indians, the order was obviously meant to hurt them. By another order the Nepal Government placed restrictions on all foreigners in Nepal on their purchase of houses and immovable property in general.[4] This was also designed to hurt the Indians. Any sovereign nation is entitled to lay down conditions for employment in its territory and on holding of property by foreigners but then sovereign nations have also to honour their treaty obligations.

Specially when India has been extending the Nepalis equal treatment with Indian citizens in the matter of jobs under the Central Government and in respect of properties and other things Nepal could not have discriminated against Indian citizens resident in Nepal. It is a mystery why India never held Kathmandu to its treaty obligations but is it justified on the part of Nepal always to shout foul whenever the treaty is mentioned? The problem is humanitarian in nature. Where will the five million Nepalis in India go if India retaliates?

One of the reasons why King Mahendra dismissed the B. P. Koirala government, barely 22 months after it had won a massive mandate from the people, was that Koirala wanted a few of the excesses against India and Indians to be undone. He had his limitations under the 1959 constitution laid down by the King who had the final say although the government was said to be based on the will of the people. King Mahendra had, of course, won the sympathy of some Nepali elite and intellectual groups and the Nepali establishment, mainly the civil servants and diplomats, who relished his assertion of authority against India. Koirala had, therefore, to walk cautiously and assume a stance of equality between the two powerful neighbours. In that period, which was the worst for India's relations with China, (and it finally led to China's aggression against India in 1962) this policy was bound to hurt India more than China. But Koirala did not mince words when the

Mustang incident took place in 1960 with the Chinese troops on the border killed a Nepali soldier. Koirala's friendly relations with New Delhi helped him to get a better treaty with India in the matter of trade and transit in 1960. This reminds us that along with the Treaty of Friendship a treaty of Trade and Commerce was also signed by the same two signatories, Prime Minister Mohan Shamsher and Ambassador C. P. N. Singh in 1950. The Trade treaty came into force on November 1, 1950, as provided in Article 10. Under it, the Indian Government recognised Nepal's right to commercial transit of all goods and manufactures through the territory and ports of India.

Subsequently, treaties of Trade and Transit were signed between the two countries in 1960, 1971, 1978 (extended upto 1989) and 1991. Nepal's desire for separate treaties of trade and transit was acceded to by India in 1978. All the treaties have a history of their own, generally indicating the prevalent mood in Kathmandu and/or New Delhi. For example, the 1960 treaty was entered into when B. P. Koirala was at the helm, before he was dismissed and jailed by King Mahendra later in the same year. The 1978 treaty was signed when the Janata government was in power in Delhi and was known to be particularly friendly to Nepal, and the 1991 treaty was signed when popular government was restored in Nepal and G. P. Koirala was Prime Minister and the Narasimha Rao government in India continued the friendly policy of the Janata Dal government and gave up the strong tit-for-tat policy of Rajiv Gandhi (1984-89).

In Nepal, however, the section ot people who have made India-baiting their constant preoccupation, the pro-Chinese Communists and the students guided by them have been agitating against most of the treaties of trade and transit as they have done in respect of the treaty of friendship. There is total failure on their part to appreciate the anxiety of the country which lends them the transit facilities to ensure that these must not be misused by the people of the country to which they are extended and also of the country extending the facilities. It is common knowledge that unscrupulous elements in trade (and some others) have been even otherwise misusing the facility of the open border between India and Nepal and smuggle foreign goods imported into Nepal from third countries into India and essential articles from India into Nepal. We have already referred to the existence of this undesirable activity which has not been hampered by the treaties and agreements in force from time to time.

In their standard book on India's foreign policy, Appadorai and M. S. Rajan have summed up the issue of trade and transit which have sourced relations between the two countries in the following words:

"What had become a major constraint in relations between India and Nepal by 1970, however, was the question of trade and transit, particularly in view of the ten-year term of the 1960 Trade treaty coming to an end. Problems on this issue had been growing through the years since the first Treaty of Trade and Commerce was signed in 1950. The problems centred not only on obtaining better terms but also (perhaps ) on India's desire to protect its trade interests, as against Nepal's desire to diversify its trade.... It (India) also objected to the competition placed on Indian interests against imported goods which were imported by Nepal from third countries and re-exported from Nepal to India. The problem moreover, was largely aggravated by smuggling on a large scale".[5]

What is surprising, the Nepali desire for diversification of its trade was never hampered by the various trade treaties. According to a study made by a Nepali economist, the bilateral trade between India and Nepal has declined drastically from 97.7 per cent of Nepal's total trade in 1956-57 to as little as 28.3 per cent in 1993-94. If the treaties were standing in the way, as alleged by many vocal Nepalis, how could this steep fall be accounted for, even allowing for the large scale smuggling of goods both ways, which obviously does not find a place in the official books of trade. To quote the economist :

> "However, in Nepal's total volume of trade, India's share was as much as 97.7 per cent in 1956-57 which declined marginally to 54 per cent in 1969-70. But afterwards India's share in Nepal's total volume of trade began to decline fast. In 1975-76, the share in Nepal's total volume of trade plummeted to 67 per cent which fell to an all-time low of 22.5 per cent in 1989-90 when there was a trade dispute between the two countries but it improved to 28.3 per cent in 1993-94."[6]

The trade dispute referred to above was the squeeze applied unjustly by India when Nepal had done some unpleasant things in relation to India in contracting arms from China and India wanted to have it out on Nepal in the economic sphere. Unfortunately the ordinary people of Nepal suffered with long queues for kerosene and petrol. The situation was retrieved when the Janata Dal government came to power in India in 1989-90 and simultaneously democracy was restored in Nepal.

This aspect will be gone into in some further detail in the next chapter. There is one more important treaty between the two countries which we have to refer to here. This is the Treaty of Extradition between the Government of India and the Government of Nepal signed at Kathmandu on October 2, 1953. It was signed by the Indian ambassador, Bhalchandra Krishna Gokhale for India and by Matrika Prasad Koirala (B. P. Koirala's elder brother) for Nepal when he was Prime Minister. The treaty came into effect one month after the signing without ratification. (This shows that when it suits the high contracting parties, they dispense with the procedure of ratification.)

The treaty clearly specifies that it has been entered into by the two countries "on a basis of strict reciprocity" and requires each country to deliver to the other those persons, who being accused or convicted of a crime committed in the territory of one government, shall be found within the territory of the other government, under the circumstances and conditions stated in the present treaty. In other words, the treaty is as between two equals and not between one superior party and another inferior in status to it. In India under British rule for a long time, Indian judges could not try Britons and when the first case of its kind came up in Calcutta the Europeans resident in India launched an agitation. Of course, it is easy to argue that extradition treaties are generally entered into between two equal and sovereign nations. But the relevance of the point made here is in the context of the continuous Nepali propaganda that treaties are imposed on Nepal by the big brother India and attributing to this country the attitude of a bully. They forget that a bully is essentially a cowardly person and is not sure of his strength. The treaty was entered into at a time when Indo-Nepali relations were at their best and were in the phase of "special relations" when India could have got away with anything but she did not even try. All the treaties referred to here and some others which are relevant are reproduced in full in the appendices.

Going back to the main treaty, the Treaty of Peace and Friendship, there have been few formal requests for its revision or scrapping it altogether although from time to time some Nepalis, even in high offices, fulminated against it and others took potshots at will. On the other hand the Treaty of Trade was often sought to be amended and the first such request was made in 1958. The ascending to the throne of Nepal by King Mahendra marked a big change in Nepal's overly friendly relations with India. India also contributed to this situation to some extent by entering into the Tibet treaty with China which some in Nepal perceived as a sign of weakness on India's part in relation to China.

The first discordant note on the Treaty of Friendship between

India and Nepal was struck by the newly appointed Prime Minister, under Mahendra, Tanka Prasad Acharya, who was a self-proclaimed Sinophile. He was appointed to the high office on January 27, 1956 and lost no time to tell the world that Nepal wanted direct relations with other countries and would welcome economic aid from them. This was meant for China more than any other country and the Chinese envoy to India, who was concurrently accredited to Kathmandu, rushed to the Nepal capital from Delhi to announce his country's readiness to offer aid without any strings.

The treaty of friendship had been conceived as a bulwark against any threat to Nepal's security and tacitly recognised that Nepal was part of the Indian security system. In the early fifties when it was signed the main threat to the security was perceived to be from China, both by New Delhi and Kathmandu, but Nepal, under Mahendra, wanted to proclaim to the world that it did not regard China as a threat, although the controversy over the world's highest mountain and over the status of Tibet erupted even later. At the same time the King and his chosen Prime Ministers, one after the other, would want the world to believe that the Friendship Treaty with India was a hindrance to Nepal, or a nuisance. Nepal wished to be totally undependent on India. But this was easier said then done because there were so many ties between the two countries and Nepal knew that China was far away while India was near and there was the open India border.

This, of course, has never prevented sections of Nepalis from carrying on a whispering campaign against the treaty which often erupts into the open. The series of King-nominated Prime Ministers and the Communists, under different faction labels, have been in the forefront of this campaign, although only the latter, in office for a while in 1995, asked for a formal revision. The fact that people like Tanka Prasad Acharya, Tulsi Giri, Kirti Nidhi Bista and Marich Man Singh Shreshtha (who was finally sacked by King Birendra after he had been installed in office by the same dignitary) have carried on a campaign against India would show that they did so with the tacit or explicit or implicit approval of the King. Both Mahendra and Birendra (who took over where his illustrious father died in 1972). They certainly had the King's approval for their actions and utterances. Both Mahendra and his Prime Ministers blew hot and cold. They spoke of close ties with India and claimed they prized equal friendship with India and China. Perhaps they believed in the doctrine that some were more equal than the others. When it suited them they roundly abused India and Shrestha even poked his nose in Indo-Srilankan affairs and criticised

India for stationing troops (IPKF) in the island republic although the troops went in at Sri Lanka's request and were withdrawn when Sri Lanka asked for it. [7]

The Communists, on the other hand, were openly pro-Chinese from the outset. In October 1951, the Communists sent greetings to the great helmsman, Mao Tse-tung (later called Mao Zedong) and wished him "ten thousand years" of life in typical sychophantic manner practised in many developing countries. When the Communists staged a revolt in 1952 and were suppressed by the Nepali government they fled to China and were readily afforded asylum by the Mao regime. They were even granted broadcasting facilities from Chinese soil to persuade the Nepali people to overthrow the "reactionary" regime of Nepal which by then had emerged from Ranacracy and taken its first steps in democracy also. [8]

**Koirala's Protest**

China, of course, changed course in a few years and tried to win over the Nepalis who fell for gimmicks but only B. P. Koirala protested against the Chinese claim on the world's highest mountain and pointed out that Tibet was a tributary state of Nepal but the main role in this transformation was played by King Mahendra himself. When it suited them, the Communists joined hands with the Nepali Congress leaders and tried to mobilise the people against the so-called democracy of the Panchayat system. They played a leading role, side by side with the NC in the 1990 struggle, in which the Nepali security forces killed some 50 demonstrators in Kathmandu alone.

In the first elections held under Nepal's genuinely democratic constitution in 1991 the Communists, by now united under the Communist Party of Nepal (Unified Marxist Leninist) banner, won only 66 seats against the NC's 110 out of a total of 205, which gave the latter a clear majority. Even in the 1994 elections, occasioned by factionalism within the NC, the latter won the position of the largest single party but the Communists had some outside support and were able to form the first elected Communist government in the world after the 1957 victory of the Communists in India's Kerala State, but could not last even a year. Even during this unstable rule of theirs, their leader, Prime Minister, Man Mohan Adhikari, a veteran politician of Nepal, asked for a revision of the Indo-Nepal treaty without specifying what really pinched him. But before meaningful exercise by the senior diplomats of the two sides could be undertaken, Adhikari was voted out of office by the Pratinidhi Sabha, the lower house of the Nepal Parliament.

Those elements, including some in India, who think that the mere label of Communism means a progressive outlook have much to ponder here. When Beijing wanted it the Nepali Communists were sychophantic, as in 1952, and when Beijing did not object they also fought shoulder to shoulder with the NC against the despotic rule of the King. But they always remained hostile to India. Obviously, the Communists enjoy a considerable measure of support among the people of Nepal (and certainly the King would have them rather than the NC in his government as Birendra showed when he allowed Adhikari to continue in office after dissolving the lower house at his instance, all of which was overturned by the Nepal Supreme Court in August 1995) but there are many inconsistencies in their stand. They are a party to the system of which a Monarch is the head, they are openly against India while avowing that they are holding the scales even between India and China and they denounce the Indo-Nepal treaty when they are out of power but seek only a revision of it when in power.

Of course, the Nepali politicians in general find in the treaty a good bogey with which to play on the sentiments of the people, by calling it unequal but not explaining how, by suppressing the fact that five million of their fellow-Nepalis could lose their livelihood if the treaty were scrapped and so on. This does not prevent them from sniping at India and some from faking shots openly. For example, in 1977 when the Janata government came to power in India and was showing all the signs of friendship towards Nepal without concealing its desire to see democracy restored in the Himalayan kingdom, four prominent persons issued a public statement for scrapping the 1950 treaty because they said it was unequal. The signatories were three former Ministers or Prime Ministers, S. P. Upadhyaya, T. P. Acharya and D. R. Regmi, and another politician, K. J. Raymajhi.They did not ask for closing the border though.

As for the Nepali government, it had at no time called for scrapping the treaty. Under the treaty, all Kathmandu has to do is to give a year's notice and terminate the treaty. Article 9 of the treaty, the last article, says, "The Treaty shall remain in force until it is terminated by either party by giving one year's notice." Instead of taking this straightforward course, the two Kings and the Communists, when in power for a few months in 1995, have relied on propaganda tactics, innuendoes and the strategy of spreading dissatisfaction against India. The issue of revision was, as we have seen, taken up for the first time by the Man Mohan Adhikari government but the two Kings also took it up through their

Prime Ministers from time to time but on an informal basis. India, of course, pointed out that the treaty was a bedrock of Indo-Nepal security.

In a diversionary move, King Birendra came forward with a Zone of Peace proposal on February 25, 1975, on the occasion of his coronation. He could never get India's endorsement for this plan although some 86 countries ultimately supported it. Even the Janata government which was more responsive to the needs and fears of Kathmandu refused to endorse the proposal. The plan was born after Nepal resented the merger of Sikkim with India in 1975 after the Sikkim Congress, a body largely of people of Nepali origin, won an overwhelming majority in the elections in the state in 1974 and asked for the merger of their state with India. The 1974 Nuclear explosion made by India, which placed the country in the exclusive club of nuclear powers and India's victory in the Bangladesh war of 1971 were also not liked by the Nepali establishment. Nepal did not realise that the Nepalis in Sikkim were being empowered and were getting their right to rule themselves instead of remaining as subjects of the Sikkim Maharaja. Nor did Nepal resent the nuclear explosions by China continuously since 1964.

So much for Kathmandu's claim that it treats the two countries equally and is "non-aligned" between Beijing and New Delhi. If one country, China becomes a major nuclear power and goes on holding explosions even as late as 1995, Kathmandu is happy. But, if on the other hand, India holds only one explosions and thereafter puts its nuclear programme under wraps, obviously under American pressure, Kathmandu feels its security threatened. If China launches an attack on India, as in 1962, the Nepal government does not raise its little finger in India's support, but if India recovers from the shock and recoups its strength which is then deployed in the cause of the suffering people of Bangladesh the Nepali establishment feels threatened. Is this a demonstration of friendship or equal distance between India and China? The Indo-Nepal border is open; the Nepal-China border is closed. Is this equality?

The Zone of Peace proposal was pursued vigorously by King Birendra who made refinements to the policy of his father. But when India sought clarifications and asked Kathmandu from which source it perceived a threat to itself so that a Zone of Peace assurance would become necessary it could not provide a proper answer. But there was an indirect gain in the form of one of the clarifications which said that Nepal would continue to honour the obligations under all existing treaties it had signed if they were valid. This made it clear that Nepal stood by the 1950 Treaty of Friendship. The King's advisers failed to realise that the treaty and the Zone of Peace could not co-exist.

It is a painful story on the whole of a country realising that the treaty cannot be done away with but never stopping to make anti-Indian propaganda about an "unequal treaty" and after some time never asking for its termination. Fortunately, during the rule of the NC things have been much better and the issue receded into the background.

What has India has done to safeguard her interests and put the Nepali leaders wise about the true character and import of the Friendship Treaty? Nepal's behaviour has always been shifting, although for the long period of 35 years the two Kings were in absolute control, the basic attitude of hostility towards India has not changed. So, when the opportunity presented itself, India brought to Nepal's notice certain fundamental truths. Kirti Nidhi Bists, one of the most vocal critics of India when in power, had described the treaty as "outdated" in 1969, the year when he did his worst to harm India's interests. But when he visited India in 1972, as Prime Minister, just four months after India secured the surrender of over 90,000 Pakistani troops in Bangladesh and won the liberation war, he told the Indian government that Nepal desired to reactivate the process of political consultations envisaged in the letters exchanged along with the signing of the friendship treaty. The trend of bilateral discussions was continued for some more time.[9]

When Prime Minister Indira Gandhi visited Nepal in February 1973, with the aura of the Bangladesh victory still largely undiminished, she reminded her counterpart that under the provisions of the treaty "we have to appraise each other of important developments." In view of this commitment she urged the then Nepali Prime Minister Bista to brief her on the latter's visit to China the previous November, Bista was reluctant to do so at first but later realised that he had to comply with Mrs Gandhi's request and apprised her of the outcome of his talks in Beijing. [10]

Such developments were transitional in nature as the permanent feature of Nepal's policy towards India was one of unfriendliness and could not be altered except when the Nepali Congress was in power. But whenever the occasion demanded it, India did not mince words. Nepal's Foreign Minister Karki made a frontal attack on India on the Sikkim merger issue in 1974, and said, "It is our irrevocable policy that there should be no outside interference in the internal affairs of any nation. Sikkim's interest lies in the unity and mutual cooperation of her people." India strongly retaliated: "We will reply to friendship with greater friendship, but we also know how to deal with hostility." Nepal was told to keep off and not to be too concerned about the internal affairs of India. It is said that King Birendra then reined in his Foreign Minister and declared that "we should not allow the Sikkim affair to cloud the totality of Indo-Nepal relations." Karki's successor Rijal visited India and subsequently the anti-Indian propaganda on Sikkim ceased[11].

The Sikkim affair showed that the people in power in Kathmandu are not only hostile to India but also shortsighted. The fact that the main elements of the Sikkim population are people of Nepali origin and it is they who took the initiative for merger of the protectorate of Sikkim into India was lost on them. The interest of the empowered Sikkim population seemed not to bother them at all.

## REFERENCES


1. *Politics of Revolution 1945-54, in Nepal Strategy for Survival,* Leo E. Rose, *op. cit.*
2. *Ibid.*
3. He was again in India in October 1995, see *The Hindustan Times,* Oct. 8, 1995, when he said he was happy to sing in Agra. Naturally.
4. *Policy towards India,* S. K. Jha, in *Nepal : An Assertive Monarchy,* Chetana Publications, New Delhi.
5. *India's Foreign Policy and Relations,* A Appadorai and M. S. Rajan, South Asian Publishers, New Delhi.
6. *Duty Free Border Trade and Special Economic Zone between Nepal and India,* Hari Bansh Jha, Centre for Economic and Technical Studies (CETS), Kathmandu.
7. *Asian Recorder,* 1989, Vol. XXXV.
8. *Perspectives on Nepal's Foreign Policy,* Rai Singh, in *Contemporary South Asia* , ed. M. D. Dharamdasani, Shalimar Publishing House, Varanasi.
9. *Policy towards India,* S. K. Jha, in *Nepal : An Assertive Monarchy, op. cit.*
10. *Perspective on Nepal's Foreign Policy,* Rai Singh,
11. *Ibid.*

# 5

# SPECIAL RELATIONS

The shifting sands of Indo-Nepal relations have passed through five distinct phases during which, as we saw in earlier chapters, certain significant developments were noticed, mostly adverse to India. These can be summed up as:

1. The Rana Phase of appeasement of India and general friendliness;
2. The Tribhuvan Phase of close friendship and "Special Relations";
3. The Mahendra Phase of sustained anti-Indianism and playing of India and against China and the other way about;
4. The Birendra Phase in which the Mahendra policy was continued with some refinements and modifications; and
5. The Democracy Phase of general friendliness under the Nepali Congress interspersed with hostility during Communist rule.

In this chapter we will deal with the first two phases through which the relations have passed between the two closest neighbours with an unparalleled open border across which neither passport nor visa is required. The uneasy relationship came into being with Mahendra's succession to the throne of Nepal on the death of his father Tribhuvan in 1955. Until then the relations were not only friendly at the people-to-people level but at the government level too.

The Ranas had been hereditary Prime Ministers and commanders-in-chief of the Nepal army (even now Nepal has only a token air force and the question of having a navy does not arise as Nepal is completely land-locked) from 1846 and had enjoyed the support and protection of the British rulers in India. With them, the Ranas had a 'I scratch-your-back-you-scratch-mine' relationship. The British exercised a kind of suzerainty over Nepal and afforded protection to the country at a time when the Chinese rulers were weak and the situation to the north of Nepal was full of uncertainty. The Indian government after independence assumed a somewhat similar role in relation to Nepal, but free India and (now free) Nepal had a close relationship of historical and cultural-relations and social ties without any parallel in the world. India not only recognised Nepal's sovereign status, which the British rulers in India never had, but also entered into a Standstill Agreement under which the provisions of the 1923 treaty between the Rana rulers and the British were continued until a new treaty was entered into between the two countries.

**Convergence of Views**

India realised that the northern frontiers of the country really lay through Nepal and thus both the rulers of Nepal and of free India found their views converging on the theme of mutuality of interest. While India had recognized the new Communist regime in China, which seized power from the Kuomintang nationalists in October 1949, the Tibet policy was a source of concern for both India and Nepal. Jawaharlal Nehru, India's Prime Minister and also Minister of External Affairs (1947-1964), declared in 1950 that "any possible invasion of Nepal would inevitably involve the safety of India."[1]

While there was thus a common concern about security, India's insistence on reforms in Nepal and suggestion for association of the popular forces with the administration irked the Ranas. One section among them was amenable to the Indian suggestion and even invited an Indian team headed by a senior Congress leader, Sri Prakasa, who later became Governor of Bombay province, to draft a new constitution based on democratic principles for Nepal. This was the time when Padma Shamsher was Prime Minister but his policy met with stiff opposition from another Rana group, led by the Commander-in-chief Mohan Shamsher. This group was ultimately successful in the tussle among the Ranas and Mohan Shamsher replaced his brother Padma Shamsher as Prime Minister. But he was equally concerned about the nation's security and the finalisation of a treaty of friendship with India, which had been already initiated, was pursued vigorously.

The treaty was eventually concluded and the two nations bound each other in ties of friendship and pledged eternal peace between them. Contrary to the feelings of resentment and hostility against the treaty, which later became a regular campaign, the popular leaders in Nepal were all for it and B.P. Koirala even proposed a military alliance between the two countries which was rejected by Nehru. The latter apparently abhorred military alliances and could not, therefore, make a distinction between security arrangements between two neighbours and a military alliance like the one between Pakistan and the distant United States. Any way, the point to be noted is that the treaty had the full backing of the people's leaders who had yet to gain any kind of official status as Mohan Shamsher was against their induction in the Government.

Incidentally, this was the only time when Nepal came to India's help in a matter of its internal security, much before the treaty was signed. This was in September 1948, when India launched a military action, called the police action, against the Nizam of Hyderabad, who pretended that he was sovereign when most Indian States had acceded to and even merged with India. India was also fighting the Pakistani forces in Kashmir, whose army had entered the state in the guise of tribal raiders in October 1947. Later on Pakistan had to admit before the United Nations Security Council that its regular forces were involved in the fighting in the state. The Indian army was thus fully stretched and Nepal readily agreed to send ten batallions to India. They played a useful role in maintaining peace in the country at a time when India did not have much strength of paramilitary forces like the Central Reserve Police Force (CRPF), the Border Security Force (BSF) and similar other forces.

The struggle for popular rule continued in Nepal and the fact that the Nepali Congress leaders many of whom had even participated in the Indian freedom movement were in the forefront of the struggle was an open secret. The Ranas were reluctant to support any move for the NC leaders to be inducted into their government and they were, in any case, not willing to permit any change to take place that would endanger their own existence as rulers. India was not interested in the sudden overthrow the Gurkha regiments into the British army more secure. Obviously the two countries also wanted to see which way New Delhi was going. On that score there could be little doubt because Nehru and his entire cabinet had gone to the airport in Delhi on November 10 to welcome Tribhuvan when he arrived there from Kathmandu. They wanted to demonstrate to the world and the Ranas that they regarded the King as the supreme authority in Nepal and not a figurehead that the Ranas had made him out to be.

The NC rebellion was assuming serious proportions as the arms they had received from Indian sources, although India did not involve its army in the struggle, had boosted their morals. One of Nehru's closest advisers, Rafi Ahmed Kidwai, who was also a key minister in his cabinet, had been in a British jail in India during the last struggle for independence, the Quit India Movement, waged by the Indian National Congress under Mahatma Gandhi's leadership along with Surya Prasad Upadhyaya, Secretary General of the NC. This is believed to have helped in facilitating the task of the rebel leaders as also the fact that Jaya Prakash Narayan, one of the most respected leaders of the freedom movement in India, had been close to the NC leaders. They had given him asylum from the British rulers during the Quit India Movement for some time.

The rebels captured Biratnagar in the Terai region and had also some successes elsewhere. At one place the regular Nepali army garrison went over to their side. The Ranas were still not willing to see the realities and resisted efforts to induct the Nepali Congress leaders into their government and recognise the status of King Tribhuvan as a real monarch. Mohan Shamsher's son, Bijaya Shamsher, who was progressively head of the Nepali Foreign Office and Foreign Minister, conducted the negotiations with India. Nehru made it clear that India regarded Nepal as part of its security system and warned the world powers that India's patience on the Nepal King's status was not inexhaustible. This was meant for the United States and Britain which had been approached by the Ranas to recognise the dummy minor king Jnanendra.

### Tribhuvan's Return

The Ranas finally came round and recognised the status of the King who returned to a tumultuous welcome from his people at Kathmandu airport from New Delhi on February 15, 1951 which completed the revolution. Some of the Nepal Congress leaders were not satisfied with the compromise formula under which they were to serve in an interim coalition government along with the Ranas under Mohan Shamsher as Prime Minister. But they were won over and B.P. Koirala was made Home Minister in the government. The real trouble came when his step-brother M.P. Koirala was made the first non-Rana Prime Minister of Nepal in November 1951. It is said that C.P.N. Singh, who was interfering in Nepal's internal affairs, had persuaded the King to choose the more amenable M.P. Koirala.

This, the second phase, of Indo-Nepal relations was at once a most cordial and also an ominous one for the future of the relations between the two close neighbours. Cordial because there was little or no friction and there was complete understanding between them, and portentous because C.P.N. Singh interfered in all major decisions by the Kathmandu authorities. He is reported to have attended a conference of district officials and while Nepal was seeking India's help and even guidance there were limits to the envoy's functions which were often overstepped. The fact that Singh sometimes conducted his own foreign policy has been noted by sympathetic Indian and other observers and recorded by them.

"...Nepal's heavy dependence on India and the resultant Indian presence in its affairs invited criticism of Nepal's India policy and also engendered suspicion about New Delhi's intentions in some quarters in the Kingdom. The overbearing attitude of the Indian diplomats, particularly the Indian ambassador, C.P.N. Singh, was sharply resented by many of the prominent Nepali leaders", says S.K. Jha, a scholar of Indo-Nepal relations.[2] The king and the leaders of the government did not see in Singh's activities any sign of interference, because often they sought Indian advice and help, but there were disgruntled elements, some of whom could not be accommodated in the cabinet or had to leave it, who indulged in anti-Indian propaganda. The foundations of the suspicion that India wanted to dominate the affairs of the small neighbour were thus laid and the hands of those who wanted to exploit the feeling were strengthened. The envoy was mainly instrumental in this matter and whatever good he had done for India and Nepal was not only washed away but the seeds of discord which soon began to appear when Mahendra ascended the throne in 1955 were sown.

King Tribhuvan was the first Constitutional Monarch of Nepal and greatly valued Indian cooperation with the country. But, as we have seen, it was believed that the King had overlooked the more popular and important Nepali leader, B.P. Koirala, in favour of his brother, M.P. Koirala, as the first commoner head of government in November 1951. Even B.P. Koirala charged C.P.N. Singh "with taking undue interest" in Nepal's internal affairs. This is stated in Giri Lal Jain's *India Meets China in Nepal.* As a perceptive writer Jain recognised that "India's concern over the developments in Nepal is only natural. Geography is a compelling factor. The social, economic, political and historical ties between India and Nepal are so intimate that their destinies are indissolubly interlinked... Nepal does not possess any natural boundary with India."[3]

But even Girilal Jain has recorded the charge of interference which India had to bear because of C.P.N. Singh's unwise role. Quoting a sympathetic foreign correspondent, in Delhi, also covering Nepal, Robert Trumbull of the *New York Times*, he notes, in Trumbull's words: "It is said openly in Kathmandu that the real ruler of Nepal today is the Indian Ambassador, Mr C.P.N. Singh".[4] While this may be an exageration and the kind of gossip which all foreign correspondents gather, while hurriedly "doing" a country in a few days visit, the truth underlying it has to be recognised.

Of course, Singh was succeeded by a more or less correct envoy, B.K. Gokhale of the former ICS, Indian Civil Service, created by the British to rule India to which Indians were admitted in the latter part of their rule and several of whom were inducted by Nehru into the newly emerging Indian Foreign Services (IFS), which now means most of the diplomatic posts in India and abroad. Gokhale put the ties on an even keel and stopped the interference in Nepal's internal affairs which the Nehru chosen Singh had been practising. It was Gokhale who signed, with M.P. Koirala, the Indo-Nepal extradition treaty in October 1953. Singh who had an advantage over several others because he was from Bihar State of India, Closest to Nepal, belonged to the landed aristocracy and combined wealth with education which Nehru obviously valued.

Much of India's involvement, as we have seen, was at the invitation of Nepal. In particular, the help extended by New Delhi in the training and modernisation of the Nepali army turning it from a somewhat old-fashioned army with a meagre salary for the lowest ranks, into a regular fighting army ready to go into instant action was of immense advantage to Nepal. It was unfortunate that the Indian military mission people who rendered yeoman's service to Nepal later became the centre of a controversy. Between 1951 and 1953 the Nepal government requisitioned the services of the Indian army thrice to help it in maintaining law and order. Not only were Indian advisers called in to make suggestions on the reorganisation of the administration but also the services of some Indian civilians were taken on loan. Indian planning specialists were also invited to help the country in assessing planning and developing its resources and large scale Indian economic assistance was also received. It remained a major component of foreign aid for a long time.[5]

All this was part of the building up of "special relations" which the two countries had embarked upon and which, under King Tribhuvan, the Nepal government was consciously cultivating. There was complete coordination between the two governments in foreign policy and defence and the Nepal rulers know that what they did was in the interest of their country. It was patently clear that while India was keen that Nepal should recognise the security concerns and its foreign and defence policies were shaped accordingly, no sensible person in India was in his wildest dreams thinking of treating Nepal except as a sovereign nation and never considered its absorption in India.

But hostile elements with Indophobia as their principal pastime were already active and only waiting for an opportunity to cause damage to Indo-Nepal relations. It has been India's misfortune that several of its neighbours have a strong sense of inferiority complex. Their desire to assert themselves in the affairs of the world and secure for their countries a place of honour is legitimate. But what is not so is the constant habit of Indo-baiting. They fail to realise that India has enough problems of its own without taking over those of the neighbours.

In the world which respects power but makes feeble protests about its misuse, the only superpower in the world now, the United States, has often walked into countries which it looks upon as being in its sphere of influence. For others like Iraq, which are physically half way around the globe from Washington, it takes shelter under a so-called United Nations mandate, like a mafia don seeking approval of his action from his lackeys. Grenada in the West Indies is a considerable distance from North America, but Washington looks upon it as part of the American sphere of influence. It had committed a crime in the eyes of the United States because it had some communist leanings. So, one day in the early eighties the Americans walked into the country while the world looked on, including the mighty Soviet Union. India has done nothing of the kind even in respect of its closest neighbour, Nepal. But voices have been raised against India over the years by Nepali "Intellectuals", disgruntled and out-of-office politicians and above all, the two Kings, Mahendra and Birendra, operating through their chosen politicians holding the office of Prime Ministers. More of it in the following chapters.

Finally, what the Ranas practised in Nepal, for a little over a century (1846-1950), was a unique system. They exercised all the powers of a supreme authority and worked in the name of the King who was reduced to a figurehead until the winds of democracy began to blow in Nepal in the wake of the freedom of India and with India's help the Monarchy was restored. The Ranas also established their own hereditary system and power was retained in the family, whether India acted wisely in leaning towards the King will have to be decided by history because after the honeymoon with Tribhuvan came to an end with his death in 1955 India had to endure a hostile neighbour during the rule of his son and grandson for more than three decades. Of course, the Ranas could not have lasted for ever but the democratic forces could have gradually taken over from them without the Monarchy coming in between. Once it was restored with India's help Tribhuvan's successor behaved like a typical ruler wedged between two powerful neighbours and never raised their little finger in favour of India.

There is a historical parallel in the Maratha kingdom in western and south-western India founded by the great Shivaji. With a series of weak Rajas succeeding him, the Peshawas, the Prime Ministers of the Maratha King, took over and by their powers in the field of battle and their administrative and diplomatic skill they established themselves as the hereditary Maratha power with its headquarters in Poona, now called Pune. They ruled over a large area of India in the eighteenth and part of nineteenth centuries directly or through their Subedars in Indore (the Holkars), Nagpur (the Bhonsles), Baroda (the Gaekwars) and the Scindias in Gwalior. Things went well as long as there were illustrious Peshawas like Bajirao and Balaji Bajirao at the helm but with a succession of weak or scheming Peshawas the system collapsed. While all the Subedars, except the Bhonsles at Nagpur, survived until freedom arrived in 1947, the Peshwas were liquidated by the British rulers early in the 19th century.

## REFERENCES

1. *The Political Revolution 1945-54*, in Leo E Rose's *Nepal: Strategy for Survival.*
2. *Policy Towards India*, S.K. Jha, in *Nepal an Assertive Monarchy*, Ed. S.D. Muni, Chetana Publications, New Delhi.

3-4. *India Meets China in Nepal*, Girilal Jain, Asia Publishing House, Bombay, New York, p.96; pp. 94-95.

5. *Policy Towards India*, S.K. Jha, in *Nepal: An Assertive Monarchy.*

# 6

# FRIENDSHIP IN DECLINE

At the beginning of this book we have placed prominently a quotation from Kautilya's *Arthasastra* on the position of a King wedged between two powerful kings and how he should conduct himself so that no harm comes to him. Sanskrit being the common heritage of India and Nepal (and several other countries), one should not be surprised if King Mahendra had himself seen this piece in the original or a translation of the great work or any of his advisers had done it. In any case, what Mahendra did now on assuming the kingship of the Himalayan state in March 1995 has a remarkable resemblance with what Kautilya had taught 2,300 years ago. (That Kautilya flourished in nearby Bihar is another significant circumstance.) "Nepal's relations with India entered a phase of confrontation when on December 15, 1960, King Mahendra took over the government by a royal proclamation, "says S.K. Jha in his piece "Policy Towards India" in the book *Nepal: As Assertive Monarchy* which we have referred to earlier. In fact, the confrontation began the day when Mahendra assumed kingship in 1955, not five years later after the sudden end of the B.P. Koirala democratic interlude during which there was a temporary bright phase.

The era of special relations was over and Mahendra was assertive as one who wanted to be a real monarch, one who not only reigned but also ruled. He made it apparent soon that he was a different personality from his father who was openly friendly with India. This relationship of close friendship was not acceptable to him but he did not act in indecent haste. He toured India extensively which should have convinced him that the people and government of India were extremely friendly towards Nepal but if that was so the King did not show it in his actions. Diplomatic relations with China were established in August 1955 but Mahendra did not give India any inkling of it and the question of consulting New Delhi, of course, did not arise. Nepal and China declared in a joint communique on August 1, 1955 that diplomatic ties would be established and ambassadors exchanged.

The Chinese lost no time and their man in Delhi, Ambassador Pan Tzu-li, was promptly accredited to Kathmandu and presented his credentials to Mahendra on August 3.

Since India was among the first non-communist countries to recognise China and the Indian ambassador to the previous Kuomintang regime, K.M. Panikkar was promptly accredited to the Communist regime, this could not have affected Indo-Nepal relations. Also, New Delhi had recognised Tibet as part of China and entered into an agreement with Peking on Trade and Intercourse with the Tibet region of China in April 1954. This was interpreted in Kathmandu as a sign of Indian weakness.

**Shocked for India**

What could have hurt New Delhi was that Nepal had not thought it necessary to consult it or give it a hint of what was coming. A further shock was in store for India when, in another five months, Mahendra set up a government under the India-baiter Tanka Prasad Acharya. Soon after the establishment of diplomatic relations between Nepal and China, Acharya visited China in September 1955 and toasts were drunk to the eternal friendship of two neighbours. Chinese Premier Chou En-lai made the astounding statement that China's socialist system "completely precludes" aggression against any country.[1] In the light of India's experiences in October 1962 this hyperbolic statement was obviously meant for Acharya's ears for whom any Chinese words were sweet music. Acharya had said in his first press conference as Prime Minister that he would end the special relations with India and modify them into "equal friendship" with all countries.

The Indians were, of course, partly responsible for a change in Nepal's perception of its special position in Tibet but the powers in Kathmandu now went ahead speedily and recognised China. In 1954, M. P. Koirala, as Prime Minister, had spoken of special ties with Tibet and earlier in 1953 a big delegation of Tibetans had arrived in the Nepali capital bearing the annual tribute of Rs. 30,000. That was, of course, before the Indian government, under Nehru, recognised Tibet as a region of China under the Treaty of April 1954. Nepal, under King Tribhuvan, believed in close coordination of its foreign policy with India's so the talks for the recognition of China by Kathmandu had been initiated but moved rather slowly. They received a big boost under Mahendra's regime and the pro-China Tanka Prasad Acharya was naturally all for establishing ties with Peking which also opened the doors for economic and other aid from China to Nepal.

Nepal's traditional view was that Tibet was not a part of China and it had a kind of suzerainty over Tibet. This was now undergoing a radical change in favour of China because of Mahendra's policy of strengthening the ties with China so that he could snap his fingers at India. Under a treaty signed in September 1956. Nepal signed away its rights and Kathmandu agreed that "all past agreements between Nepal and Tibet were abrogated." The letters exchanged along with the treaty were even more explicit in China's favour. Nepal agreed to withdraw its military escorts in Lhasa for its different offices and all the extra territorial rights enjoyed by Nepali residents were abolished.[2]

In a way this was a recognition of the reality on the ground but Mahendra did it in order to spite India, a case of cutting one's nose to spite the face. The Chinese cleverly paved the way for it by generous economic aid which was interpreted even more generously by the pro-pating elements in Nepal which were now in command of the destiny of the country. The details about Nepal-China relations and treaty obligations would be covered at length in part four of the book but insofar as these things impinge on Indo-Nepal relations we have to recognise that Mahendra's principal motivation was to place himself in a position of strength in dealing with India. During the B. P. Koirala interlude, in 1959-60, and earlier during King Tribhuvan's reign, Nepal tried to salvage some of its honour but a price had to be paid for creating a tension-free situation on the northern border so that Kathmandu could deal with India and stave off its alleged interference in an effective manner.

The agreement that India had bowed to the Chinese by recognising their possession of Tibet under the treaty of April 1954 would not avail King Mahendra and his advisers. When the time came to demonstrate her strength, India offered asylum to the Dalai Lama and a horde of his officers and followers in 1959 and incurred the wrath of Peking which has neither forgotten the issue nor forgiven New Delhi for this act of interference in her "internal" affairs. A number of Tibetans resident in India often create embarrassment for the Indian government, by practising the frequently indulged habit of many Indians to hold demonstrations and defy the authorities on any issue considered important by the group concerned. The Dalai Lama has behaved like a spiritual leader at times and at times like an alleged head of State. The United States and its friends and allies in the western world are happy that India has to face the music and bear the brunt of Chinese wrath as they pamper the Dalai and boost his ego but do pretty little to get him his due, namely a free Tibet. President Clinton received and feted the Dalai Lama when he visited the United States in 1995.

Has Nepal done anything of the kind to displease the Chinese? Not even under the rule of the popularly elected government of the Nepali Congress has Kathmandu extended any help to the Tibetans in exile or given them shelter and asylum because that would provoke the rulers in Beijing, earlier called Peking. On the contrary, Kathmandu has made one concession after another to China under the impression that this would strengthen its bargaining position with New Delhi. Whether it is the question of fighting the Khampa rebels who were harassing the Chinese forces or it is the firing on an unarmed Nepali patrol at Mustang, the signing away of Nepal's rights in Tibet, the issue of the highest mountain in the world, to which the Chinese had laid claim, or the insulting notes sent by China during the Cultural Revolution in 1967 to Mahendra, he or whoever has been in power in Kathmandu has just swallowed all that and kept smiling. Of course, the Chinese tried to make amends in some cases and corrected their errors but most of that was not the result of any exertions by the Nepali elite and administration. If in the context of improved relations between India and China the rulers in Beijing find it less essential to bother about the Nepali attitude it is again a result of some fortuitous circumstances.

We have referred to the some of the anti-Indian steps, like the order meant to hurt the Indian teachers in Nepal and Indian wanting to buy property in Nepal, taken by Mahendra in this period before the B.P. Koirala interlude of democracy began. There was yet another in this series, through his chosen Prime Minister, in 1958 when he asked for the withdrawal of the Indian Military Mission which had rendered much useful service to Nepal and trained its army. India had no option but to comply with the Nepali demand and on July 16, 1958 the mission was withdrawn but a much reduced Indian Military Training Advisory Group was allowed by Nepal to continue to function.

Then came the Koirala democratic regime after Mahendra mysteriously gave the country a new constitution under which the first elections were held. The Nepali Congress won a landslide victory and Koirala began to assert himself although the King had reserved the final authority to himself. During the period from 1955 to early 1959, when the NC government came to power, Mahendra and his Prime Ministers had reoriented Nepal's foreign policy so much that Koirala had no option but to follow it. Yet he maintained a friendly posture towards India while espousing Nepal's independence and sovereignty. There was no real contradiction between them and the problem had only been created by Mahendra and his advisers and the hypersensitive Nepali elite. It was a tough task for Koirala to change the course. Since this was an extremely difficult period for New Delhi in its relations with China, as we will see in part four of the book, it was a matter of much relief for the Indian government to have a friendly regime in Kathmandu.

Koirala was able to negotiate with India a new treaty of Trade and Transit in 1960, something which Mahendra himself had sought but had not succeeded in realising. The treaty met Nepal's aspirations and was favourable to Kathmandu in the matter of trade with third countries carried on through Indian territory. He also resisted Chinese pressure on Mount Everest, as we saw in an earlier chapter, and his strong opposition to the Chinese claim to the mountain led Peking to modify its attitude, although China was able to secure Nepal's agreement on the boundary between the two countries going through the mountain. (The Chinese Premier even quoted Indian maps in support, something China has not done in its boundary dispute with India.)

B. P. Koirala also prevented the Chinese from coming closer across the northern frontier by their proposal to build a road to Kathmandu from the town of Kodari on the Nepal-Tibet border. As we will see later, this policy was reversed by Mahendra.

**Indian Leaders' Utterances**

Some of the pronouncements made by Indian leaders created a problem at this stage. Nehru, in the course of a speech in Parliament on the India-China conflict, said in November 1959 that "any aggression on Bhutan or Nepal will be considered an aggression on India". This was naturally criticised by anti-Indian elements in Kathmandu and created a difficult situation for Koirala. He, however, tried to sooth the feelings aroused against India by people who either failed to understand what Nehru had said or deliberately misinterpreted his concern for the security of Nepal as being bound up with that of India.

In a press statement two days after Nehru's speech, Koirala said: "Nepal is a fully sovereign independent nation. It decides its external and home policy according to its own judgment and according to its own liking without ever referring to any outside authorities. Our Treaty of Peace and Friendship with India affirms this. I take Mr. Nehru's statement as an expression of friendship that in case of aggression against Nepal, India would send help if such help is ever sought. It could never be taken as suggesting that India could take unilateral action"[3] . Nothing could be more categorical and clearer than this statement of the Nepal Prime Minister and it did help in quelling the ill feeling sought to be created by the hostile elements.

Nehru had made a stronger statement on India-Nepal friendship and identity of interests in security in the Himalayas in 1950 and he was now only reiterating what India and Nepal had agreed to in the past decade of close relations. There was no hint in his statement that India would take unilateral action, although he should have had prior consultations with the Nepali leaders specially when a friendly person like B. P. Koirala was Prime Minister. Perhaps, because of the strain under which the Indian Prime Minister was then functioning, with Indian politicians, including many in his Congress party, strongly critical of the way he had handled the China problem and general public opinion in the country highly adverse to him, such niceties were not observed. But there was nothing wrong he was propounding as Koirala said in his press statement.

Nepali elements hostile to India were leaving no stone unturned to attack India at the slightest pretext and assumed interference in their affairs. In October 1956, the first Indian President, Dr Rajendra Prasad, a great scholar of history and as a native of Bihar closely aware of Nepal's problems, was on a visit to Nepal as part of the frequent tours undertaken by the heads of state of India and Nepal to each other's country and by their heads of governments. At a banquet hosted by King Mahendra he made a rather obvious statement. He said, "Any threat to the peace and security of Nepal is as much a threat to the peace and security of India. Your friends are our friends and our friends yours."[4]

Even this innocuous statement was commented upon critically in Nepal. What is wrong if the head of state of your neighbouring country says "Your friends are ours and our friends yours?". He is not imposing India's friends on Nepal without accepting Nepal's friends as India's. But the atmosphere within a little over a year of Mahendra's coming into the picture was such that Nepal or the elements hostile to India in that country were ready to take offence at any remark which could remotely lend itself to the theory of interference. The succession of Indian ambassadors were not only a friendly but an understanding lot, all different from the one who had created more problems for India than he had solved, C.P.N. Singh.

Koirala had resisted Chinese attempts to encroach on Nepal's territory and even referred to the time when Nepal had a kind of suzerainty over Tibet, as we have seen in a previous chapter. But he tried to follow the King's pro-China policy as far as possible and in doing so he even tried to justify Nepal's refusal to give any moral support to India in the dispute with China which was smouldering then and was soon to erupt into a big fire. He adopted the specious Nepali argument that the country was "neutral" or "non-aligned" between India and China. Speaking to newsmen in Chandigarh during a goodwill visit to India, in January 1960, Koirala said that his government would adhere to "the policy of neutrality enunciated by Mr. Nehru. In the context of the Sino-Indian dispute we are friendly to both the countries. We want an amicable settlement between the two."

Nehru, in fact, had never endorsed neutrality and had said on more than one occasion that non-alignment did not mean neutrality and equated it with cowardice. It was one thing for Nepal not to take sides in the India-China border issue but to justify this selfish approach as being "non-aligned" or "neutral" was the height of absurdity, bowing to the bully and leaving your own friend in the lurch. But this was the policy which Mahendra wanted pursued and even an elected Prime Minister could not do much about it except to say Nepal wanted an amicable settlement.

Mahendra, however, was not satisfied with Koirala. He found the Prime Minister was not identifying himself with the King's views and dismissed the NC government on December 15, 1960, imprisoned Koirala and some of his colleagues and justified his autocratic action in the name of "safeguarding nationalism and sovereignty." That things like an elected Prime Minister being dismissed even while his majority is in tact was akin to a military coup, as often happens in countries like Pakistan (Prime Minister Zulfikar Ali Bhutto was overthrown by Gen. Zia-ul Huq, the army chief, in July 1977 and executed after a "trial" in 1979) was the reason why the King's action was aptly called a *royal coup*.

Nehru's strong reaction to the dismissal of Koirala and his imprisonment helped Mahendra to rally the anti-Indian elements in his country which were overjoyed by the fall of the democratically elected government because it was friendly to India. Nehru said the dismissal was a complete reversal of the democratic process. The allegations against Koirala and his colleagues were dubbed by him as vague charges. Mahendra tried to justify his action by pointing out that there was interference by a foreign power. The nationalist sentiments of the younger generation of Nepalis were thus being exploited. He had difficulty in making the people swallow this bitter pill because they had voted overwhelmingly for Koirala less than two years ago. There were no serious charges against him, even by the routinely vocal opposition politicians. So, the King took recourse under the nationalist sentiment and said he was seeking to safeguard Nepal's sovereignty and prevent a foreign power from interfering and hurting his country. The "foreign power" was naturally India but he did not have the strength to say so. Indeed, he could not do away with India altogether because Nepal depended on her in many respects.

Mahendra relied on anti-Indian and pro-Chinese politicians like Tulsi Giri, Kirti Nidhi Bista and others to mouth anti-Indian utterances and pursue vigorously his anti-Indian policies to the maximum extent possible. They played the role of Mahendra stooges admirably but this did not prevent the King from throwing them into the dustbin of have-beens when his purpose was served and even resurrecting them if their services were required again. Mahendra himself undertook an extensive tour of China from September 28 to October 15 in 1961. It was during this visit that the Chinese "persuaded" the Nepali King, if such persuasion was at all needed, to sign an agreement on the construction of a highway from Kodari, on the border of Nepal and Tibet, to the capital city of Kathmandu. The proposal had been made by Chou En-lai to Koirala in 1960 but was turned down by the latter on the ground that it was not justified on economic considerations. Now it found a willing acceptor in Mahendra because he could kill two birds with the highway stone: he could please the Chinese and put pressure on the Indians and make them accept his autocratic regime lest he became a total Chinese stooge. There was a third motive too. The King wanted to tell the people of his country that he could win projects from China for Nepal's benefit, since a highway could be useful to Nepal, sooner or later.

**Pose of 'Neutrality'**

This was a time when a conflict between India and China over the boundary issue was reaching the climax and the hostilities broke out in October 1962 when Nepal assumed its famous pose of "neutrality"

To add insult to injury, the Foreign Minister, Tulsi Giri, told a Nepali paper: "Nepal's relations with India will remain close, ...Nepal has a six hundred mile border with China. China has now emerged as a great power. Friendly relations with the northern neighbour should be the natural aim of the country's foreign policy."[5] Mahendra in a consolation gift to India, however, said that the Nepali people are not ungrateful and treachery is totally alien to their values.[6] Nobody who knows the Nepali people could disagree with the royal observation but there was nothing in concrete terms that Kathmandu did which could have brought some solace to a harassed and humiliated New Delhi.

On the contrary, the King, who had already disregarded the Treaty of Peace and Friendship, which required consultations at a time when either side faced aggression, as India now did, followed by Nepal coming to India's help, extracted several concessions from New Delhi. First, Nehru had to forget that there ever was any Koirala in office in Kathmandu. Economic benefits were secured for his country by the King on transit trade with third countries and on access to the Indian markets. Mahendra also signed an agreement with Britain and the United States in 1964 on supplies of arms which were duly received in 1965. Both the western nations were, of course, aware of the Indo-Nepal Treaty under which Nepal had to get its arms supplies from India only but they were already seeking to dictate terms to New Delhi in the wake of the Chinese aggression of October-November 1962. India was, however, able to put its foot down and make Mahendra enter into a secret deal on arms needs of Nepal being met by New Delhi and only to the extent these could not be so met imports were made with India's help.[7]

The war with Pakistan in September 1965 again saw Nepal take a spine-like posture, although it could not maintain even for the sake of argument, that it could remain "neutral" or "non-aligned" between India and Pakistan. The fact that a professedly Islamic nation had invaded a predominantly Hindu but secular nation and Nepal itself had a 90 per cent Hindu population did not move Mahendra. Power politics and the balancing act could not have gone any further. After all, Kautilya had spoken of a weak King, wedged between two powerful kings also taking the help of a third country. So, what was wrong for Nepal to see India in distress even if the attacker was a Muslim nation?[8]

There is nothing on record to suggest that South Block, the headquarters of India's External Affairs Ministry, ever reminded

Kathmandu of its treaty obligations requiring it to come to India's help. We have already seen how during the Rana regime in 1948 Nepal sent some army contingents which were deployed by India on internal law and order duties and relieved the pressure on its own army at a time when the Nizam of Hyderabad had been seized by a day dream and wanted to be recognised as a sovereign King. The same Ranas were overthrown largely with Indian help and, of course, only India could restore the monarchy in Nepal which made it possible for Mahendra to seek friends elsewhere to spite India.

In 1969 Prime Minister Kirti Nidhi Bista thundered against India and openly sought the withdrawal of the Indian Military Group operating from the army headquarters in Kathmandu and of the Indian military personnel stationed in the checkposts on the northern border of the country with Tibet. All this could have been accomplished within the diplomatic system but Bista, under obvious Mahendra pressure, wanted to humiliate India and show to the Nepali people that the King was asserting Nepal's independence. India accepted the Kathmandu demands as she had no other option but often India has sought to retaliate by using the trade and transit leverage, as it did again in 1989 when a kind of blockade was enforced. The 1960 transit treaty was due for renewal but the renewal was prolonged and it actually came off in August 1971. The most favoured nation concept was introduced for the first time.

Both the King and his nominated Prime Ministers blew hot and cold as it suited them. The same Bista, back in power after a gap, signed with India in June 1972 the biggest foreign aid project of Nepal for the construction of the central sector of the east-west highway of Nepal bringing it to the Indian border town of Birganj. It was then estimated to cost Rs. 35.89 crore. The western sector was about to be completed linking Kathmandu with the western parts of the country. Bista incidentally had become Prime Minister again in April 1971 after a gap of a year. Bista's cabinet resigned in a few months in August 1971 because the King did not like the handling of the Rashtriya Panchayat elections, the system of sham democracy that Mahendra and his son imposed on the country for thirty long years. Bista was, however, back in power soon thereafter. His first resignation was occasioned by his failure to get elected to the panchayat.

The year 1971 saw India's regional prestige fully restored with the victory registered by its armed forces and by Indian diplomacy in the Bangladesh war of liberation against the Pakistani army. This was a crucial moment for Nepal which had so far taken advantage of a weakened India after the 1962 war with China and the Pakistani invasion of 1965. Nepal, of course, had made no secret of its support and sympathy for the dictatorial regime in Pakistan during the years and India had to protest against the Pakistan mission in Kathmandu being allowed to become a base for anti-Indian propaganda by Pakistan.[9] Many nations, their media and the people had showed open support for the Bangladeshis suffering under the jackboots of the Pakistani army but Nepal kept a discreet silence which signified that it was "neutral" or friendly to Pakistan. Mahendra also took a fairly long time to recognise Bangladesh. Surprisingly, Dhaka and Nepal became friendly later, after the assassination of the founder Mujib-ur-Rahman, and missed no occasion to needle New Delhi over issue like river waters. There are no permanent friends, only permanent interests, as they say.

Once again the question of any consultations with India, as provided in the treaty of friendship and the letters exchanged along with it, did not arise so far as Nepal was concerned. In another context we have noted how India brought off a diplomatic coup by entering into a treaty of friendship with the Soviet Union which bolstered India's position vis-a-vis Pakistan, China and the United States. The latter two wanted to help Pakistan in some way or the other when it was fighting a life-and-death struggle against the Indian armed forces but could not. The Chinese were, in fact, giving Kathmandu a lesson in "neutrality".

## REFERENCES

1. *China-South Asian Relations, 1947-1980,* Vol. II, R.K. Jain, p. 295.
2. *Nepal: Strategy for Survival,* Leo E Rose.
3. S.C. Nayak in *Nepal's Perception of India's role, in contemporary South Asia. ibid.*
4. *Ibid.*
5. *Gorkhapatra,* as quoted by S.C. Nayak.
6. *Ibid.*
7. *Ibid.*
8. That Nepal is not immune to the Hindu-Muslim problem can be seen from the extensive riots between the two communities in October 1971 in the Terai region; officially 19 persons were killed but local newspapers said 60 were killed, *Asian Recorder,* 1971, Vol. XVII.
9. *Asian Recorder,* 1971, Vol. XVII.

# 7

# SON FOLLOWS FATHER

The saying child is the father of man may not have proved true in the case of King Mahendra, who was as different from his father Tribhuvan as chalk is from cheese, but it came true in the case of Birendra who succeeded to the throne on Mahendra's death in January 1972. Some scholars have been inclined to treat him differently because of his western education and sophisticated approach. But if you go by actions and results rather than labels you have to recognise that Birendra carried on from where Mahendra had left. The only difference was the changed circumstances like the liberation of Bangladesh in the December 1971 war which strengthened the Indian position in the South Asia region immensely. Some of these changes, leading to Kirti Nidhi Bista even recognising the validity of the 1950 Friendship Treaty with India, which only in 1969 he had described as outdated, have been noted in the earlier chapter. It must be pointed out that the policy of partyless "democracy" in which the Rashtriya Panchayat, introduced by Mahendra, was looked upon as the embodiment of all the virtues of people's rule, was carried on by Birendra for 18 years.

India had invited Nepal to the March 1947 Asian conference convened by Nehru in New Delhi which showed that India considered Nepal as a free and independent country, although at that time the treaty of 1923 between Nepal and the British rulers of India was in force and Nepal was under British Indian suzerainty. By the treaty of friendship in 1950 India recognised Nepal as a sovereign, independent nation. With Bhutan India had signed a treaty in 1949, which is still in force and under which Bhutan is required to be guided by India's advice in its foreign relations. There is no such provision restricting Nepal's independence of action in the Indo-Nepal treaty. Yet assertion of an independent foreign policy has been a recurring theme of the pronouncements of Nepali rulers. This is more an indication of hypersensitivity and a failure to understand the true meaning of independence.

Birendra sometimes made statements to the western press which contradicted history and geography while they constituted the familiar assertions of a Nepali position intended to hurt India. Thus in 1973 he told the American magazine *Newsweek*: "The concept of a buffer state has become outmoded. Nepal is an independent country with independent relations with more than fifty countries of the world[1]. Nepal is not a part of the subcontinent. It is really that part of Asia which touches both China and India."[2] If you take this literally the King has no ground to stand upon in SAARC (South Asian Association for Regional Cooperation) of which Nepal is actually a proud member and has got even the permanent secretariat allotted to itself. If Nepal is not a South Asian nation what business has it got to be in SAARC? Like Afghanistan, it can be a good neighbour of some of the countries like India but certainly not in South Asia.

**The Equidistant Theory**

Birendra also forgot that while Nepal has a common frontier with China its almost entire trade passes through India and more than 25 per cent of it is with India itself. The statement is almost a parrot-like repetition of the old Nepali formula that the country is equidistant from India and China. These are the kind of statements which some scholars have taken up to make the point that Birendra had a different outlook from that of his father. Difference of degree yes, not of substance.

The statement was actually for American consumption and the consumption of the non-aligned nations which were to hold their 4th summit although the sentiments voiced were old cliches. In any case, this was not the sort of statement which would be welcomed by India.

Birendra lost no opportunity to assert his independence and to attack India for alleged "big brotherly" attitude while he had nothing but praise for China, belying the oft-repeated Nepali claim that it looked upon the two neighbours with an attitude of equality. He paid an extended visit in the company of the graceful Queen Aishwarya Rajya Lakshmi Devi to China and had meetings with Mao and the energetic and shrewd Chou En-Lai in December 1972. He visited India, along with the Queen, in October 1973 and made the usual platitudinous statements about Indo-Nepal relations. He had told the Chinese that Nepal would never permit its soil to be used against another country, an assurance to Mao that India could not hope to use Nepal as a base against China.[3] (These were the days of lack of cordiality between China and India and the Peking press picked up reports and comments from obscure Nepali journals and lifted other anti-Indian comments from time to time.) In India, the King spoke of the "common cultural and religious heritage of the two countries." He gave India no assurance on the score of security.

The Indian leaders were, of course, effusive in their statements of friendship for Nepal. President V. V. Giri (not to be confused with Nepal's own Tulsi Giri, off and on Prime Minister and Foreign Minister of Nepal, always anti-Indian and pro-Chinese) spoke at the banquet in honour of the King of the "open border of friendship between the two countries." In his reply, Birendra made no secret of the differences between the two countries but tried to rationalise them. He said: "With contiguous borders such as ours it is natural that differences arise from time to time. ... We should constantly endeavour to resolve our problems in a spirit of peace and amity keeping the friendship between our two countries in perspective." The officials put a brave face on the proceedings by referring to the "community of interests and similarity of approach" in the joint communique issued at the end of the King's visit.[4]

In an interview given to a pressman in Kathmandu in March 1974, Birendra claimed that there was now much more understanding between Nepal and India and the relations had improved after the exchange of visits. He wanted the relations to be mature and sober. He said Indians and Nepalis had played a part to make the revolution in 1950 a success (when King Tribhuvan was restored and democracy given an indirect recognition when a few Nepali Congress ministers, including B.P. Koirala were inducted into the government) but afterwards, "the big brother attitude "had developed. If the King was complaining of the days when the Nehru-appointed ambassador C.P.N. Singh was ruling the roost in Kathmandu, he was right. But with his replacement by the correct B.K. Gokhale and his successors behaving like normal envoys there was no complaint on that score. If the Indian foreign office sought to drive some sense into Nepali heads this could not be called a big brotherly approach. Yes, the tightening of the economic screw by India sometimes whenever the Nepali rulers and elite behaved in an anti-Indian fashion was a tit for tat policy and was, in this writer's view, not justified as it hurt the ordinary people more than the elite. But surely, action to protect one's interests cannot be termed as a big brother's approach.

**India's Rejection of Partyless Democracy**

The King himself recognised the validity of this truth when he added, "Perhaps that was inevitable. But we got over that." He had, however, another grievance, the one which the Nepali anti-Indian elements have always harboured against India. They have never made a secret of their dislike of the Indian media reporting or commenting on the suppression of democracy in Nepal, as they would do in any country relevant to India. Birendra said: "When my father abolished the party system in the sixties the repercussions and comments were not what the Nepalis expected from the Indian side."[5]

He was right in saying that the Indian side (meaning the Indian government) had reacted unfavourably to the partyless "democracy" which Mahendra and Birendra kept going for thirty long years in their country. Only to the extent that an elected Prime Minister was dismissed by the former in December 1960 and then had him immediately imprisoned had Nehru, as Indian Prime Minister, commented, as he had done when Gen. (later Field Marshal) Ayub Khan seized power in Pakistan in 1958. The Indian press is free and liberally exercise that freedom, often some sections of it attacking India, as we have seen. It would naturally be expected to criticise the seizure of power by the King in the famous "royal coup". That certainly is not an indication of unfriendliness towards Nepal as a country. The Chinese media are government owned and entirely under the thumb of the government and if they endorse every action of the King or keep silent on the murder of democracy in Nepal, that, per contra, is not a sign of friendship. In fact, the Chinese, like the Americans, prefer to deal with dictators rather than with elected representatives in their relations with foreign countries.

Nepal's hypersensitivity, as we have seen, led it to attack the internal affairs of India in Sikkim. This they regard as their privilege as the "small brother" perhaps. In any case, if the abolition of party government and dismissal and incarceration of an elected Prime Minister are internal affairs of Nepal then the developments in Sikkim, with the Sikkim Sangram Parishad, a Nepali outfit at that, campaigning for merger of their state with India and getting the approval of the government and Parliament in New Delhi to it, are surely India's internal affairs. But Nepal thought it wise to come out with official comments. Foreign Minister G. P. Karki said that Nepal was opposed to outside interference in the internal affairs of any nation[6]. Of course, Karki failed to realise that he was interfering in India's internal affairs.

The Chinese have been protesting off and on over the Sikkim merger and if the Nepali government of the day and some sections of the press also did it, it is easily understandable as reflex action. What was pinching the Nepalis was, of course, not merely the verbal Indian criticism, both at the government level and by the media, but the presence of the Nepali exiles in India. They were operating from Indian soil against the Nepali government and protesting against its suppression of democracy. This was indeed happening and often B.P. Koirala was in India whenever he was out of prison or released from detention in his home country. As we have noted, there has been a close connection between the Nepali nationalists and the freedom movement in India and if India can grant asylum to the Dalai Lama and his entourage and incur the wrath of the mighty Chinese it could also offer the hospitality of its soil to the Nepalis struggling to restore democracy in their country. Moreover, the Indo-Nepal border is an open one.

But it would be wrong to conclude that the democratic struggle was being waged from India. To be effective and successful the struggle has to be fought in Nepal and the student community which has always been in the forefront of any democratic movement was straining every nerve to see democracy restored in their country. The alumnus of the Tribhuvan University in Kathmandu were quite active and there was a mysterious fire in the Singh Darbar, the Nepali Government Secretariat in the capital, apart from other developments. The struggle was eventually a long drawn out one and largely a democratic peaceful movement, in which the Nepali Communists also joined. It finally led to the abolition of the partyless system of which Birendra had spoken so fervently. There was no talk of outside (Indian) interference when this happened in 1990 and even the hypersensitive Nepali leaders did not complain of it. The biggest change in Nepal after 30 years of dictatorial rule was brought without even a suspicion of the "ever-present" Indian hand.

The partyless system was a sacred cow of the Nepali Kings, Mahendra and Birendra, and the politicians who enjoyed its fruits becoming Prime Ministers or Foreign Ministers without any base in the country. Some scholars have written articles and books about this system although it was nothing but a negation of democracy. Thanks to it, Messers Bista, Tulsi Giri, Karki, Shreshtha and so on could hold forth against India so long as the King did not dismiss them from office. Of course, they headed the administration for a number of years and helped the two kings to carry on the affairs of the state at home and abroad but the fact remains that they represented nobody except themselves and they held office at the pleasure of the King in truth, not merely in a constitutional sense.

The Nepali people's affection for Indian leaders like Mrs Gandhi became fully manifest when she visited Kathmandu in February 1973 after a lapse of five years, while the euphora of the great victory of Indian arms in Bangladesh in December 1971 was still visible and in the wake of which the treaty of friendship was concluded between India and Bangladesh in March 1972. She was given a big ovation and the civic reception in her honour at the Tundikhel open air theatre was attended by a huge crowd of 80,000 odd people. She told a luncheon meeting, organised by Prime Minister Bista that there were no major outstanding problems between the two countries. "Our rich cultural heritage is the same. Many of our social and economic problems are similar." Even Bista had to recognise that, "We have remained good friends through all strains and stresses of current international history." It would be pertinent to ask Mr Bista how much he had contributed to this "good friendship"[7].

The elan of the relationship was, however, gradually lost sooner rather than later. Even a discreet person like Mrs Gandhi had to tell Tulsi Giri, now Prime Minister, on his visit to New Delhi in April 1976, that "our friendship with other countries need not come in the way of the friendship with between India and Nepal." Obviously she was trying to remove Nepal's unfounded misgivings over India's close ties with the Soviet Union which pinched Nepal because its Chinese friends did not like the Soviets at all. Also, she was telling Giri that India and Nepal could remain friends even while he hobnobbed with Peking. That there was a treaty of friendship between New Delhi and Kathmandu she had pointedly told Giri's predecessor Bista when she visited Kathmandu in February 1973.

Giri had obviously in mind the renewal of the trade and transit treaty which had expired and for which official level talks had been held but without any result. Nepal actually wanted two separate treaties on trade and transit at a time when Mrs Gandhi had imposed an internal emergency. All opposition was totally suppressed by her and she was looking askance at the world in general. The Nepal government had to wait for the Janata government to come to power in India following her defeat in the Lok Sabha elections in March 1977.

The Janata government not only believed in and practised good neighbourly relations with all of India's close neighbours in its bid to build bridges of friendship but some of its top leaders were also personal friends of the Nepal Congress leaders like B.P. Koirala. This led to some apparent friction at first because the hypersensitive Nepalis did not like even the highly respected Jayaprakash Narayan, the father of the anti-authoritarian movement which led to the Janata Party coming to power, telling them that Koirala must no longer be persecuted.

So, before the relations could become better they took a turn for the worse when Tulsi Giri made ablistering attack on India at a press conference in Kathmandu on May 24, two months after the Janata party came to power in New Delhi under Morarji Desai. He alleged that a full-speed "hate campaign in responsible circles" in India was under way "showing undue concern for the political system in Nepal". Without naming any Indian leader, Giri said that in recent weeks "the Indian press and other media of communication and prominent leaders of the erstwhile Socialist party have shown undue concern for the political system of Nepal, the alleged lack of democracy here and the fate of the people charged with criminal offences, whose cases are *sub-judice* and sundry matters." He was obviously referring to the continued incarceration of B. P. Koirala and some 1,100 other political prisoners. Trumped up cases were registered against them to justify the suppression of democracy, just as Zulfikar Ali Bhutto was executed after the military coup of Zia-ul-Haq in Pakistan on a charge of murder. Giri added that "these were matters of our internal jurisdiction and Nepal as a self-respecting nation could not tolerate interference from external sources."

**More Royal than the King**

This was a typical reaction from the Nepal leadership, open and bitter criticism of friendly neighbour India, refusal to see facts which indicated that the Janata government wanted more friendly and easy relations and was prepared to accommodate Nepal in most matters. Something which could have been settled through diplomatic channels was thus converted into a public issue. Giri wanted to show to the King that he was more royal than him, to the hypersensitive among his countrymen that he could be counted upon to stand for Nepal's self-respect, and indulge in the favourite Nepali pastime of India-baiting. This was amply proved because only a fortnight ago, on May 9, Foreign Minister Atal Bihari Vajpayee had declared that India had no intention of interfering in Nepal's internal affairs and this statement had been welcomed by the Nepali government.

This point was made when an official spokesman in Delhi reacted to Giri's attack. In highlighting an imaginary hate campaign Giri had made a statement which had certain ingredients "which could lead to avoidable misunderstandings". He also said that the Indian press was free and of late the public media were not controlled in their news reporting[8]. (He was obviously referring to the temporary freedom which AIR enjoyed at the time, something which was short-lived even while the Janata Party was still in power.) There was a clear distinction between the views of Jayaprakash and some of the other leaders in the heterogeneous and undisciplined Janata party. Its government did not wish to interfere in Nepal's internal affairs even in the matter of Koirala's release from detention.

Curiously, the King, who had mouthed the same parrot-like formulations about non-interference, in an interview with a Hong Kong weekly, the *Far Eastern Economic Review,* quitely released Koirala and let him go abroad for medical treatment (he was now suffering from cancer) to any foreign country of his choice after Jayaprakash had issued a public appeal to the King. But Birendra paid no attention to the latter's call for initiating the process of democratisation in his country.

Vajpayee visited Nepal in July 1977 and it was the first country he had gone out to for bilateral talks. He emphasised that India and Nepal had unique relations "founded in history, culture, tradition and religion, social and economic ties.[9]" He told the Lok Sabha in New Delhi on July 26 that he had told Tulsi Giri, now Foreign Minister as Bista had bounced back to Prime Ministership in the musical chair constantly played by the King. "The government of India would not interfere in the internal affairs of Nepal, for that matter, of any other country."

Not only the relations were getting better but the most controversial part, the Treaty of Friendship, was once again proving to be a source of strength to the two sides. Vajpayee told the Lok Sabha that during his talks in Nepal, "I reaffirmed that there is a treaty of peace and friendship between India and Nepal which has accepted that both countries would live in perpetual peace. The treaty and subsequent actions fully reaffirm the independence, sovereignty and territorial integrity of Nepal. I was happy to hear from my counterpart that Nepal would continue to honour that treaty and other commitments which both our countries have jointly entered into.[10]"

The Prime Minister Morarji Desai visited Nepal in December 1977 for two days during which many steps were taken to the satisfaction of Nepal. Desai set the tone for his visit by declaring at the Kathmandu airport that India would not falter in its resolve to be friendly to Nepal. Departing from the prepared text of his reply to the welcome speech, he said, "Even if people here or in India or elsewhere try to do anything to create misunderstanding between the two countries, India would not falter.[11]" His reference to those in India trying to create a misunderstanding was obviously an allusion to his own party leaders who were frequently issuing statements about Nepal's internal affairs. The joint communique on Desai's visit welcomed the fact that there was an "improved atmosphere conducive to beneficial cooperation in the entire Indian sub-continent.[12]"

The Indian side acceded to Nepal's long standing demand for two separate treaties, one on trade and another on transit to replace the 1971 treaty which had been due for renewal for two years and was hanging fire. The new treaties were signed in New Delhi by the Indian Commerce Minister Mohan Dharia, and his Nepali counterpart, Pitamber Dhajakhati, Minister of Industry and Commerce. There was also an agreement to control unauthorised trade which pinches India more than Nepal. The trade agreement enlarged the scope for Indian preferences for Nepali manufactured goods. The treaty of transit allowed Nepal the facility of overland routes for trade with Bangladesh. Nepal exported rice to that country in the same year.

The Indian government also broke with tradition and honoured a distinguished Nepali Gandhian leader. Tulal Meharji Shreshtha, who had done pioneering work for the uplift of the downtrodden in Nepal, by giving him the prestigious Nehru Award for International Understanding. So far it had been given to many western personalities or those who had earned honour in the western world, like U Thant (UN Secretary General), Martin Luther King, Yehudi Menuhim, Marshal Tito, Andre Marlaugh, Raul Probisch, Guiseppe Tucci, Mother Teresa and so on. Khan Abdul Ghaffar Khan, a great leader of the Indian freedom struggle, who had to remain in Pakistan as his North-West Frontier Province became part of Pakistan on the partition of the country, was one of the few exceptions. There are also some elder statesmen like President Nyerere of Tanzania. Now a Nepali commoner was honoured and that could not have but helped in making the Nepalis feel that India cared for them.

On one important matter, however, the Desai visit to Nepal failed to satisfy the Nepali ego, specially that of the King who had invented for his country on his coronation in February 1975 a Zone of Peace. This had been hawked by Kathmandu in world capitals and by now some 80 or more countries have said `yes' to Nepal's request for agreeing to the zone. It costs them nothing to do so. India has steadfastly refused to accept the proposal as it is in conflict with the provisions of the treaty of friendship. Both cannot co-exist. A treaty of peace has no meaning if India has to accept that Nepal is a zone of peace when it is India's duty under the treaty to ensure peace in the zone. The joint communique issued at the conclusion of Desai's visit to Kathmandu in December 1977 merely recorded the views of both sides. In other words, the differences were politely recorded. According to the communique, Nepali Prime Minister Bista recalled the proposal for a zone of peace which Desai said that he was fully of the view that peace must prevail in the entire area to which India and Nepal belonged.

After the idea was mooted by King Birendra in 1975 India's approval was sought on more than one occasion. It was clear that Birendra had come forward with the plan to counter the treaty which for some mysterious reason pinched the Nepali elite wanting to show off in the world. Several governments under the two kings have asked for a revision of the treaty informally but only in the era of democracy the short-lived Communist government of Man Mohan Adhikari formally asked for the revision without specifying in public what areas of it required to be revised. But before anything concrete could be done Adhikari lost his majority in the house. The King obliged him by dissolving the house at his request. This was overruled by the Supreme Court after which in September 1995 a coalition of the Nepal Congress and two other parties, under Sher Bahadur Deuba, of the NC, was formed. More about it in the next chapter.

Some scholars are of the view that the success of the Indian army and the air force which pulverised the Pakistani army in Bangladesh in just 14 days leading to the surrender of over 90,000 Pakistani troops and the creation of a sovereign Bangladesh, while China looked on, prompted the Nepali King to come forward with his peace zone proposal. He was keen that India should be checkmated in the South Asia region. Nepali hypersensitivity was again at play. India maintained that Nepal should clarify from which source it perceived a threat to its security. There has been no satisfactory reply but as we saw earlier the Nepali government had to clarify that the country would continue to honour its treaty obligations under the 1950 Indo-Nepal treaty, if these are valid.

There is no doubt that India has not tried to expose the real intention behind the Nepali plan in the world but has sought to diffuse it completely by not accepting it. But India's refusal to endorse the pet plan of the King only strengthened the resolve of Kathmandu to pursue the matter and portray itself as a victim of Indian highhandedness.

However things at home were getting too hot for the King to handle as he was cut off from the ground realities. But before we go on to that aspect, we have to take note of two developments having a bearing on Indo-Nepal relations. In November 1977, Bista opened the Indian-aided Kamala bridge, the second longest road bridge in Nepal, near Janakpur in the Terai region of the country. The bridge cost Rs. 4 crores (a fairly substantial amount at that times) and cut across the 1000 km-long east-west highway of Nepal which was another Indian aided project. The bridge is 638.50 metres long.

Bista made an extended visit to India in April 1978 and had talks with Desai and Vajpayee. He also visited a number of other places like Lucknow, Hyderabad, Trivandrum, Madras, Calcutta and Patna before leaving for home. The joint communique issued at the end of his stay in Delhi spoke of the "qualitative improvement" in the relations which were now characterised by trust and confidence[13].

**Things Hotting up in Nepal**

By 1979 things were getting hot in Nepal, Kathmandu was issuing restrictive orders and effecting arrests as the anti-Panchayat system agitation was gathering momentum. B. P. Koirala's movements were confined in April that year to Kathmandu valley which meant he could not go to the Terai region of his country nor indeed leave Nepal. Later that month senior leaders of the Nepali Congress, Krishna Prasad Bhattarai and Ganesh Man Singh, were arrested as reports of students in revolt against the autocratic rule were coming in. The Tribhuvan University closed its colleges in the capital and in Biratnagar in the Terai. The closure of the colleges came about after a fortnight-long strike by the students. As expected, there was violence in the capital and in some other towns.

Chandra Shekhar, Janata Party President, still the ruling party in India, in a statement condemned the house arrest of Koirala and the arrests of the other leaders. In a reflex action, Nepal lodged a protest through its ambassador, Vidyanand Jha, who handed it over to Foreign Secretary Jagat Mehta. But within just nine days, on May 9, Kathmandu reversed its arrests orders against Bhattarai and Ganesh Man Singh and they were released. The restrictive orders against Koirala were also withdrawn and his house detention was lifted. Koirala was firm in his views despite his declining health and said after his freedom was restored: "It is a delusion on the part of the King if he thinks that he can maintain his throne by sheer armed force.[14]"

All this should give the readers a fair idea that the Rashtriya Panchayat system was without any credibility and the people were yearning for a return to democracy which was smothered out of existence in 1960 by King Mahendra.

Meanwhile the brightest star in Nepal's democratic firmament, B.P. Koirala, died on July 21, 1982 within hours of his return home from Bangkok where he was undergoing treatment for his cancer. He had to prefer Bangkok because the United States was costly and India was ruled out because he would be accused at home again of being an Indian stooge if he was admitted to one of India's famed hospitals. He had striven for democracy in his country and played a leading role in the restoration of the monarchy in 1951 after which he became Home Minister in the coalition government. When Mahendra, for some inscrutable reason briefly played with democracy in 1959 and 1960, Koirala's Nepali Congress won 76 of the 109 seats in the Pratinidhi Sabha (where were the Bistas, Tulsi Giris and others at that time?) and he was Nepal's first elected Prime Minister for a year and ten months. He was then dismissed and imprisoned and the musical-chair politicians, functioning as King Mahendra's chosen Premiers, hounded him out of politics and finally the country. He, however, continued to be in the forefront of the struggle for restoration of democracy which was crowned with success eight years after his death.

Incidentally, another Nepali politician, who had gone to Bangkok for medical treatment, Dr. K.I. Singh, considered a maverick, also died in just three months. He was also a former Prime Minister.

There was much going and coming between the Nepali capital and New Delhi as contacts were kept up despite uneasy ties. King Birendra visited India soon after Indira Gandhi bounced back to power as the Janata party dissipated its strength in factional quarrels. President Zail Singh also visited Kathmandu and warned Nepal that unless South Asian nations built up mutual understanding and cooperation "outside forces would continue to exploit our differences." At a civic reception in Kathmandu he spoke of the binding religious and cultural relations but wanted that this legacy of history must be added to continuously.

An important outcome of Zail Singh visit was the agreement in principle to the setting up of a joint commission to strengthen the ties between the two countries but modalities were to be worked out later.

Giani's visit took place in July 1986 and within less than a year, in June 1987, an agreement was signed by the foreign ministers of the two countries, Shailendra Kumar Upadhyaya and N.D. Tiwari, for creating the commission to promote and coordinate economic cooperation between the two countries. The Commission met for the first time in Kathmandu in the following year and three sub-commissions were set up to on trade, economic and industrial cooperation and water resource management. India also persuaded Nepal in 1986 to drop the proposal to entrust to China the construction of the 200-km-long Kohalpur-Mahakali section of the east-west highway which was an India project from the outset. India provided, under an agreement, Rs. 50 crores worth economic aid for the project to compensate Nepal which decided not to avail of a World Bank loan for it. India was at that time still keen that China should not come too close to the Indian border under the guise of economic assistance to Nepal.

The make-believe world of India-Nepal relations in which one side hurls open or veild abuses against the other while some friendly activity continues to take place and the people-to-people ties are always good, was shattered by a series of developments in 1989. The trade and transit treaties between the two countries signed during the time of the Janata party rule were being extended from time to time but in March that year India informed Nepal that the two issues would have to be considered together. (The two treaties expired on March 23, 1989.) Nepal had been asking for two separate treaties and only during the Janata's rule this was acceded to. Nepal had entered into a deal with the Chinese for purchase of several anti-aircraft guns and other weapons which was a violation of the Indo-Nepal Friendship Treaty of 1950.

Now followed a series of retaliatory measures. The Kathmandu authorities had already introduced a work permit for Indians in Nepal working in hotels, factories and the trades. Both skilled and unskilled workers were affected and for good measures the Nepalis had also thrown in the Tibetans so as not to appear to be discriminating against the Indians. But restrictions on Indian workers in Nepal were against the letter and spirit of the friendship treaty. Now after India announced that only a single treaty would have to be negotiated, the Kathmandu authorities introduced a new tariff schedule for imports on April 11, 1989. This made Indian goods dearer than third country goods imported by Nepal through India territory. The economic restrictions introduced by India resulted in considerable hardship to the ordinary people of Nepal as kerosene and petrol became scarce commodities and petrol rationing was introduced. Indian supplies of these and other essential commodities were now routed only through two checkpoints.

The official spokesman of the External Affairs Ministry said in New Delhi that there was no intention "to cause discomfort or hardship to the people of Nepal" and it would be ensured that supplies of medicines and babyfoods as well as other essential items were not affected. Even if the intention was not to hurt the man-in-the-street the fact was that there were large queues even in Kathmandu for purchase of essential goods. The Nepali leaders, of course, blasted India and Foreign Minister Upadhyaya said India was "flexing its muscle at a small country like Nepal". He conveniently did not refer to what Nepal had done to snap its fingers at the big fellow, the work permits, discriminatory tariffs, and purchase of military equipment from China in violation of the treaty. Nepal, in fact, had withdrawn the import preferences for Indian goods. With the new restrictions as many as 100 commodities of export from India were affected including cotton textiles, powder milk, bus and truck chassis, tea, coffee, hand tools, bicycles and rickshaws. We have seen in an earlier chapter that Indian share in the bilateral trade has declined perilously from a peak level of 90-100 per cent to a quarter or a little more of Nepal's total imports.

The return to democracy in Nepal in 1990 and the formation of a non-Congress Janata Dal government in India (December 1989) had to be awaited for this vicious cycle of anti-Indian measures and an economic squeeze to be ended.

## REFERENCES

1. Nepal now has diplomatic relations with some 100 countries but many of them prefer to accredite concurrently their ambassador in New Delhi to Kathmandu.
2. As quoted by S. C. Nayak, *ibid*. The interview was carried by the *Newsweek* magazine of September 10, 1973.
3. *China-South Asian Relations, 1947-1980* ed. R. K. Jain, Radiant, Delhi.
4. *Asian Recorder*, 1973, Vol. XIX.
5. *Ibid*., 1974, Vol. XX.
6. S. C. Nayak, *ibid*., quoting *Rising Nepal*.
7. *Asian Recorder*, 1973, Vol. XIX.
8. *Ibid*., 1977, Vol. XXIII.
9. *Ibid*.
10. *Ibid*.
11. *Ibid*., 1978, Vol. XXIV.
12. *Ibid*.
13. *Ibid*.
14. *Ibid*., 1979, Vol. XXV.

8

# AGE OF DEMOCRACY

How the people rose in revolt against the Panchayat system finally in April 1990 has been referred to in previous chapters. The Nepali Congress took the lead in the movement for restoration of democracy, reminiscent of the MRD agitation in Pakistan against the dictatorship of Zia-ul-Huq. The Communists of different hues participated in it and thus reaped the benefit of popular support in the two elections that followed, the second one giving them the position of the largest single party leading to their brief honeymoon with power under Man Mohan Adhikari for a nine-month period in 1994-95. The NC, first under Girija Prasad Koirala, the third Koirala brother after Matrika Prasad and then Bisheshwar Prasad to become Nepal's Prime Minister, and then under the comparatively youthful Sher Bahadur Deuba, as Head of a coalition government, ruled for much of this period.

But first, there was an interim government under the elderly politician of the party, Krishna Prasad Bhattarai, soon after the popular agitation in April 1990 overthrew the Panchayat system. Deuba had been in the forefront of student agitations in the past and had been the founder of the Nepal Students Union. The students had always been active in the struggle for democracy in the past also and were the strongarm of the NC in the agitations launched under its auspices against the Panchayat system. That events in India influenced Nepal and vice versa has been seen by us in the previous chapters. The fall of

Rajiv Gandhi's Congress(I) party in the 1989 elections, leading to the formation of the Janata Dal government in India in December 1989 gave a thrust to the democratic movement in Nepal, although it may not be expedient for some people to point it out.

There had been several uprisings against the partyless system in the past and even a referendum had been held on it during the eighties. The nominees of the King merrily kept on ruling by flexing their sovereignty muscle at India and constantly playing the China card in relations with India. As in the days of Mahendra so in the time of Birendra the Prime Minister kept on changing after a few years although Tulsi Giri and Kirti Nidhi Bista managed to come back from oblivion. The people's anger was rising all the time and finally a massive agitation was launched in 1990 when even the Panchayat building was attacked and set on fire. Several of the members faced the fire of the people and the security forces had to ire upon the agitators killing some 50 of them in Kathmandu alone.

**Elections in 1991**

The Marich Man Singh Shreshtha government was dismissed by the King who installed a stopgap government under L. B. Chand while he invited Bhattarai, as the senior leader of the NC, to head an interim government before the first ever elections under a new and fully democratic constitution were held in 1991. His government included representatives of the Communists and two independents. Relations with India being a matter of top priority Bhattarai visited India in June 1990 and held talks with Vishwanath Pratap Singh who was then Prime Minister. The burning economic issues were settled and the *status quo ante* was restored in trade and transit as it existed before April 1981. On its part, Nepal cancelled the unfulfilled part of the contract for purchase of Chinese anti-aircraft guns.

The joint communique referred, for the first time in three decades, to the "unique, friendly and brotherly" relations between the people of the two countries and said these should be normalised and imparted "new dimensions and dynamism so as to elevate them to ever-rising levels of cordiality".[1] Both sides adhered to *Panchsheel* and said: "Nepal and India will fully respect each other's security concerns... Neither side will allow activities in its territory prejudicial to the security of the other. The two countries shall have prior consultations with a view to reaching mutual agreement on such defence-related matters, which in the view of either country, could pose a threat to its security."[2]

As noticed earlier, the troublesome economic issues were sorted out and the *status quo* was restored, pending the "finalisation of comprehensive arrangements", meaning new treaties which, as we will see, took some more time. But all the 22 points of entry for goods from one country to the other were restored along with routs specified for movement of goods. Nepal, on its part, agreed to restore tariff concessions for Indian goods and exempted Indian goods from the levy of additional customs duty. The work permit regulations were withdrawn.

As noticed earlier, the two countries had reaffirmed their commitment to the Friendship Treaty when the Foreign Minister of Nepal, Shailendra Kumar Upadhyaya, visited India and met I.K. Gujral, Minister of External Affairs. The two ministers agreed that the treaty would remain a bedrock of bilateral relations. Gujral visited Nepal in July and some more points were agreed to including additional points of entry into Nepal for third country tourists.

During his short-lived premiership, before the Congress(I) which had brought him to power pulled the rug from under his feet, Chandra Shekhar managed to pay a visit to Nepal which had a special place in his scheme for things. He dispelled Nepal's suspicions that India would interfere in its internal affairs or undermine its sovereignty. He and Nepal Prime Minister Bhattarai decided to set up a high level task force to prepare long term plans for bilateral economic cooperation. They agreed to restore some rail links. In his breezy style he told a newsman that India would have no objection to Nepal's purchase of arms from China but was wise enough to add, or prompted by a diplomat to say, he felt that there would be no need for it[3].

The two main factions of the Communist movement in Nepal, the Man Mohan Adhikari led Communist Party of Nepal (Marxist) and the Communist Party of Nepal, led by Madan Bhandari, merged in January 1991 into one unified party, called the Unified Nepal Communist Party (United Marxist-Leninist), and became a formidable force in the politics of the Himalayan Kingdom. But it failed to win a majority in the first elections in Nepal under a real democratic constitution. That honour went to the Nepali Congress but since Bhattarai himself failed to get elected, being defeated by Bhandari, G. P. Koirala became the Prime Minister. In a broadcast after assuming office Koirala spoke of maintaining strong ties with India as well as China but the Communists, the second largest party, attacked the treaty of friendship with India and called it an unequal treaty. The Nepal communists have always been pro-Chinese and generally anti-Indian whether in or out of office, although when inside the government they had to act more responsibly and speak with restraint.

Koirala made a fitting rebuttal in his reply to the motion on the King's address. He told the Communists to see the spirit of the 1950 friendship treaty and the 1960 trade and transit treaty rather than its letter. Nepal had equal friendly relations with India and China but because of the open border with India, religious affinity, cultural and social intercourse, high weightages in trade and commerce besides the age-old ties between the people of the two countries, the relations with India were more important. But he added: "Our relations with India and China will be guided by pragmatism."[4]

Towards the end of the year, G. P. Koirala visited India for a few days from December 5, 1991, when all the pending issues were settled. The Indo-Nepal joint commission had met two days before and when Koirala met Prime Minister P. V. Narasimha Rao the modalities of economic cooperation were worked out. Both Prime Ministers agreed to fight terrorism propelled from across the frontier, in which Pakistan specialises, and they showed awareness of each other's sensitivities in matters of security of their countries and in political developments. In concrete terms, once again Nepal was able to get two separate treaties, one for trade and the other for transit. The treaties came into effect immediately and met a long standing Nepali demand that trade and transit facilities be separated and governed by separate treaties.

In 1987, things were pretty bad and a kind of economic war was fought by the two countries when Nepal unleashed a series of measures including defiance of India by purchases of Chinese anti-aircraft guns and higher tariffs on Indian goods, apart from the work permit restrictions for Indians, all in violation of the 1950 treaty, and India enforced rigid restrictions on supply of essential commodities to Nepal, like petrol and kerosene, which badly hit the ordinary Nepalis. The Janata party, during its 2½ years rule had acceded to Nepal's request for two separate treaties but in the highly surcharged atmosphere of 1989 the Rajiv Gandhi government warned Nepal that only a single treaty would now be negotiated. Under Narasimha Rao, the Congress (I) party, however showed a changed and more relaxed approach and the fact that there was a democratically elected government in power in Kathmandu, as opposed to the autocratic regime of the King and his nominees, designated as Prime Ministers, contributed to this modified approach.

The Trade Treaty, now signed, is to be valid for five years, 1991-96, and contains the provisions of the earlier treaties. New facilities and concessions for Nepal's trade, have been incorporated in it. Customs duties have been reduced. The Transit Treaty is valid for seven years, 1991-98. The transit treaty incorporates simplified customs and other provisions for Nepali importers and exporters using Indian ports and other facilities. The two Prime Ministers also reached agreement on the hydel projects like Karnali, Pancheshwar and Saptakoshi which were hanging fire for years. An Indo-Nepal foundation to honour the memory of B.P. Koirala was agreed upon[5].

The bonhomie and relaxed nature of the relationship was evident not only in the extent and depth of agreements reached but also in the joint press conference addressed by the two Prime Ministers at the end of their talks. The statement issued to mark the end of the visit spoke of the utmost warmth, friendship and sincerity, as the hallmark of uniquely close traditional relations which were revived after a period of sustained anti-Indian propaganda. The foundations of this understanding and close relationship were actually laid when Bhattarai visited India in June the previous year and met Prime Minister V. P. Singh but the actual working out of details took time. The political situation in India was also volatile as Chandra Shekhar and his supporters collaborated with the Congress(I) to overthrow the V. P. Singh regime and install Chandrasekhar in power for a brief period. That brief delay gave a handle to the anti-Indian elements in Nepal to unleash some of their fire against New Delhi as the two trade and transit treaties took time in finalisation. But it must go the credit of the Narasimha Rao government, which came to power in June 1991, that within six months it sorted out all the problems and gave Kathmandu whatever it asked for.

Rao said: "We agreed on everything we discussed. This is a happy augury for working together in all possible fora." Not only Rao said that G. P. Koirala's visit had been very successful but the latter himself declared that he was going back home with great satisfaction. He said there was a package of agreements and something concrete to offer to the people of Nepal.

The NC government got involved in an internal feud between Bhattarai, who was out of office but had control of the party machine, and the Prime Minister. This led to the fall of the government as Koirala resigned fearing defeat in the lower houses of Parliament. In the resultant elections to the house in 1994 the Communists emerged as the largest single party and managed to form a minority government. When the NC, the Rashtriya Prajatantra Party, and the Sadbhavana Party forged an alliance and the Man Mohan Adhikari government of the Nepali Communists realised that its days were over Adhikari recommended to the King dissolution of the house so that he could continue as Prime Minister until fresh elections to the house were held in the end of 1995. Meanwhile the Supreme Court was approached and in a landmark judgement it struck down Adhikari's recommendation to the King to dissolve the house and the King allowing him to head a caretaker government. Following this judgment, in August 1995, events moved fast and Adhikari was voted out of power by the restored lower house. Under a younger leader, Sher Bahadur Deuba, a coalition of the three parties was installed in office by the King on September 4, 1995 and it also won a vote of confidence from the house, in the face of grim predictions of instability, including some in sections of the Indian press[6]. Deuba won a majority in the Pratinidhi Sabha, as the house is known, in September 1995 and the coalition continued in power thereafter.

To recapitulate, Nepal has had three governments since the first democratic elections and the formation of the NC government, under G. P. Koirala, on May 29, 1991. The Communists were at its throat throughout the period it was in office until it resigned to avoid defeat in the lower house and fresh elections were held on November 15, 1994, while a year and six months of the full term of the house was still to run. The Koirala government had to go, not because the Communists were accusing it at every step of being pro-Indian, but because of dissensions within the party.

**Communists came to Power**

In the mid-term elections in November 1994, the Communists emerged as the largest party and the NC supported them from the outside. For a minority government dependent on the goodwill of the NC, in particular, the Man Mohan Adhikari government showed remarkable ability to lay down new foreign policy objectives and went to the extent of asking for investment from Pakistan, of all countries. Islamabad had, of course, little to offer except more ISI agents who were already in Nepal in sufficient strength and the communists were going all out to promote anything which would embarrass India and indirectly help Pakistan.

All their calculations, however, went away when the NC decided to withdraw its outside support and the consequences have already been noted in the previous pages. The dissolved house being restored by the Supreme Court, a coalition of the NC, Rashtriya Prajatantra Party and the Sadbhavana Party under Sher Bahadur Deuba, was installed in power on September 11, 1995 and subsequently won a vote of confidence. Of the three parties in the coalition, the NC is pronouncedly pro-Indian although it stands for an independent foreign policy which Nepal can call its own. Of the other two, the RPP was critical of India when it was in the opposition as this posture comes naturally to many politicians and also evokes a good response in the anti-Indian press in Kathmandu. A statement lambasting India on some real or imaginary issue is sure to receive headline treatment in some vocal sections of the press. But now that it is in office and one of its senior leaders is Nepal's Foreign Minister, Dr. Prakash Chandra Lohani, it is remarkable that there has been no anti-India outburst from him or any other responsible person in the government. This was a common phenomenon under the late minority government of Man Mohan Adhikari. The third partner in the coalition the Sadbhavana Party is pronouncedly pro-Indian.

Nothing has particularly changed in Indo-Nepal relations except what we noted earlier when Koirala and Narasimha Rao reached agreement to Nepal's satisfaction in 1991. But scheming politicians do not need an excuse to make a provocative statement against a bigger neighbour as they used to do in the past. That this has not happened shows that anti-Indianism no longer pays. Even the Communists having been badly bitten by events which saw them temporarily in office have perhaps learnt a few lessons and would be able to see the events in their proper perspective.

One of the factors which may influence their thinking and that of others in Nepal is that India no longer feels threatened by China's presence in Nepal as it used to be in the past. India-China relations have seen remarkable improvement in the past few years, specially since the Janata government first made a move for improved ties and under the wise guidance of Deng Xiao-ping, the elder statesman, China began making friendly overtures at the about the same time and then Rajiv Gandhi, as Prime Minister, made a successful visit to China in 1988. One cannot call it a sea change and the troops are still in position almost check by jowl on the eastern, northern and western frontiers and the border problem has not yet been solved but the ties are certainly free of tension.

There is thus nothing which a Nepali politician can seek to exploit by accusing India of some anti-Nepal move or action and no government in Kathmandu can now try to play one against the other. The China card is thus not available to the Nepali leaders as the Indian security perception has considerably changed. Even if Kathmandu were so cussed as to award a contract to a Beijing corporation which would bring some Chinese in the Terai, close to the Indian border, it is unlikely to cause any ripples in New Delhi's South Block as India would no longer consider some Chinese presence close to its border as hostile activity.

This does not mean that everything is honky dory in Indo-Nepal relations. The denial of the right to own property in Nepal to Indians and other forms of discrimination that we have mentioned earlier continue to gall Indians and also the government although it may not react as a matter of policy. As it is the Narasimha Rao government has followed a weak-kneed policy with almost every country and if it puts up with insults from Nepal also it would cause no surprise among the knowledgeable. But, in reality, things are more or less on an even keel after a long time, although the pin pricks and insults which the big fellow has to put up with sometimes to keep the little man in good humour continuous to exist. Only a sustained programme to educate the people about India's role can help to exorcise the ghost of anti-Indianism from some Nepali minds and the media.

India will not only have to be large-hearted but also appear to be so. At the same time, firmness to protect Indian interests, if it is displayed in regulated measures, would help in restoring the image of this country. By way of economic aid and measures to help the people of Nepal, India has already done a lot but wherever a feeling of injustice or of taking advantage of a small neighbour persists that should be removed, if it is possible to do so.

Under an agreement between the two countries when Prime Minister Narasimha Rao visited Nepal in October 1992 the revolving or standby credit extended by India to Nepal was increased from Rs. 350 million to Rs. 500 million with a highly concessional rate of interest. For India, which herself is a developing nation and where about 35-40 per cent of the people still live below the poverty line, this is something of a sacrifice. Nepal must have received economic assistance from India worth Rs. 15,000 million, much of it for major infrastructural projects like Kosi and Gandak river valley schemes and the highways. Nepali students are studying in Indian Universities and colleges in large numbers and the Indian government has provided as many as 350 scholarships, although the preference seems to be for the expensive educational system of the United States. Essential goods have been supplied to Nepal at considerable cost to the Indian taxpayer and strain on Indian foreign exchange reserves, including petrol, kerosene, sugar, baby foods and the like. There is even a quota system for the supply of some of the essential commodities as though Nepal were a part of India and meeting its needs were an Indian responsibility. The trade has been highly preferential which is non-reciprocal, although elements in Nepal would always complain of Indian big-brotherly treatment[7].

There is a long and open border of 1,774 km between the two countries and this is the only international border of its kind in the world with no passport and visa requirement of any kind. People go in and out at will along with their accompanied baggage and some five million Nepalis work and live in India on terms of equality with Indian citizens. They can even compete for all jobs under the Indian government, except a few top jobs, while the 150,000 Indians in Nepal feel as though they are not wanted there. They are not allowed to open bank accounts. Indians cannot own property, as we have seen, register their vehicles or run businesses. As we have noted, some people circumvent the law and do it under a `benami' transaction, or a local name with a local frontman, but that is a matter of enforcement of law which is slack in many developing countries, including Nepal. There are cases where Indian firms have won contracts in open international bidding but they are deprived of these contracts. The letter and spirit of the Indo-Nepal Treaty of Peace and Friendship have been systematically violated and Indian representations to the Nepalis often fall on deaf ears. Not surprisingly, sections of the Indian press, which excel in sensationalism and even take potshots against their own country, endorse Nepali complaints that India is taking advantage of its bigness.

By 1967, when India had completed two decades of its existence as a free nation, as many as 13 road projects were completed in Nepal with Indian aid and participation, six airport projects, 15 irrigation and 24 water supply schemes along with three intensive river valley development programmes. Indian help has extended to education, with several major projects in Nepal's only university, the Tribhuvan University in Kathmandu, veterinary services, local development projects, geological and forestry services and so on[8].

**The Basic Facts**

People who talk of India taking advantage of Nepal in joint river projects—King Birendra himself once referred to it—are not aware of the basic facts. Some six thousand rivers and rivulets flow down from Nepal into India. Every year they carry away 174 million cubic metres of water and the total potential of hydroelectricity of these river flows in Nepal is about 83,000 mw but only 239 mw is generated so far. The first major project undertaken by India was the Kosi barrage in 1963 followed by the Gandak project in 1970. Both projects made a substantial contribution to the solution of floods in India and Nepal, apart from the irrigation benefits they conferred on both countries.

At Trishuli in Nepal India built a major hydroelectric project in 1962 when it began producing 21 mw. This was at a time when the total hydroelectric generation in Nepal was just 4.56 mw. In 1983, India also built the Devighat hydroelectric project to generate 14 mw of electricity. There are several other projects which are under study and some have also been taken up. As we said earlier, there could be cases in which the Indian side as the much bigger country took or appeared to take advantage of the smaller neighbour but to take a sweeping view and call it discrimination is, to say the least, not borne out by facts. Mostly it is a product of ignorance, prejudice and bias.

The criticism is fairly old but it would be interesting to note what the Nepal Prime Minister, M. P. Koirala, had to say about it. In a press interview he said, on June 5, 1954:

"If one is determined to misunderstand a very plain situation, nobody ever can help him realise the fact. India could have very well put the barrage a couple of miles below the present agreed site, if it had no consideration for Nepal. The sovereignty and territorial rights of Nepal have not been impaired by the Kosi project." He explained that Nepal had purchased land in India for a railway project just as India had purchased land in Nepal for developing the Kosi project dams without hurting Nepal's sovereignty."

Regarding the question of alleged interference by India, what M.P. Koirala had to say, in the same interview, is interesting: "Granting even (that) there were (Indian) advisers, it is for the Government of Nepal to accept their advice or reject it. I definitely know that those people who shout at the top of their voice about India's interference had sought the help of Indian advisers themselves to the extent of taking them into Cabinet confidence and associating them in every administrative execution. During recent times these practices have completely stopped and it ill behoves these very gentlemen now to cry about Indian interference."[9]

What Prime Minister Jawaharlal Nehru had to say about this interference at a New Delhi press conference—Nehru, unlike his successors, met the capital's press regularly, once a month—on February 18, 1952 is even more interesting: ... there are in Kathmandu at present numbers of small groups, may be, not more than half a dozen in a group. They call themselves political parties and some of these small groups criticise the government or talk about Indian interference. I do not think they really mean much by it except that they frankly say that they want to be taken in the government."[10]

## REFERENCES

1. *Asian Recorder*, 1990, Vol. XXXVI.
2. *Ibid.*
3. *Ibid.*, 1991, Vol. XXXVII.
4. *Ibid.*
5. *Ibid.*
6. See Ajit N. S. Thapa's letter to the Editor, *The Times of India*, Sept. 6, 1995, Correcting a number of wrong statements in its editorial of Aug. 31
7. This and other information in this chapter on Indo-Nepal economic relations based on data supplied by sources in Kathmandu.
8. *Documents on Nepal's Relations with India and China*, 1949-66, ed. A. S. Bhasin, Academic Books, Bombay, New Delhi.
9. *Ibid.*
10. *Ibid.*

# 3

# NEPAL-CHINA

# 9

# A BRIEF SURVEY

That Nepal lies between two big Asian nations, India and China, has by now become a cliche but one which remains valid all the same. To its south lies India, wherefrom it derives its religion and culture, to both of which Nepal has made a significant contribution. To its north lies Tibet with which it has had extensive contacts because of trade, history, ethnic and other similarities. In the eighteenth and nineteenth and part of the twentieth centuries, Nepal had more to do with Tibet because of the disunity and political instability in the country to its south at first. Then the British who got a firm foothold over the entire country sealed it off more or less from the north. The British even acquired the status of an overlord in respect of Nepal but paid some regard to its independence. Apart from Thailand, Nepal was one of the few Asian nations which was not ruled by the European colonialists.

Nepal, as it is known today, was founded in 1769 by King Prithvi Narayan Shah from whom the Nepali monarchs are descended. Prithvi Narayan was a powerful ruler, a conquerer and a consolidator in the sense that Sardar Patel united India after independence when he brought under the Indian flag 526 princely states ruled by the Rajas, Maharajas and Nawabs, and Bismark united Germany. From the kingdom of Gorkha in western Nepal he moved to Kathmandu. After his death in 1774 his successors pushed both towards the north and towards some adjoining parts of India in the south. In their southward push, they not only captured Kumaon and Garhwal hills and the Dun valley, now parts of India's Uttar Pradesh state, but also the Simla hills of the present Himachal Pradesh state of India. They also took possession of large parts of Sikkim, now a state of India. That Nepal could take a hand in Indian affairs was established long before some Nepalis started a campaign against "Indian interference." By the beginning of the 19th century the Union Jack was rising in the plains and hills of India and after their defeat in the Anglo-Nepal War of 1816 the Nepalis had to turn their attention more to the north than they had been doing. The British made them return to India the Kumaon and Garhwal hills, the Dun valley, the Simla hills and made them vacate Sikkim. The expansionist British also took away the Terai region from Nepal but it was returned after some time. This happened when the Ranas, ruling the country from 1846 to 1950, became friendly with the British and sent troops to help put down the armed rebels during the first war of Indian independence in 1857.

**Nepal's View of Tibet**

The descendants of Prithvi Narayan Shah made a thrust towards the north as Nepal always regarded Tibet as a kind of vassal. Tibet, on its part, was zealous of its independence of China and there was a kind of musical chairs when Tibet would only acknowledge the authority of the Chinese emperor in name and at times the Emperor would assert his authority. In 1791, the Nepali forces threatening Tibet were thwarted by China which came to the rescue of Tibet at its request. Consequently, the Chinese were able to force a treaty on Nepal in 1792 under which Nepal acknowledged the superior position of China and agreed to send a mission to Peking every five years. The treaty clearly said, "China should henceforth be considered as father to both Nepal and Tibet who should regard each other as brothers." [1]

In this context, the generally held Chinese view that all the countries on China's periphery, like Nepal and Tibet, were part of China was expressed by no less a person than Mao Tse-tung in 1939. He said that Nepal was among the territories taken away from China by the imperialist British. In his words :

"In defeating China in war, the imperialist powers have taken away many Chinese dependent states and a part of her territories. Japan took away Korea, Taiwan and Ryuku islands, England seized Burma, Bhutan, Nepal and Hong Kong; France occupied Annam and even an insignificant country like Portugal took Macao."[2]

The Nepalis of the eighteenth and nineteenth centuries were not the ones to take Chinese threats lying down and avenged their defeat in a war with Tibet in 1856 following which a humiliating treaty was forced on Lhasa. We will examine this and related developments in a subsequent chapter in greater detail. Suffice it to say here that the Ranas, who had put the real rulers in cold storage, were reasserting Nepal's traditional overlordship over Tibet.

By 1947 India became independent and the British authority departed. The situation to the north was full of uncertainties but in October 1949 the Communists were victorious in China and within a year they even "liberated" Tibet. A totally new situation was to be faced by the Nepalis, whether they were from the Rana clan or freedom fighter like B. P. Koirala and his associates. The Ranas were overthrown with India's help although they had signed a treaty of friendship with India. Indo-Nepal relations were close and cordial during the regime of the restored King Tribhuvan and during the 22-month interlude of democracy in 1959-60.

India had reaccredited its ambassador to China who was already accredited to the old Kuomintang regime in China when the Communists came to power and India recognised them within just two or three months. Nepal had no ambassador in China who could be reaccredited in this manner. In any case, Nepal had to recognise the red regime first. The Americans, the mightiest power on the earth, took full 23 years to say that Taiwan was not China and to recognise the Communists. For Nepal, however, the problem could not be shelved since China was sitting right on its border as by now Tibet had been taken by the reds. By 1953 the annual tribute of Rs. 10,000 paid to Nepal by Lhasa since 1850 was also stopped and under the new dispensation Tibet was not the same region that Kathmandu had known for many years.

It is in this context that the Nepali policy of balancing one country against another has to be viewed. For Nepal both the major countries to its north as well as south are relevant but it is often forgotten that India and Nepal have a common open border and the Nepalis freely move into and out of India as, indeed, Indians are free to enter and leave Nepal without passport or visa. There is no such free entry for Nepalis when they travel to Tibet or China. During all the time that both countries have vowed to be friendly to each other, neither has proposed that the border also be kept open. Neither has Nepal asked India to close its border. So where is the much flaunted "equality" the Nepalis say they practise in their relations with India and China?

Of course, the rules of rational thinking do not govern conduct of individuals or of nations and communities. Nepal was neither under any compulsion to recognise China, although it is a close neighbours. There is the example of Thailand and some other countries which are almost as close but which have thrown their lot with the Americans and finally took their own time to have dealings with China.

India was, of course, not opposed to Nepal having direct relations with China. After it had given up its rights in Tibet and recognised it as a part of China and even signed a treaty with China in April 1954. India told Nepal, as if the signal was not enough, that it had better mend its fences with Peking. The groundwork was laid during the time of King Tribhuvan for establishing diplomatic relations with Peking. But the coming to power of King Mahendra, who always saw India as a thorn in his side, speeded up the process. A new chapter opened in Nepal's external relations as in its domestic affairs with his accession to the throne. He viewed China not merely as a country with which Nepal must have friendly and good neighbourly relations but also as a card. Which he could play against India just as the Congress (I) and some other political parties in India, think of the Muslim voters as a card, not as individuals. Nepal has always looked at the problem through tinted glasses, not in a natural way.

**No Formal Ties**

When the Communists emerged in China in October 1949, Nepal had diplomatic ties only with India, Britain and the United States. If it is argued that China being its next door neighbour Nepal must have diplomatic ties with it, then how come so long Nepal had no formal relations with China? It could have had relations with any country, unlike India which was under colonial rule until 1947. But relations had to be established and after India entered into an undignified treaty with China over Tibet, Nepal had also to make peace with the Communists in China and recognise the "liberation" of Tibet. When the much bigger India had abandoned its rights in Tibet and bowed to the Communists how could Nepal lag behind in doing its obeissance to the Chinese Communists. Mahendra's advent hastened the process and he had other ideas. He and his Prime Minister, the leftist and China-loving Tanka Prasad Acharya perceived China as a key with which they could unlock the imaginary Indian grip on Nepal's foreign policy. Mahendra thereby opened the doors of his own foreign policy of baiting India with his contacts with China while he could extract the maximum benefits from India.

Many scholars have fallen for the balancing theory and the strong willed Mahendra trying to get even with New Delhi by using the China bogey. Not many have, however, bothered to find out if the king was upto something more. He knew that however much he disliked India he could not wish away the facts of geopolitics. So he made full use of India and exploited its relationship with Nepal to the best advantage of his country, using the friendship with Peking as a card with which to beat down the Indians and extract from them the best benefits. It was not merely a question of survival of a small and weak state trying to make the best of a bad situation. India, as a matter of fact, has been treated by Mahendra and those who think along his line as a milch cow which begins to lactate the moment it is made aware of the presence of the red dragon.

The diplomatic relations were established in 1955 and thus followed regular visits by the VIPs of both sides and a number of others who are much lower down in the protocol. The fact that this opened the main door of keeping India under check was never lost sight of by Mahendra and his son Birendra. Geopolitics need not have the same meaning for everyone. It has substantially different meanings for different people, including the main players.

## REFERENCES

1. *China-South Asian Relations*, Vol. I, R.K. Jain, Radiant, Delhi.
2. *Ibid.*, R. K. Jain. References to Nepal, Bhutan, Burma, Korea the Ryuku islands and Annam were deleted in the subsequent editions of the Mao book. Annam is the old name of Vietnam. Like all well educated Chinese, Mao also had a proper imperialist outlook but politics and diplomacy dictated that the neighbours need not be unduly frightened. Incidentally, Communist China has not bothered to take back Macao, from the "insignificant" Portugal in the last nearly 50 years.

# 10

# TIBET : TRIBUTARY STATE

In 1791-92, the Chinese Emperor in Peking came to the aid of Tibet when it was under repeated attacks by Nepali forces. His officers and representatives, more aware of the ground realities, were apparently not in favour of rushing military help to the Tibetans but the Emperor finally sent down a force from mainland China and a trusted commander, Fu Kang-an, which even invaded Nepal. Chinese history which Mao Tse-tung relied upon in his famous observation we have referred to earlier, has several such examples where the central Chinese authority has sought to establish its hegemony over the neighbours.

The force inflicted heavy losses on the Nepalis who fought back and succeeded in bogging down the Chinese Tibetan combined force. But both sides were exhausted, the Nepalis more than the Chinese-Tibetans, and finally the treaty of 1792 was signed. The proud Nepalis were able to ward off the Chinese demand that the minor Raja and his regent go in person to sign the treaty. But Nepal recognised Chinese overlordship and sent a mission every five years, agreed to under the treaty, to Peking as acknowledgement of it. This practice was continued for a long time and after diplomatic ties were established between China and Nepal in 1955 the practice was continued in another form—the frequent visits of the head of state and government to Peking, offset by the Chinese President and Premier's trips to Kathmandu.

The history of the late eighteenth and nineteenth centuries clearly establishes that the Nepalis were trying to seek new pastures north and south of their country. In the South, however, the rise of the British power thwarted their moves and the rulers made peace with them. But the Nepalis, however, could not reconcile themselves to the status of equality with the Tibetans and renewed their efforts to bring Tibet back under their thumb. The powerful Jang Bahadur, who assumed overall powers in Nepal and established the Rana regime which lasted until 1950, mounted an invasion of Tibet and the army reached Lhasa by way of the Kuti and Kerong districts which hold the easier of the many mountain passes between Nepal and Tibet.

**Treaty of 1856**

China did nothing this time and the Nepalis were able to force their terms on the Tibetans under a treaty in 1856 which included an annual tribute of Rs. 10,000 from it. Tibet regularly paid this tribute to Nepal right up to 1953 but after that the Nepalis were told to contact Peking for future payments. By that time, India had made a treaty with China on Tibet signing away all its special rights in Tibet and is believed to have advised Nepal also to follow suit. Jang Bahadur had discontinued the five-yearly mission to China for a while in the mid-nineteenth century but later on he realised that Nepal must not lean too much on the British which was his policy, and contacts with China must be maintained. Additionally, the ruling elite also knew that they were allowed to take a number of duty-free commodities for sale in China and this was a highly lucrative business. (Very much like the entourage of some West Asian dignitary bringing in gold into India in the early years of independence and selling it at high profit to the gold-crazy Indians.)

The 1852 Nepali mission to China carried with it opium worth Rs. 300,000,[1] a sizeable amount those days, for sale under its diplomatic privileges. So, after all the British and other western colonialists were not the only ones who sold opium to China. How else could the Nepalis show their affection for the friendly Chinese except by selling opium to them, just as Pakistani drugs reach China nowadays, via international routes, as a token of the eternal friendship between the two countries.

Quite apart from it, the fact has to be recognised that when the Nepalis feel that Tibet was their tributary state for a long time they cannot be faulted. We have referred in an earlier chapter to the Nepali view, as expressed by no less a person than B. P. Koirala, when he was Prime Minister, on how the people of his country viewed Tibet. In a statement at a press conference in Kathmandu on August 11, 1959, Koirala said:

> "Nepal could no longer afford to ignore the defence of her 500 mile-long northern border. Before the situation changed in Tibet (evidently referring to the changes brought about by the advent of the Chinese there), the northern border did not pose any problem even from the defence point of view. Tibet paid us a tribute and we enjoyed extraterritorial concessions there. Historically speaking we had some suzerainty over Tibet. We have now to look after two frontiers. The defence of the north would cost more than that of the southern frontier with India. The army personnel has to be paid special high altitude allowance and they had to be specially equipped to withstand the rigours of the climate at high altitudes".[2]

What we are concerned here is with the popular concept in which is embedded the feeling that Tibet had been for a long time a vassal of Nepal, something which the treaty of 1856 and the annual tribute paid by Tibet right up to 1953 fully testifies. What happened subsequently is part of contemporary history as both India and then Nepal made their peace with the Chinese over Tibet and acquiesced in the Chinese occupation of Tibet by recognising it as an "autonomous" region of China.

The 1856 Nepal-Tibet treaty is an interesting document (which is reproduced in the appendices). It also contains a clause about extradition although only the offence of murder is mentioned under Article 8.

> "A Gorkha subject who goes to the country of Tibet after committing murder of any person of Gorkha shall be surrendered by Tibet to Gorkha; and a Tibetan subject who goes to the country of Gorkha after committing murder of any person of Tibet shall be surrendered by Gorkha to Tibet."

Incidentally, Nepal was still known only as Gorkha in that period. Under this clause both parties have been granted equal rights and both are referred to as countries or states in some translations. In another clause which is, in fact, the preamble to the treaty, China is referred to although China had no role to play in the war which the treaty brought an end to. It says, "The Emperor of China shall continue to be regarded with respect as heretofore." In another translation this is rendered as "We further agree that the Emperor of China shall be obeyed by both States as before." China is thus the overlord for both. The situation was a shifting one insofar as Tibet was concerned and as for Nepal the only sign of overlordship was that a five-yearly mission used to be sent to Peking by the Nepalis.

Another interesting detail of the treaty is that disputes relating to trade between the merchants from both countries were supposed to be settled jointly but the fees and fines realised from the Nepali merchants were to be taken by the Nepal representative only.

"... In the event of dispute between the subjects and merchants of Gorkha and those of Tibet the Bharadars of both Gorkha and Tibet shall sit together and jointly adjudicate the cases. All incomes (fines, etc.) from such adjudications realised from the Gorkha subjects and merchants and Kashmeries shall be taken by Gorkha" [3].

The mention of "Kashmeries" among the merchants of Nepal would indicate that the doughty traders of the beautiful valley of Kashmir from India were present in Nepal and were going to Tibet from there, selling goods manufactured by their famed craftsmen and by others in India which they would buy before going on to Nepal. Being climatically from an extremely cold region the rigours of the weather in Tibet would pose no problem for them. This was, of course, not the case for the hardy Sikh soldiers in the Nepali army who fought alongside the Nepali troops against the Tibetans. They hailed from a region of India which is quite cold in winter but not so cold as are the high mountain reaches of Tibet. In the relevant article on the return of prisoners of war the treaty says:

"Tibet shall return to the Gorkha government all Sikh soldiers held as prisoner and also all officers, soldiers, women, and guns of Gorkha that were captured and taken during the war and the Gorkha government shall return to Tibet all the soldiers of Tibet captured in the war as also all the arms yaks...."

Tibet was also forbidden to levy any duties and taxes on the Nepali merchants and that would certainly include the Kashmiri merchants coming from Nepal into Tibet. The treaty is a curious mixture of equality in several respects and special treatment to the Nepalis in some others. The equality is only a reflection of reality. For example, the goods of any trader plundered in either country were to be returned to him by the efforts of the government concerned and if necessary the plunderer was to be compelled to restore the property.

All this goes to emphasise the importance of trade in the relations between Tibet, as it existed then, and Nepal. The Nepali traders and others like the "Kashmeries" listed in the treaty of 1856 were interested in bringing goods from India and Nepal to Tibet and carrying its produce for sale in these countries. Even the trade between Tibet and India was to be a Nepali monopoly. A number of people in Nepal depended on the trade with Tibet for their livelihood and while in the case of the British the general policy was that the flag would follow the trade (the British would come in as mere traders and stay as conquerers) in the case of Nepal trade by itself was certainly an important factor in its traditional relationship with Tibet.

Tibet has however, been more or less a closed book for the Nepalis since the Chinese came to power and sealed off all routes of trade and commerce. When the Dalai Lama fled his country and sought asylum in India, along with a body of his officials and followers, some refugees also went to Nepal. Thus S. P. Upadhyaya, Home Minister in the B.P. Koirala Ministry, told the United Nations General Assembly on October 20, 1959, while opposing the motion for placing Tibet on its agenda (an obvious American move to embarrass China) :

"The Dalai Lama has left Tibet and gone to India and received political asylum there. There has been an influx of Tibetan refugees into India and Nepal. For example, about a thousand refugees have come into Nepal from across the Tibetan border. These are the events that lie in the background of this question of Tibet. It is the Government of the People's Republic of China that is believed to be responsible for these events, but that government still remains unrepresented in the United Nations."[4]

Now instead of trade, Nepal had to face the problem of providing for these refugees from Tibet. The situation was sought to be remedied somewhat by a treaty which Nepal signed with China, now the supreme authority in Tibet, in May 1966 for a ten-year period, extended further in 1976. Under this agreement, movement across the border is regulated by passports and visa, except in the case of border residents who also must report at the border checkposts or the nearest officials. In the past, the real trade was carried on between the Nepalis merchants in Kathmandu and other major centres and the Tibetans of Lhasa or important border towns. But even in 1960 there was not much trade between the two. Thus B. P. Koirala told the correspondent of the *Far Eastern Economic Review* of Hong Kong on May 26, 1960, in Kathmandu when questioned about his reaction to the proposal for a Chinese-built highway from Kodari, on the Nepal-Tibet border, to Kathmandu:

"I have on various occasions explained that road building projects are undertaken with reference to the economic benefit which each project may produce. We have not yet received any proposal from China to build a road from Nepal to Tibet. Such a project will be initiated when our trade grows to such an extent as would justify a road. The question of reacting coolly to the Chinese proposal does not arise in this context".[5]

Koirala stated in plain language that trade between Nepal and Tibet did not justify a road (and he was not interested in a road for propaganda purposes). In fact, the trade had declined and that was bound to happen with the Chinese seeking to meet themselves the needs of Tibet and there were several hindrances in the way of the Nepali traders wishing to enter into trade relations with their counterparts in Tibet. Trade, in fact, was a major casualty of the arrival of the Chinese in Tibet. That the road was eventually built by the Chinese and the question of economic necessity was ignored after the Koirala regime was overthrown and King Mahendra became supreme is a different matter.

Trade has thus been a major casualty of the Chinese occupation of Tibet, apart from the suffering of the Tibetans themselves. No doubt, the special privileges enjoyed by the Nepalis and some by the Indians would have been abolished sooner or later, as they were not consistent with the modern concept of equality of nations, but the trade between Nepal and Tibet need not have been reduced to almost nothing. Yet, the anti-Indian elements in Nepal have never been known to have objected to this development. Once their forefathers went to war with Tibet and secured trade rights in particular. Now their extinction was not even mourned. Long articles and books have been written about Chinese economic assistance to Nepal but not much has been said about the deprivation of this legitimate livelihood of many Nepalis by the fact that Tibet is now under China and the fact is accepted by Nepal and India.

On the other hand, the Indo-Nepali border has continued to be open and trade not only flourishes but Nepal has also been enabled to develop and diversify its own international trade to India's detriment as we have seen. Indian trade with Nepal, which was once almost 100 per cent of Nepal's total trade, has been reduced to a little over a quarter. Some increase may have been recorded in the recent past but that does not explain or offset the decline the trade has suffered. Hari Bansh Jha, a Nepali scholar, says in his book *Duty Free Border Trade :*

"... despite the concessions given by India to Nepal, India's share in Nepal's total volume of trade has declined .... Between 1956-57 and 1993-94 the deficit in the balance of trade shot up spectacularly by nearly 2.6 fold, which by all accounts in an unhealthy development .... One of the reasons for substantial decline of India's share .... is the policy of trade diversification that Nepal has adopted, since 1962-63.

The policy which was politically motivated laid emphasis on diversifying the country's trade away from India to third countries." [6]

Jha goes on to argue, with facts, that the huge trade deficit in Nepal's trade with India has been met to a great extent by the invisible earnings of Nepal from India like the remittances made by the Gurkha soldiers of the Indian army, other Nepalis working in India, the earnings from the Indian tourists, who throng Nepal all the year round and the excise refund. He also makes the point that the trade treaties on which successive Nepal administrations have laid so much emphasis and at times made them the subject of a political struggle against India have not helped Nepal very much. This he says is due to the lack of integration of the economies which hurts both countries.

## REFERENCES

1. Leo E. Rose, *Ibid.*
2. *China-South Asia Relations*, R. K. Jain, *ibid.*, p. 301.
3. R. K. Jain, *Ibid.* Bharadars are the high civil and military officers under either government.
4. *Ibid.*, R. K. Jain.
5. *Ibid.*
6. *Duty-free Border Trade and Special Economic Zone between Nepal and India*, ed. Hari Bansh Jha, Centre for Economic and Technical Studies, Kathmandu.

# 11

# NEPAL'S CHINA CARD

Coming to modern times, King Mahendra, who ascended the throne on his father's death in March 1955, was keen to play the China card as soon as possible to cut India to size. For that Nepal had to have diplomatic ties with China the ground for which had been prepared even earlier. The first official indication that the ties were to be formalised came in Chinese Prime Minister Chou En-lai's report to the first session of the first National People's Congress of China on the work of his government. That was in Peking on September 23, 1954. Chou said: "Contacts are being made with a view to establishing normal relations between China and Afghanistan as well as between China and Israel. Our country is also ready to establish normal relations with Nepal."[1] Interestingly, he did not make any cordial reference to Nepal and called the country just "Nepal".

It was obvious that in Mahendra's scheme of things the establishment of relations with China would have top priority. He built upon the favourable ground created during his father's time and the matter now received the necessary fillip. Within five months of his assuming the monarchy, the delegations of Nepal and China which were discussing the modalities of the establishment of relations reached accord on August 1, 1955 and a joint communique was issued in Kathmandu. It said the negotiations between the two delegations carried on in the Nepali capital on the issue had "now concluded successfully[2]". The two countries agreed to exchange ambassadors and, apparently as a concession to Chinese propaganda, they swore by the five principles of peaceful coexistence, saying these "should be the basic principles to guide their relations." The five principles are : mutual respect for each other's territorial integrity and sovereignty; non-aggression; non-interference in each other's internal affairs, equality and mutual benefit and peaceful coexistence. The Chinese already had an ambassador in Delhi who was immediately accredited to Kathmandu on a concurrent basis. He presented his credentials to Mahendra on August 3, two days after the joint communique on the successful conclusions of the negotiations was issued. (The envoy had actually helped fashion that accord.) The usual platitudes of friendship were mouthed including a bow to the five principles. Realising that the establishment of embassies would take some time, they agreed on September 20, 1956 that "for the time being" their respective ambassadors in India would also be their envoys to each other's country. The setting up of embassis seems to have taken somewhat longer and when the two countries were engaged in the bitter controversy created by the Mustang border incident in which the Chinese troops killed a Nepali soldier, the two Prime Ministers, Chou and B.P. Koirala, lamented that they did not have full-fledged embassies in each other's capital. This deficiency was perhaps made good when Mahendra made a state visit to China in October 1961. In any case, the road from Kathmandu to Peking lay through Delhi.

**Nepal's Sinophiles**

The lack of the facility, however, did not dampen the spirits of ardent Sinophiles like Premier Tanka Prasad Acharya whom Mahendra had chosen to head the government after he became King. Within days of taking over in January 1956, Acharya sounded the deathknell of "special relations" between Nepal and India at his first press conference. He was shrewd enough not to annul the open border with India. The Nepalis have always had self-interest at heart and did not wish to throw the baby out with the bathwater. Acharya announced that Nepal would have direct trade relations with third countries.

Acharya undertook an extensive tour of China from September 26 that year. But a few days before that a treaty was signed by the two neighbours in Kathmandu on Trade and Intercourse between Nepal and the Tibet region of China. This wats the first of two such agreements and Nepal thereby signed away its rights and the rights of its merchants who had extensive trade with Tibet. Now they had to hold passports and obtain visas before venturing out on trade but mercifully the border people were exempted from this rigorous provision. On the contrary the border with India was and is still open, although some elements would talk of "equality" between the two neighbours and accuse India or maltreating Nepal.

Nepal had to agree to the withdrawal of its military escorts from Lhasa and other places in Tibet. This was to be accomplished within six months of the treaty being signed. Nepal ordered the withdrawal of its personnel within the stipulated period although the treaty was not yet ratified. Such was the concern which Kathmandu had for Chinese susceptibilities and such was its anxiety to prove that it would abide by the treaty obligations even before it had received ratification. The treaty itself was in the form of letters exchanged between the Nepal's Foreign Minister, Chuda Prasad Sharma, and the Chinese envoy Pan Tzu-Li, who was apparently in such good books of Peking that he could negotiate major treaties like this one.

Acharya's first visit to China resulted in some economic aid and the pro-Peking elements made much of this bounty conveniently forgetting the sad blow to Nepal-Tibet trade. The pattern made familiar during the regime of Mahendra and later by his son King Birendra was now followed and Acharya was sacked after he had fulfilled his assigned role and was replaced by Dr. K. I. Singh who was more pro-India than pro-China. However, he also lost his coveted office when Mahendra mysteriously opted for democracy for a while in 1959-60. Since democracy is no respector of former nominated or elected Prime Ministers, Acharyas and their ilk fell by the wayside as the Nepali Congress party of Koirala swept the polls in the elections. Koirala became Prime Minister but he did not enjoy full powers as he had to fall in with the King's wishes on many matters.

He had to hold the balance even between India and China but he made no secret of his close links with India. When Nepal's interests demanded it, he took a strong stand on such issues as the Chinese claim to Mount Everest and the Mustang incident about which we will speak in detail in subsequent chapters devoted to them. Obviously, Koirala's pro-Indian approach did not suit Mahendra's grand scheme of playing India against China and he was dismissed on December 15, 1960 even while Koirala had a big majority in Parliament. He and his colleagues were arrested and Mahendra made it plain that he did not like democracy at all. His dislike of Koirala was also obvious but to what extent Koirala's stiff attitude to Chinese aggressive postures contributed to it is difficult to say.

Koirala's tenure as Prime Minister laid several important steps in developing relations with China which we have to take note of here. He visited China in March 1960 and this was reciprocated soon after, in April that year, by Chou En-lai. During his Peking sojourn, Koirala and Chou signed a Boundary Agreement under which a joint committee was set up to work out a detailed boundary agreement to be signed after the delineation and demarcation of the boundary on the ground. Importantly, it was also provided that a 20-km wide demilitarised zone would be created on the border but China violated it even before the ink on the accord had dried out, on June 28, 1960, at Mustang. Perhaps while the Boundary Agreement adorned the Chinese foreign office's Nepal Bureau the soldiers on the border had not been told of it.

Chou's visit in April saw a more detailed and elaborate peace and friendship treaty between the two nations on the 28th of that month. The spree of signing treaties confused some people and this was reflected in a question put to Chou En-lai at a press conference he addressed in Kathmandu a few hours before he and Koirala signed the treaty.

"*Question* (Ramesh Nath Pandey, Correspondent of *Janata, Commoner* and *Nepal Times*): In 1956, China and Nepal (had) already signed a treaty on the basis of the five principles and now they are going to sign a new one. Does this mean that the previous treaty is no longer valid ?

*Answer*: In 1956, China and Nepal only concluded an agreement on trade and intercourse between the Tibet region of China and Nepal. The treaty of peace and friendship to be signed now is a political treaty of a broader scope between the two countries. It will bring the relations of friendly cooperation between China and Nepal to a new phase[3]".

The new treaty, signed by the two Premiers, bound the neighbours to "maintain and develop peaceful relations". Twice the treaty mentions that disputes will be settled by negotiations but the second time this is mentioned in the context of interpretation of the treaty, and the negotiations are to be conducted through normal diplomatic channels. The treaty did not specify for how many years it would be in force but it provides for a notice of a year for termination of the treaty by either side. The question, quoted above, to Prime Minister Chou by a Nepali journalist, however, indicated not only the confusion caused by a plethora of treaties but also the mental make-up of the educated Nepali who was keenly aware of the treaties entered into by his country with important neighbours. If you ask an average educated Indian how many treaties India has signed and with whom, he might not be able to quote more than one, at best.

Koirala believed in advancing the cause of his country and while he entered into the two treaties he did not mince words when the occasion demanded it. His predecessor, Tanka Prasad Acharya, was different. While in Delhi in September 1956, four weeks before he was to go to China on his first ever trip, he claimed that his "coming visit to China would not affect the neutrality of his country". But the moment he set foot on Chinese soil he was gushing with words which only a fellow traveller could utter: "The Chinese revolution of our times has attracted the attention of the whole world. But what has produced a deep impression on the people of Asia is the resurgence of China and the awakening of the Chinese people.... the tremendous national reconstruction that China has done in the course of these few years and her great achievements in the field of national development."[4]

Not surprisingly, the hard headed Chinese also responded in kind to such expressions of servility and made some astounding statements in response. At a banquet in honour of Acharya in Peking Chou said: "... our Socialist system completely precludes the possibility for China to launch aggression against any country. In our relations with Nepal in the future, we will prove by deeds that we will strictly adhere to the five principles of peaceful co-existence, *Panchshila*."[5] His thesis that socialist countries never commit aggression was disproved by China's attack on India in October 1962 and the claim that the five principles would guide China in its relations with Nepal was set at nought by what happened at Mustang.

**Mahendra's First Pilgrimage**

King Mahendra, after he had quietly put Koirala and his associates in prison, paid the first of several visits to China in October 1961. This was the time when the relations between India and China were at their lowest ebb and within a year a regular war was to be fought between the two big Asian nations but Nepal maintained its "neutrality" which was another name for selfishness. Although the Indo-Nepal Treaty of peace and friendship required mutual consultation in the event of aggression on either party, actual or feared, Nepal continued with its policy of forging new ties with China. Even after the Chinese aggression Nepal never publicly expressed its disapproval of the action nor any sympathy for India. Non-alignment or neutrality was here equated with cowardice and justification of attitude of aggression and the actual act of aggression by Nepal's northern neighbour. Nobody expected Nepal to come to India's help in terms of men and materials but a word of cheer or an expression of sympathy was called for in such cases. In another three years, China's close ally, Pakistan was to test India with its own brand of aggression but even then the Nepalis, under Mahendra, kept their counsel, although the Pakistanis were no neighbours and could not have caused any harm to Nepal's by their voicing of sympathy with India. If the aim was to feel happy at India's dire predicament, this was now ensured.

Mahendra's visit to China was notable not only for the many expressions of solidarity with China and studied avoidance of mention of the "friendly nation of India", which he did only in a message to his people on the eve of the sojourn to Peking, but also for two major agreements signed in the course of his visit, one by himself. Any word of disapproval of China's threatening postures towards India was, of course, out of question for the Nepali King. The agreement Mahendra signed was the Nepal-China Boundary Treaty, replacing the treaty signed when Koirala had gone to Peking in 1960. The new treaty was signed on behalf of China by its President Liu Shao-chi, Chairman of the People's Republic of China and by Mahendra for Nepal.

Any settlement of national frontiers on a permanent basis is highly desirable as it is conducive to peace and the physical demarcation on the ground removes all doubts where one territory ends and the other begins. It also prevents the trigger-happy border guards from killing foreigners. But Mahendra went to the extent of claiming to his people that he had returned to Nepal from China with gains in his pocket and Mount Sagarmatha, or Everest as it is known, had been secured by him for Nepal. He said at a civic reception in his honour in Kathmandu on October 27, after he had signed the treaty with Liu Shao-Chi in Peking:

"By the Northern Boundary treaty, the Kingdom of Nepal has gained three hundred square miles and I feel that all the Nepalis will experience a sense of glory when I state that Sagarmatha, on which the eyes of the world seem to be focussed, continues to be as it has been, ours and within our territory."[6]

What does the treaty say about the mountain? As we would see in one of the subsequent chapters, the Chinese had at one time claimed the mountain but it was B. P. Koirala who took a strong stand and finally it was agreed that the boundary runs through it, thus making it possible for the Chinese to claim the northern side of the world's highest mountain. The treaty signed by Mahendra records:

"... then runs generally southwards along the mountain ridge, passing through Cho Oyu mountain, Pumoli mountain (Gaire Langur), Mount Jolmo Lungma (Sagarmatha) and Lhotse ...."[7]

Thus the treaty just says that the mountain is as it was earlier in the time of Koirala who had resisted the Chinese attempt to grab the world's highest mountain. The King had performed no miracle nor made any notable achievement for his country.

It would be recalled that Koirala had specifically opposed the Chinese proposal for building a highway linking Lhasa with Kathmandu and said roads have economic linkages and when the trade developed to an extent that a road was necessary the issue would be looked into. Now the King swallowed all that and signed, or asked his Foreign Minister, Tulsi Giri, another pro-Peking politician chosen by the King to head an important Ministry, to sign it along with the redoubtable Marshal Chen Yi, China's Foreign Minister. China was to provide substantial economic aid for the major part of the road falling in Nepali territory and, what is important, send "experts and technicians". Such experts and technicians are, indeed, required for a special type of road passing through mountainous terrain but the moot question was whether they were all experts and technicians or ones who were also burdened with other responsibilities. The change in the Nepali perception, within a year, could perhaps be understood as dictated by economic reasons but such a sudden change could also have been caused by the policy considerations of Mahendra who wanted to cause the maximum annoyance to India.

There was much bonhomie between the two sides now and the Chinese lost no opportunity to rub salt into India's wounds knowing that Mahendra's Ministers would find the words sweet music to their ears. Foreign Minister Chen Yi not only sent Tulsi Giri a message on the first anniversary of the boundary treaty, on October 5, 1962, but also made a thundering speech at a reception thrown by the Nepali embassy in Peking the next day. He said:

> "We are now in the sixties of the 20th century in an era in which the national independence movement is surging forward; all manifestations of great nation chauvinism and all activities of interference and subversion against other countries go against the current of the times and will surely end in failure.
>
> "The Chinese people regard the Nepali people's struggle against foreign interference and subversion and for equality and friendship with all neighbouring countries as a struggle for

principle(s). The Nepali people can rest fully assured that should any foreign power dare to attack Nepal, the Chinese government and people, together with all other countries which uphold justice, will forever stand by Nepal[8]."

History does not record it but one can be sure that Chen Yi's speech must have been received with thunderous applause by the employees of the embassy. Only three years earlier, when Nehru gave expression to almost similar sentiments that India would regard aggression on Nepal as aggression against herself, a veritable storm was raised by the anti-Indian elements in Nepal. Koirala had to come out with an explanatory statement but now Chen Yi was giving expression to similar views and the Nepalis were not saying a word of protest against it. The voice of the real Nepal was suppressed through the ban on democracy. The value one can attach to the Chinese promise of assistance can also be seen from the fact that in 1971, only nine years after the valuable words were uttered by Marshal Chen Yi, China made many verbal statements and gesticulations in favour of its protege, Pakistan, but did not raise its little finger in support when Islamabad was engaged in a life and death struggle against India in the Bangladesh war.

We have referred earlier to Nepal's attitude of accepting the Chinese aggression against India. It must be recorded here that King Mahendra uttered a few words of gratuitous advice to both sides to settle the dispute when the Chinese invaders were still in India. He told the Nepali news agency, the Rashtriya Sambad Samiti, RSS (not to be mistaken with the Khaki-clad volunteers of the Hindutva organisation in India Rashtriya Swayamsewak Sangh): "So, this being a dispute between India and China, Nepal deems it most appropriate that they should resolve it through mutual understanding".

This was at a time when countries like Egypt and Ghana as well Burma and Ceylon were trying their best to bring about a cease fire and truce. Nepal was happy with a bare statement that the dispute should be settled "through mutual understanding". After all China would not mind such an innocuous statement. Even Nepal's representative in the UN, Rishikesh Shaha, generally considered friendly to India, twisted facts, in the General Assembly on October 26, 1962, when the Chinese attack on India was at its peak: "Whatever the merits of the case (of the India-China border dispute and the Chinese aggression), the argument (that UN membership is open only to peace-loving states) loses all its weight because India itself is one of the greatest champions of the lawful rights of China in the United

Nations."[9] That was correct but not in the context of the current agony that India was subjected to by Peking. China's lawful rights was one thing but its aggression, on which Rishikesh Shaha had nothing to say except expressions of the usual hope of settlement of the dispute, was another.

The Chinese missed no opportunity to tell the Nepalis and others that they had demonstrated their sincerity by solving the boundary problem and signing a treaty with Nepal on the subject, implying thereby that the Indians were unreasonable. How unreasonable they were and who was really unreasonable, would be examined in part four of this book. Even with Nepal they had tried their tricks by claiming Mount Everest and by the attack on the Nepalis in Mustang but they realised that they should not fight a battle with both India and Nepal. Suffice it to say here that the dispute with India is over a much larger area and the Chinese never expressed regrets for the killing of the Indian policemen in October 1959 in Ladakh which aggravated the tension.

We have said earlier that China, like the United States, prefers to deal with autocrats rather than the elected representatives or with democracies in general. This was no idle observation as can be seen from the following comment in the *People's Daily*, the mouthpiece of the ruling Chinese Communist Party :

"The people of China and Nepal have always lived in amity. Since the formal establishment of diplomatic relations between the two countries, the traditional friendship between them has registered even greater development. The economic and cultural ties between the two countries have, in particular, become increasingly closer after King Mahendra personally took over the helm of the state. Now the Lhasa-Kathmandu highway is being constructed at an accelerated pace ..."[10]

**Recurring Themes**

The Chinese leaders' speeches and comments in the controlled press had certain recurring themes, such as the traditional friendship, the peaceful settlement of the boundary question, China's generous economic aid to Nepal and so on. There was yet another point which regularly recurred, the manner in which, according to the Chinese, Nepal had suppressed the "rebel Tibetan bandits" in 1959. As we have seen Nepal had even told the UN General Assembly that as many as a thousand Tibetan refugees had entered Nepal after the Dalai Lama's escape to India. But the Chinese claimed again and again that they were not refugees and Nepal did not show any sympathy for them.

Thus the *Peking Review* said in an article by Mao Tung on January 25, 1963, while welcoming Tulsi Giri, Nepal's Foreign Minister, to China : "When a handful of Tibetan reactionaries staged a rebellion in 1959, Nepal adhered to her correct stand of non-interference in China's internal affairs".[11]

Earlier, Foreign Minister Chen Yi himself gave expression to his country's admiration for Nepal's "correct stand" on November 23, 1962 in his speech of welcome to Rishikesh Shaha who had been doing extremely well defending China in the United Nations. "When a handful of reactionaries in China's Tibet region launched a rebellion in 1959 Nepal persevered in its correct stand of non-interference in China's internal affairs." Mao Tung and his ilk have only to echo what the mighty Marshal had to say.

Chen Yi never let go an opportunity to lavish praise on King Mahendra which only goes to show that the Chinese leadership realised his usefulness to them and the valuable role he was playing in strengthening China vis-a-vis India. Thus visiting Nepal in March 1965, he said at a banquet hosted in his honour by the Nepal government: "His Majesty King Mahendra is an outstanding statesman. He is filled with lofty aspirations to bring prosperity to his country and the determination to safeguard independence and sovereignty."[12]

Mahendra was playing his anti-India card by strengthening the ties with China and exploiting the sentiments of the elite which wanted greater access to the world. Even a dispassionate observer of the scene like the American scholar Leo E Rose was constrained to remark:

"... the China factor has been a vital ingredient in Kathmandu's calculations on a broad range of issues, both internal and external," and, "China continues to be the only plausibe counter balance to a dominant Indian influence.[13]

Again, "King Mahendra was able to exploit the nationalist sentiments of the hypersensitive Nepali elites by stigmatising the opposition forces as puppets of a foreign power. Indeed, it would appear that on occasions Mahendra gave a deliberate twist, an anti-Indian orientation to his foreign policy in order to solidify popular support to the royal regime."[14]

When China exploded its first nuclear bomb in 1964 the men under King Mahendra were apparently happy. There was no popular reaction in the press resembling the anti-Indian feelings which were voiced in 1974 when India exploded its first and only peaceful nuclear device. The Chinese one was viewed as a great achievement but the Indian explosion was looked upon as a threat to the small neighbours. China has kept on exploding its bombs and there were tests conducted in the Lop Nor desert even in 1995. But when the first explosion was made in 1964, the Nepal Foreign Minister, Kirti Nidhi Bista, who later became Prime Minister under Mahendra's system of musical chairs for pliable politicians, told the UN General Assembly: "The People's Republic of China which has recently entered the group of nuclear powers, has so far not been invited to participate in any disarmament conference. It is difficult to conceive of general and complete disarmament or of any meaningful steps towards it, without the participation of all nuclear powers in the negotiations."[15]

Bista was thus conferring on China the status of a nuclear power already and speaking of the Chinese explosion with approval and apparent glee.

The real Chinese perception of the game that the Mahendra-nominated politicians were playing with their great neighbour was expressed in the strongest possible language when the Red Guards of the Chinese Cultural Revolution seized temporary control of China's Foreign Office and insulting notes were addressed to Nepal. Chou En-lai was able to recapture the Foreign office before long but before that could happen there were official notes and articles written in the Maoist-controlled press attacking Kathmandu in the most blatant language.

Thus, on July 14, 1967 the *Peking Review* carried a commentary in abusive language on an incident alleged to have taken place in Kathmandu where a Chinese propaganda photo exhibition was being held. The article accused the Nepali government of approving and supporting the "outrage" by some demonstrators, described as hooligans, who had forcibly entered the hall and "clamoured hysterically" for the removal of the portrait of Chairman Mao. Dutifully, the Chinese envoy, Yang Kung-su lodged a "serious" protest on July 5 (the alleged incident took place on July 1) with the Nepal government warning that the great socialist China was not to be bullied and those indulging in the anti-China campaign would suffer the consequences of their actions. Here is the opening part of the article which would show the kind of language used and the real feelings of the Chinese towards Nepal:

> "On the evening of July 1, a group of Nepalese hooligans, instigated and directed by US imperialism, Soviet revisionism and the Indian reactionaries, and with the connivance of the Nepalese government carried out anti-China activities in front of the Chinese

photo exhibition hall in Kathmandu. They made several attempts to break into the exhibition hall, clamouring hysterically for the removal of the portrait of the Chinese people's great leader, Chairman Mao, and of the Chinese national flag. They shouted anti-China slogans and viciously insulted Chairman Mao...."[16]

This was followed by a Nepali denial of its involvement in the incident and professions of friendship for China, a recurring Nepali lullaby, which failed to put the Chinese to sleep, at least this time. The Nepali note also pointed out that the Chinese news agency, Hsinhua, had filed a wrong report. The Chinese Foreign Office then fired off a strong protest note in reply and repeated the accusations contained in the *Peking Review* article. The protest warned Nepal in the most humiliating manner! "If the Nepalese side does not care for the friendship which has taken a long time to build between China and Nepal but allows imperialism, revisionism and reaction to indulge in their evil ways in Nepal or even tails after them in opposing China, then the Nepalese government must bear full responsibility for the serious consequences arising therefrom".[17]

This was not a newspaper article which one could conveniently disown in the manner of lying associated with all diplomacy but a calculated diplomatic missive, written in the most undiplomatic language, by the mandarins of the Chinese Foreign Office. As they say, there is truth in wine, or when a man has had too much to drink he likes to brag and boast and often his true feelings and some hard facts may come out. So also, when the chips were down and the Chinese were almost wearing no clothes they liked to portray others also in their true natural colours. The Chinese had perhaps known for long that many in Nepal looked upon their friendship with Peking to be a weapon to keep India down, a kind of card to play to beat the Indians with. In those days when the polite ways of diplomacy were thrown to the winds by the Chinese they thus let the Nepalis know what they thought of them and their professions of friendship.

There is no doubt that the incident took place although the Chinese Foreign Office, much under the intoxicating influence of the Red Guards, painted it in the most glaring terms. It is possible that one of the communist factions, favoured by the Palace, opposed to the Chinese Red Guards and supporting the Soviets, had a hand in it and the Americans always ready to put their finger in other people's pie were instigating some elements. The Nepali government was perhaps not able to tackle the trouble makers who must have received enough provocation from the Chinese and their friends in Nepal while the

Indians may have played a subsidiary role in the entire affair, although in their report to New Delhi the Indian diplomats may have tried to corner the credit for it.

As we said earlier, Chou En-lai was able to wrest control of the foreign office from the extremist elements before things could get completely out of control. The Nepali leaders were making once more their usual professions of friendship with China without the fear of being rebuffed for alleged or real hypocricy.

The king himself, in his address to the UN General Assembly on November 6, 1967, referred to the "great Chinese people" and called China the "world's most populous country." A trade agreement was signed in Peking in May next year when Bista, soon to be elevated to Prime Ministership, went there and put his signature to it along with his counterpart, Chen Yi. It recognised the traditional border trade rights of the inhabitants in that region of Nepal and Tibet and the most favoured nation treatment was accorded to each other's goods.

Bista was naturally lauded by China and its controlled media when in June 1969 he made a threatening statement against India and publicly asked India to withdraw the personnel in Nepal's checkposts on the Tibetan border and the Indian military group in Kathmandu. The *Peking Review* said on July 11, 1969 that public opinion in Nepal had expressed support for Bista in denouncing India's "expansionist" policy towards Nepal to which there were frequent references in the article.

Again when the talks between India and Nepal on a new trade and transit treaty remained deadlocked in 1971 the same mouthpiece of Chinese hegemony accused India of "big nation chauvinism". It said during the talks, which had been held more than once, India had put on "big nation chauvinistic airs" and put pressure on Nepal. The article, in typical Chinese fashion, repeatedly referred to the same charge and said India was "habitually bullying small countries". The same and similar articles, of course, soon failed to carry much conviction with the Nepalis because during the Bangladesh liberation war which occurred during the end of that year, in December 1971, the Chinese studiously avoided coming to the aid of their staunchest ally, the military rulers of Pakistan, gave them false assurances which it never kept or was afraid to keep because it knew that India had now had Soviet support under the treaty of August 1971 and was also well equipped to ward off any Chinese threat on its own.

India's great victory in the war against the might of the Pakistan military came as a shock to Mahendra and his advisers who had been making friendly gestures to Pakistan in the hope that it would embarrass India and weaken it. Nepal had pretended that there was no liberation struggle in Bangladesh, then called East Pakistan, knowing that would be welcome to Islamabad. As we have noted before, Nepal had shown its brand of "neutrality" another word for cowardice and selfishness, during Pakistani aggression against India in September 1965, ignoring the provisions of the treaty of friendship. Now there was a more crucial question; what would Kathmandu do when a nation striving to be born, Bangladesh, was close to its border. Yet, Mahendra and his advisers preferred to show friendliness towards the military rulers of Pakistan. Nepal was the eighth country to recognise free Bangladesh and did it only when Burma (now Myanmar) had done it. This was at a time when Dhaka was almost daily receiving messages of recognition or the moves preliminary to it. Bhutan was the second country after India to recognise Bangladesh but Kathmandu was watching what its friends in Islamabad would say until this had lost all relevance after Rangoon (now called Yangon) granted recognition and as a next door neighbour Nepal could no longer affort to sit on the fence. That Pakistan itself faced the reality in another two years is proof that one cannot close one's eyes to reality for long.

## REFERENCES

1. *China-South Asian Relations*, 1947-1980, Vol. 2. ed. R. K. Jain, Radiant Publishers, Delhi.
2. *Ibid.*
3. *Ibid.*
4. *Ibid.*
5. *Ibid.*
6. *Ibid.*
7. *Ibid.*
8. *Ibid.*
9. *Ibid.*
10. *Ibid.*
11. *Ibid.*
12. *Ibid.*
13. *King Mahendra's China Policy in Nepal: An Assertive Monarchy, Ibid.*
14. Quoted by S. C. Nayak, *Nepal's Perception of India's Role in South Asia, Ibid.*
15. *China-South Asian Relations, 1947-1980,* Vol. 2 ed, R.K. Jain, Radiant Publishers, Delhi.
16. *Ibid.*
17. *Ibid.*

# 12

# MORE OF THE SAME

Policies need not change radically because one king or ruler replaces another if the perceptions do not alter materially and the new ruler is also actuated by the same motives as those of the one he has replaced. King Birendra Bikram Shah Dev succeeded his father Mahendra in January 1972, on the latter death is a different personality from his father. He brought a degree of sophistication to bear on his task but, as we have seen before, he carried on much in the same fashion as his father. Another group of advisers may have replaced the one which was serving his father but all advisers, save a few, have a tendency to tender the advice which the appointer likes. Birendra's advisers also saw things the same way that his father's men did. India was there to be milked and China was there to be held up as a friend.

Birendra favoured the Panchayat system of "democracy" and carried on with it for another 18 years until his hands were forced by massive demonstrations in which dozens of young men were killed. This alone shows that Birendra was moving forward from where his father had left off. He brooked no change in the foreign policy pursued by Mahendra but kept the border with India open because that alone would ensure employment for the five million Nepalis in India, nearly a quarter of Nepal's total population, and brought other economic benefits to Nepal (and some to India also) while talking of "equal" friendship with India and China.

King Birendra had visited China as Crown Prince in 1966 when he was given the best of hospitality that the Chinese are truly famous for. So when he paid a visit to China, within a year of assuming full authority, he recalled the fine hospitality offered him seven years earlier. In a speech during his 1973 visit, the first of many such he was to undertake later, Birendra said: "The happy memories of your hospitality during my last visit give me ample cause to hope that this visit will be no less successful and no less fruitful."[1] That was at the banquet held in his honour by Chou En-lai in Peking. The reason why the head of state could not host the banquet, as protocol demanded, was never explained but Chou was a powerful figure in the complex leadership pattern of China. In fact, Birendra was hosted similarly for quite some time, something which he would have found embarrassing and would have protested alone if it happened in India.

**Birendra's Barbs**

Birendra's speech was full of praise not only for the hospitality but also for the friendship displayed by China. While visiting India, it was customary for the Nepali leaders to speak of the "two great neighbours", India and China, but in his major speech in China Birendra only had barbs for India, without, of course, naming the country: "The idea of one country exerting pressure on other or (a nation) being put under pressure by others is alien and unacceptable to us. Your understanding and appreciation of the principles to which we adhere are matters of deep satisfaction to us."[2] Birendra left his audience in little doubt as to which country he was referring to when he was talking of pressure being exerted. A fine way of maligning another country without naming it.

Before Birendra could undertake his first trip to China as King, his Prime Minister, Kirti Nidhi Bista, had already done so. During the regime of Mahendra, every possible agreement was signed between the two countries—a treaty of friendship, a boundary treaty in both its temporary and final versions, a treaty about trade and intercourse with Tibet again in temporary and final versions. There was thus nothing for Bista or his King to sign. After his coronation in 1975, Birendra visited China in 1976. Once again the banquet in his honour was hosted by the Prime Minister, Chou's successor, Hua Kuo-feng, and no explanation was given why the Nepali head of state was being hosted by a mere head of government. The Nepalis would raise a storm if they were treated in such a manner in India, although they know that the real authority vests in the Indian Prime Minister, not the President. In China the authority is diffused and people like Deng

Xiao-ping, who holds no formal position, is still powerful and the Chinese Communist Party wields a great deal of authority. But protocol is protocol.

By this time Birendra had come out with his famous but ill-fated "Zone of Peace" proposal about which we have had occasion to speak earlier. The Chinese had had no hesitation to endorse the proposal straight-way as it cost them nothing and also served their purpose of keeping Nepal in their "zone of influence" and embarrassing India. To quote Huo from his speech at the banquet in honour of King Birendra:

> "The proposal put forward by His Majesty King Birendra to declare Nepal a Zone of Peace reflects the strong desire of the people of Nepal to safeguard national independence and state sovereignty. The Chinese government firmly supports this just proposition. The Chinese people will, as always, stand together with you for ever in the struggle against hegemonism and expansionism."[3] Again, Hua left no one in doubt whom he meant by the favourite attributes of hegemonism and expansionism.

For Nepal to allow India to be thus maligned on foreign soil had become a habit. While they referred to India as their friend when in India they subjected the same friend to abuse in China and often in their own country. Hua was, of course, discreet and did not name India while attacking it. But the Chinese media were under no restraint. In an article on December 6, 1974, the *Peking Review* abused India in the context of the difficulties experienced by it in the relations with Nepal: "India has tried to put an end to Nepal's sovereignty and independent existence."[4]

Earlier, in an article on May 17, 1974, the same magazine reported that 100,000 people from all walks of life held a mammoth demonstration and rally in Kathmandu on March 25 to denounce anti-national elements and India for engineering an incident of an explosion in Biratnagar when Birendra was visiting the Terai town. If that were true, how come millions of Nepalis voted election after election for the Nepali Congress which stands for the utmost friendship with India. About 100 or say 1,000 demonstrators could appear to be 100,000 when the Chinese report an anti-Indian demonstration but the reality could be substantially different.

The relations between India and China still being strained, it was not uncommon for the media in China to exploit a petty demonstration staged mainly by its own agents. We have quoted several comments from these media earlier also. But the notable part is that Nepalis relished such writings and the speeches in the presence of their great leaders at so formal an occasion as a banquet. By Nepalis we, of course, mean the anti-Indian elements in that country which remained on top throughout the regime of the two kings. The task of the Chinese media looking for anti-Indian material was made easier by first publishing anti-Indian reports and writings in obscure Nepali journals which the Chinese papers could quote without specifying their popularity. This is a familiar propaganda device of planting stories which then could be picked up for reproduction and further comments which would also be made to look credible.

During Mahendra's rule, Nepal had not only diversified its trade but also began to receive economic aid from the major aiding nations besides the close neighbour India. According to a Nepali scholar[5], the country was getting aid worth only Rs. 19 million when Mahendra ascended the throne but by the time he died in 1972 the amount had risen to Rs. 352 million. Despite the fast that the United States, the Soviet Union, Britain, China and the World Bank was among its donors now, India remained the highest donor, notwithstanding its own straitened circumstances and the knocking it had received at the hands of Mahendra.

The aid giving nations, of course, kept a finger in the Nepali pie although the King deftly played one against the other. India had not succeeded in adopting a coherent attitude of firmness while safeguarding her national interests in dealing with Nepal. It was a case of muddling through and keeping a smiling face while Nepal kept on heaping one insult after another. India's dilemma was real. If it withdrew the economic aid it was providing and closed the border this would only hit the man in the street and would drive Mahendra (and later Birendra) more and more into the hands of the Chinese. It would also help the elite, which was already anti-Indian to turn round and say: we told you so. India also could not allow a close neighbour to be so isolated and driven away from itself.

From time to time, the economic squeeze was applied with results which were not uniformly favourable to India. The high point of this policy was reached during Rajiv Gandhi's rule in 1989 a little before he was himself thrown out by the electorate in the 1989 elections and the people of Nepal uprooted the Panchayat system. The squeeze was neither humanitarian nor a wise diplomatic move because it hit the ordinary people most while the elite made political capital and worked up another wave of anti-Indian hysteria. India never tried the policy of going to the extreme and closing the border which could have had serious repercussions in Nepal and exposed the people who claim that a policy of equality between the two big neighbours was best for their country. The irony of the "equality" policy is that while a Nepali can just walk across into India he has to use a circuitous route, via India and Hong Kong to enter China. He cannot hope to cross into Tibet and reach Peking (or Beijing) in less than two weeks, if at all. The point has not been grasped by many knowledgeable people even that India and Nepal have to have close relations, including security and economic coordination, because of the fact of geography, not to use the bombastic word geopolitics. The people in Nepal who have sought to exploit the situation to India's disadvantage have not realised this fact and only an extreme step by India would drive some sense into them. Fortunately, the relations between the people of the two countries have always been cordial and once democratic rule is restored things are always bright and cheery.

The period of the sixties, particularly its latter part, and the seventies was one of intense rivalry between the Soviet Union and China. During this period India's ties with the Soviets became very close and they did not seek a new or independent approach towards Nepal, different from that of India. The United States had always had a low profile in Nepal and once Nixon and Kissinger and their successors got fully involved with China they got less interested in buttressing a state close to China, although they were never disinterested. Pakistan has been a comparatively small player except to use the ground in Nepal to plan and execute its anti-Indian spying and other hostile activities. The two kings always thought of Pakistan as a force which could balance India but their wishes were not fulfilled. All the same, Pakistan was treated with kidgloves by them and by the Communist regime in the country which was in power for a few months in 1995

**Haven for Criminals**

Nepal has always been a haven for criminals from India like Babloo Srivastava, involved in cases of murder and intimidation, and the Dawood Ibrahim gang of criminals from Bombay now hiding in Dubai or Pakistan. It is not surprising that when Yusuf Memon, brother of the arch criminal Tiger Memon, responsible for the Bombay blasts of March 1993 in which some 300 persons were killed in explosions set off by the Memon gang, wanted to surrender he chose Nepal after his stay in Dubai and Pakistan. Yusuf had fled India along with Tiger and other members of the family after setting off the blasts or laying the ground work. Dawood Ibrahim is one of the prime accused in the trial still going in Bombay. Pakistan's ISI was fully involved in the dastardly explosions.

India, of course, has a treaty of extradition with Nepal and there has been no difficulty in its operation. But the open border is taken advantage of by the mafia gangs and even by petty criminals who can easily escape to Nepal after committing a crime. This imposes another reason on India to keep Nepal in good humour and deal with it as a friend, even at the cost of its honour at times. But the people-to-people relations are very good and once they come into the picture things change radically. They come out and voted for the Nepali Congress, NC, which stands for close ties with India. Some scholars have gone to the extent of saying India could have helped the NC in its election victory in 1959.[6] One may almost say, God save us from such scholarship! Why did the people vote for the same NC in 1991, after a gap of 31 years? Did India have a hand then also? Did India have a hand in the Communists securing the position of a large party to which the King entrusted power in 1994 and the NC supported them from the outside for a few months? The Communists are notoriously anti-Indian and South Block would have virtually committed harakiri in bringing them to power. People in Britain and the United States could, and often do, change their government in a peaceful poll but if the same thing happens in a developing society our scholars would ask. How did it happen without some intervention?

Some analysts have taken the view that even while playing the China card the Nepalis always kept the stiff upper lip. Superficially that may appear to be a correct reading of the situation. The two kings were never fulsome in their praise of China even if some of their Prime Ministers were. The Kings tried to maintain their dignity in public utterances so that the independence and sovereignty of their country were not compromised. Even while acknowledging China's friendship they spoke of mutual benefit. Thus Birendra said in his reply to Hua Kuo-feng's banquet speech on August 27, 1979: "We believe that such friendship, as we have defined, is mutually beneficial, is harmonious with the best interests of the regime and serves, in however small a way, the cause of world peace."[7]

True, the monarchs were keen not to appear to be subservient, but there are in such matters nuances and minute distinctions which only the experienced eye could catch. There is the obvious fact that both heads of state took potshots at India in the presence of the Chinese leaders, when they did not have to, and the latter were too ready and obliging with their compliments. India was often their butt of attack and criticism, with phrases like "hegemonism", "big bully" "interference in others' affairs", and so on plenty.

So when you are face to face with a situation of this kind you cannot maintain your pose of neutrality and equidistance. In fact, there was no attempt to do it and, as we have seen, India often suffered by comparison with the Chinese which was made by the Nepali leaders and their hosts or guests, as the case may be. The open border, on the one hand, and the passport-visa regime, on the other, even in the neighbouring Tibet region of China, made non-sense of the equality of friendship theory and the equidistance that the Nepali leaders claimed for themselves in relation to India and China and which many scholars have writtenabout in an expert manner. When you nurse a grievance against one side, real or imaginary, and use it to extract benefits and generally to blackmail it, while you openly profess friendship for the other you cannot but be accused of being unequal in your treatment of the two neighbours.

The Chinese played their cards well. After making rather quick amends for the Mustang killing of a Nepali and scaling down their blatant claim on Mount Everest to placate the Nepalis in 1960 they followed a conscious policy of keeping the Nepali leaders in good humour. They were thus able to exploit the leaders' sensitivity towards India to the fullest extent possible. When, however, the relations between India and China improved substantially, as we shall see later, the Nepalis did not have a card to play. Like the old Indian proverb which says when the boy and girl are happy with each other what is left for the marrige priest to do? To put it differently, if the two fighting cats see eye to eye there is pretty little for the monkey to do.

The theory that Nepal always maintained its independence in its dealings with the Chinese and did not allow the professions of friendship to sweep it off its feet has, therefore, to be taken with a large pinch of salt. It has to be accepted that the two kings chose anti-Indian Prime Ministers and advisers and allowed themselves to be influenced by them. These men played upon their sentiments and the fears of the Nepali people. The atmosphere was, therefore, conducive to the prevalence of Chinese influence. Anyone trying to point out something good in Indian policies and actions was bound to be dubbed an "Indian agent". There were no Chinese agents, not even Pakistani agents!

There was, of course, an effort not to lean too much on the Chinese side and to give them the impression that Nepal was there to be twisted by them at will. But the success of this policy was a doubtful proposition because the Nepali leaders always spoke of their difficulties with India and frequently of the smooth ties with China.

## REFERENCES


1. *China-South-Asian Relations, 1947-1980,* Vol. 2. ed. R.K. Jain.
2. *Ibid.*
3. *Ibid.*
4. *Ibid.*
5. *Role of Foreign Aid,* Pashupati Shamshere Jang Bahadur Rana, in *Nepal: An Assertive Monarchy.*
6. *Great Powers and Nepal,* Vinod Kumar in S.D. Mum, *ibid.*
7. *Ibid.*, R. K. Jain.

## 13

# THE MUSTANG INCIDENT

On June 28, 1960 Chinese troops on the border of Nepal and Tibet fired upon a group of Nepalis at Mustang and killed a Subedar, a non-commissioned officer of the Royal Nepal Army. They also took ten Nepali civilian personnel prisoner. Seven other members of the Nepali party, who were about to be imprisoned by the Chinese, fled the scene of the incident and reported back to their border outposts. The Nepali chief of Mustang also fled the place and there was naturally panic as many people evacuated their homes fearing large-scale violence after the Chinese had used their weapons. The incident was expectedly big news in the international media and news reached the Chinese in their capital whether the border troops had reported the facts to their bosses or not. Violence was used by the Chinese within a little over three months of the solemn border agreement signed by the two Prime Ministers, B. P. Koirala for Nepal and Chou-En-lai for China. Koirala was still Prime Minister of Nepal as Mahendra had not yet extinguished the light of democracy.

Mustang is in Nepali territory and the Chinese had no business to enter it. Unfortunately, the Chinese are known to have transgrassed others' territories when it suits them and afterwards they may or may not make amends for it. Under the boundary agreement, signed in Peking on March 21 that year, a twenty km-wide demilitarised zone was created into which neither side was to allow its troops. Article 4 of the treaty categorically states:

"The contracting parties have decided that in order to ensure tranquillity and friendliness on the border each side will no longer despatch armed personnel to patrol the area on its side within twenty km of the border but only maintain its administrative personnel and civil police there."

In the typical Chinese fashion, the boundary agreement was hailed by its media. The *People's Daily*, organ of the Chinese Communist Party, had welcomed it in an editorial on April 30 that year as an example of peaceful coexistence. But the Chinese forget their commitments to the five principles and other slogans of coexistence when they have a goal to secure and suddenly remember them after the goal is achieved.

Although they did not openly admit it, there was widespread opposition to their rule in Tibet and long after the Dalai Lama and his entourage had fled to India in March 1959, there was an active rebellion of many Tibetans fighting for their independence. The Chinese were naturally anxious to put it down but suddenly, after the Dalai Lama had fled a year and a quarter ago, they decided to engage in "suppression" work of the rebels whom they called bandits. Admittedly, the Tibetan rebels had been active for a long time and even the Chinese media indirectly recognised their existence, although they preferred to term freedom fighters as bandits. The *Peking Review* writing about it in September 1974[1] praised the then Nepal government of King Birendra who had appointed one of his periodical Prime Ministers to head of the government. The *Review* said: "In order to safeguard its national independence, sovereignty and security, the government of Nepal has recently taken measures to disarm the Tibetan rebels who fled to Nepal. These measures are welcomed and supported by the Nepali people and public opinion. After the failure of the armed rebellion by the self-owned reactionaries headed by the Dalai Lama in 1959, these rebels fled to India and from there, armed with weapons and other equipment, they infiltrated into Mustang and other places in the northern part of Nepal."

So, Mustang was still fresh in the minds of the Chinese although they now sought to involve India in the rebellion which was planned and executed the Tibetans who were fighting against Chinese rule. The article is also revealing for the cooperation of Birendra's government with the Chinese in putting down the Tibetan revolt. Thereby they earned a certificate of good conduct from the Peking lords.

The people in power in Kathmandu in 1960 were not so pliant and subservient to China. In a statement by its Foreign Ministry on June 30, China admitted that an incident had indeed taken place, as reported by the foreign media, in which it said "the Chinese troops killed and captured personnel of the Nepali side." The statement did not mention Mustang but admitted that the incident had taken place on the border. Mustang was omitted in the first statement but it clearly indicated that the Chinese leaders had decided to make as clean a breast of it as they possibly could. Normally the Chinese would never admit anything approaching a misdeed on the part of their men but now from the outset they wanted to play reasonable. The Chinese foreign office spokesman said the Chinese government was deeply concerned about the incident, while simultaneously saying it was "deeply surprised" by the news. How could one be both concerned and surprised at the same time?

**Strong Stand against Bullying**

B. P. Koirala, then Prime Minister, had always taken a strong stand against the browbeating attempts by the big brother across the border, in contrast with the attitude of his successors. He lodged a strong protest with Chou over the killing and capture of Nepali personnel. He demanded immediate release of the captured persons and adequate compensation for the loss suffered by his country. In a prompt reply, Chou said the same thing which the spokesman had said earlier, namely that inquiries were being made from the local Chinese authorities. But he added, "If the incident has indeed taken place my government will express regrets and if any Nepalis are captured they would be released speedily." At this stage he indulged in a bit of propaganda by saying that the attempts of the "imperialists and foreign reactionaries", meaning obviously the United States and India, to whip up anti-Chinese campaign would not succeed. It should be remembered that China was engaged in a big campaign to tell the world that it was being reasonable with India on the border issue and India was unreasonable in the matter. China had, therefore, to be as reasonable with Nepal, a much smaller country, as it could.

Before the Chinese authorities in Peking could receive a detailed report from their far-flung Tibetan border, public opinion in Nepal was inflammed by the killing of their compatriot and capture of some others. People were concerned that their kith and kin had fled the Mustang area. The Home Minister, S. P. Upadhyaya, had to make a statement to put the record straight and allay the people's fears as far as he could. He confirmed the incident and said the people from the border areas were fleeing to the south. The Home Minister also said that for some time the government of Nepal had been receiving reports of Chinese build-up on the border and taken up the matter with the Chinese government. "Every time we did that, the Chinese assured us that their troops would never cross into Nepal and stressed the friendship with Nepal." This action is typical of China, always assure the neighbours of their friendship. The assurance of friendship was repeated when Koirala visited Peking and again when Chou was in Kathmandu (in April 1960). But, the Minister regretted that "foreign bullets were fired upon unarmed Nepalis and they killed one of them."

Upadhyaya declared that no friendship was greater than "our independence" and "for the sake of friendship we cannot sacrifice our independence." There could not be a more trenchat criticism of the Chinese action and a stronger warning about future ties being affected by such incidents. The pro-Chinese elements at home, the Communists and others were behaving in their typical servile fashion and seeking to blame India for the reports about the killing of the Nepali and capture of some others. Upadhyaya warned them and said that their attempt to propagate that the Indian border checkposts had given the reports was treason. He said there were no Indian border checkposts on the Nepal-Tibetan border. All the posts were under Nepal and the reports came from them in Nepali code. Servility can descend to any low depth but to their chagrin their Chinese masters were to admit in two days the killing of a Nepali. Yet here they were talking of the Indians putting out the report.

On July 2, Chou En-lai informed Koirala that he had now received a report on the incident from the frontier guards in the Ari district of China's Tibet region. He claimed that this was a case of misunderstanding as the Chinese troops mistook a group of Nepalis as Tibetans since the Chinese were engaged in "suppression" work of the Tibetan rebel "bandits" and the Chinese troops fired upon the Nepalis. The Prime Minister admitted that one of the Nepalis was killed and ten of them were captured. He maintained that the Nepalis were within a kilometre of Tibetan territory. If that were so, the Nepalis would have penetrated not just one km but twenty-one km, including the demilitarised zone. Nothing more foolish could be done by any unarmed group, Nepali or any other.

In any case, Chou went on to offer his apologies to Koirala. Chou said "... this unexpected, unfortunate incident was due to the carelessness on the part of certain low-ranking personnel of Chinese troops. The Chinese government expresses deep regret at this, apologises to His Majesty's government of Nepal and condoles the unfortunate incident. The Chinese government has already instructed the troops in this locality to look at once into the responsibility for the incident and to escort the ten Nepali personnel detained, and send the dead body, together with the horses of the Nepali personnel... to be handed over to the appropriate Nepali officers at a specified place and time."

Koirala replied to Chou's letter on July 6 in which he appreciated the tone of the Chinese Premier's letter, offering apologies for the Mustang incident, but he strongly maintained that there was absolutely no justification for the entry of the Chinese into the demilitarised zone without prior consent (of the Nepal Government). He said that this entry was a violation of the March 1960 boundary agreement and demanded that the Chinese withdraw their troops at once from the zone. He reminded Chou, as if the latter did not know it, that no armed forces were to be deployed in the demilitarised zone under the agreement. Koirala also reiterated his view that the incident had occurred well within Nepali territory and rejected the Chinese contention that it had taken place in what the Chinese claimed was their territory.

If the tone of Koirala's letter was not sufficiently conciliatory it was due to Chou trying to justify some of the elements of the incident, despite his genuine apology, and asking the Nepalis to disarm the Tibetan rebels who had crossed into their territory. He also said that the work of suppression of the rebels by the Chinese would take a little longer, and later he specified the time as the end of July.

Some time later, on July 12, Chou sent a more detailed and more conciliatory letter to his Nepali counterpart agreeing to remit a compensation of Rs. 50,000 as demanded by Nepal. He still maintained that the incident took place on Chinese soil, not inside Nepal, as Koirala had reiterated in his letter of July 6. According to the Chinese Premier the incident took place at a kilometre north of the Kore pass in Chinese (or Tibetan) territory. He claimed this on the basis of investigations carried out by his men in the affected area. But he pleaded: "Now since the matter has concluded and the Chinese government has borne its due responsibility for the incident, I believe Your Excellency will surely agree that it would be meaningless and unprofitable for the two sides to continue to argue over the place of the incident."

He admitted that the Chinese intimation that their troops would enter the demilitarised zone "was given rather late, only one day remove from the day the Chinese troops began their suppressing operations". He added that the Nepal Government had difficulty in issuing orders in time in the areas on the Nepali side of the boundary. This, he said, "Should be deemed a shortcoming."

Koirala interpreted it as Chou's admission that it was a shortcoming that the Chinese had been late in informing Nepal about their intention to enter the demilitarised zone. It, however, could also be interpreted that Chou meant that the failure of the Nepalis to inform their local officers immediately was a shortcoming. Koirala preferred to take the first view which was more favourable to his government. In that letter, sent on July 24, the Nepal Prime Minister also thanked Chou En-lai for promptly sending the compensation amount. He said they had demanded it as a "token compensation" for the material damages caused by the border accident in the Mustang area." That the incident was described as "accident" shows the carelessness on the part of the Nepali Foreign Office which could not supply a clean draft to its Prime Minister. Koirala praised the Chinese for their "desire to maintain and further consolidate the friendship between our two countries."

This was indeed a graceful and conciliatory gesture on the Nepal Prime Minister's part. He also agreed with Chou that it would not serve any purpose to continue to argue over the place of the incident while reiterating his government's strongly held view that the incident took place in Nepali territory. He accepted Chou's view that the matter need not be debated further because "the Chinese government had stated that the incident had taken place on account of the carelessness of low ranking personnel of the Chinese army and the Chinese government have borne their responsibility." Koirala was only repeating Chou's words in his letter of July 12, with the omission of "due" as an adjective of responsibility.

How could the Chinese agree to pay compensation and apologise to Nepal if the incident had taken place on Chinese territory as Chou kept on hammering. Would any political consideration and a strong desire to placate the Nepalis persuade China to do it if China was really convinced that the incident had indeed taken place on its soil? It would then have taken the view that while the killing of a Nepali was bad he and his associates had no business to be in Chinese territory. There is also more convincing evidence that the incident did take place in Nepali territory, not on Chinese or Tibetan soil.

When the final demarcation of the Nepal-China boundary was to take place and a boundary agreement was being negotiated a joint team made an on-the-spot inspection in August 1961 of the areas on the border. The Chinese then conceded to Nepal an area measuring three miles by half a mile adjacent to Mustang. The team had been deputed by the Joint Boundary Commission. The fact that the Chinese parted with this territory, adjacent to Mustang, clearly establishes that this was Nepali territory and the firing incident by the Chinese troops killing a Nepali non-commissioned officer did occur on Nepali soil, falsely claimed by the Chinese.

## REFERENCE

1. Original letters and statements may be seen in *China-South Asia Relations*, Vol. II, R. K. Jain.

# 14

# WORLD'S HIGHEST MOUNTAIN

Lovers of adventure, sport, mountaineering and the like always nurse an ambition to climb the world's highest mountain, Mount Everest. The Tibetans call it Chomo Lungma, also pronounced Jomo Lungma, and the Nepali name is Sagarmatha. The first name means "The Goddess Mother of the world" and the Nepali name means "the head of the ocean." In 1865, the head of the Survey of India, was Sir George Everest, a highly competent British officer who had serviced both the East India Company, a trading corporation of London through which the British ruled much of India until the revolt of 1857 forced them to come out in the open and impose their colonial rule more directly, and the British government which succeeded the company.

It is said his Indian officers had discovered the peak after Everest had done a gigantic job of a trigono-metrical survey of the whole of India. It is curious that a mountain which truly lay in Nepal and about which there was a controversy for some time, between tiny Nepal and mighty China should have been surveyed and finally named after a British officer of India. But then the boundary between India and Nepal has never been looked upon as a closed international border. The Ranas of Nepal, who were then ruling the country, were on the friendliest of terms with the British in India and never complained that their mountain had been given a British Indian name. That happened in 1865 and Nepal registered no protest then or later. But everyone knew that the mountain belonged to Nepal.

Even after India's independence in 1947, it was the Survey of India, now manned entirely by Indians and under an Indian head, which established the actual altitude of Mount Everest as 29,028. As we have noted it has always been a great attraction to mountaineers all over the world who flock to Nepal year after year. In the beginning some expeditions tried to climb the mountain from the northern or Tibetan side. There were seven such attempts from 1920, all futile but great adventures all the same some of which resulted in tragedy. In 1953, a British expedition, led by Col. John Hunt, scaled the mountain for the first time, from the Nepali side in the south. The first successful attempt was, of course, the result of a British effort but the two men who set their foot on the peak for the first time were the New Zealander, Sir Edmund Hillary, who was later knighted by the British Queen and became his country's High Commissioner to India, and Tensing Norgay, a Nepali resident of Darjeeling in India. They were members of the British team. Since then, there have been several expeditions some of which climbed the mountain and some which failed, all from the southern side. The Chinese surprised the world when they claimed to have scaled the peak from the northern side in 1960.

With Mao's philosophy guiding the Chinese it was not surprising that they lay claim to the mountain. Mao, as we saw earlier, had said that almost all the countries on China's periphery (which he named) belonged to China once and were taken away from her by the imperialists. When the Nepal Prime Minister, B.P. Koirala, visited China in March 1960 this claim was put forward by the Chinese. Koirala reacted strongly, almost violently, and later told a press conference in Kathmandu, "the mountain belongs to Nepal and Nepal alone[1]." The issue was quite hot in 1960. When a correspondent of the Hong Kong Weekly, the *Far Eastern Economic Review,* met Koirala in the Nepal capital for an interview, he said, "The world's headlines have been concerned recently with the Everest question." That was in May 1960.

A month earlier, Chou En-lai was in Kathmandu to sign a treaty of friendship and for talks with Koirala after his unsuccessful trip to India to sell a package deal on the border. The Everest issue was on everyone's mind. Consequently, a large number of questions put to Chou at his press conference in the Nepali capital related to the controversy whether the mountain belonged to Nepal or Tibet. The questions were fired both by Nepali journalists and newsmen from Delhi, who had flown in to cover the Chou visit, Indian journalists and foreign correspondents stationed in Delhi. As they met Chou on April 28, 1960, they knew that he was the most important Chinese leader after Mao.

Kishore Raman Rana, chief editor of *Kalpana*, a Nepali newspaper, published from kathmandu, asked Chou : "Has Your Excellency discussed Sagarmatha in your talks with Prime Minister Koirala? Has China laid claim to the mountain?"

> Chou En-lai's reply was interesting. He said, "we have never laid any territorial claim to Mount Jomo Lungma or Sagarmatha ever since the question was raised during the talks in Peking. The delineations in the maps of the two countries are different. The Chinese maps which were drawn on the basis of the Chinese historical situation shows the mountain within Chinese territory, while the Nepalese maps which were drawn on the basis of Nepalese historical situation show the mountain on the boundary line between the two countries. At that time Prime Minister Koirala made the point that Nepal had always regarded the peak as Nepal's. Chairman Mao Tse-tung when he received Prime Minister Koirala, expressed the view that we could follow the Nepalese delineation which showed the mountain on the boundary line, that is northern half of the peak belonging to China and the southern half of the peak belonging to Nepal. Since Chairman Mao Tse-tung's talk with Prime Minister Koirala our government has all along maintained this attitude."[2]

In other words, there was a real cleavage between the two governments' views, Nepal holding that the mountain, whatever be its name, was hers and China holding that it was Chinese. Mao once more expressed the traditional Chinese view that being on the periphery of the Chinese empire the mountain was China's. But after Koirala's hostile reaction to the Chinese claim, a settlement was found with China recognising the supposed Nepali map delineation showing the mountain half and half in the two countries. Only to that extent Chou was right that China had no claim to the mountain, although that was only a technically correct statement. The correct position was that China would have liked to own the mountain but relented when Koirala took a tough stand. In fact, as we have seen, he told a press conference later that the "mountain is Nepal's and Nepal's alone."

After the final boundary settlement between the two countries, when Mahendra, who had dismissed Koirala's government without any basis, went to Peking to sign the agreement with Liu Shao-chi, Nepal quietly accepted the Chinese proposition that the mountain belonged half to China and half to Nepal. There is little doubt that after Koirala's overthrow by Mahendra the Nepalis adopted a softer line on the issue. The stand taken by Koirala that the mountain belonged to "Nepal and Nepal alone" was whittled down and the Chinese formulation that they held half of it (via Tibet, of course) was allowed to prevail.

To press their claim, the Chinese also announced on May 27, 1960 that three Chinese mountaineers had reached the summit of the mountain from the north two days earlier. Considering the excellence which China has attained in international sports and games and several world records they have achieved there is no reason to doubt the Chinese claim. However at the time of the climbing this report was taken with a large pinch of salt.

Koirala addressed his press conference to which we have referred on May 28, a day after the Hsinhua announcement of the successful scaling of the mountain. He said in reply to questions that Peking had not informed Nepal about the expedition, at any stage before its success or after, although he admitted that China was not obliged to do so. His soft pedalling of the issue was due to the fact that in the past Nepal had not taken up the question of the expeditions launched from the north. Nepal, he said, had never protested to Tibet. A protest now would not mean anything. It is too late now."

Obviously, he thought a protest was in order but since as many as seven expeditions had been reported since 1921 and his country had kept quiet about them a protest now would be somewhat odd. But he forgot that the entire border issue was taken up by Communist China on the basis of its ancient claims and maps and it blamed the imperialists for what happened in between. Nations do not give up their claims because somebody in the past erred. In any case, he reiterated at the same press conference that the mountain was Nepal's and Nepal's alone. He also remarked that the Chinese claiming the mountain from the northern side "did not limit, hinder or affect our stand with regard to Everest". That Koirala was making a distinction between a tradition of mountaineering and a territorial claim was amply clear when he told the Nepali Parliament five days later that he would consider protesting to Peking if their climbers had planted their flag to sustain their claim to the mountain as the "highest peak of their fatherland."

There was a measure of aggressiveness in the Chinese climbing of the highest mountain of the world at a time when the two sides were debating the issue and, as Koirala told the press, he was in correspondence with Chou. Despite the facade of unity, the possibility of there being conflicting views in China on such matters should not be ruled out. It could have manifested in the expedition being launched by a fanatical wing of the ruling clique to embarrass Chou, who cried to project a softer and more pleasant face to the neighbours and the world in general. Anyway, the Nepalis themselves were to keep silent on their claim and soon accept the Chinese claim to half the mountain when Mahendra visited Peking to sign the boundary agreement. They both reigned and ruled at that time.

**World Concern**

The world's concern about Mount Everest was reflected in the flurry of questions shot at Chou at his press conference in Kathmandu we have referred to earlier. After the Nepali journalist had had his turn, an American correspondent who had flown in from Delhi, asked whether the mountain was being divided. Chou denied that any division was being made. "We shall continue to conduct friendly consultations." The friendly consultations apparently resulted in Nepal accepting the Chinese formulation that they owned half of the mountain. When the Chinese Prime Minister denied that there was any question of dividing the mountain, he was obviously stressing a point too far.

When an Indian correspondent, stationed in Kathmandu, asked Chou what Koirala's attitude was to the Chinese proposal for accepting the delineation of the mountain in the Nepali maps, he replied: "My answer to you is that we can accept the location of the mountain Jomo Lungma as drawn on Nepali maps. You know that the delineation on Indian maps is also the same. "That was an interesting remark because China has never accepted Indian maps on the crucial India-China border issue. Obviously, he could quote Indian maps when they were presumed to be supporting a Chinese claim. When they did not, they were to be countered by Chinese maps which were the last word on the subject."

When an Indian correspondent from Delhi, who had arrived in the Nepali capital to cover the visit, asked the Chinese Prime Minister whether the Mount Everest issue would also be referred to the joint Nepali-Chinese boundary committee (or commission), as all disputed issues were to be referred to it under the 1960 preliminary treaty, he replied: "No, my Indian friend, you cannot find any loopholes on this question." Under Article 2 of the treaty which Koirala and Chou had signed in March 1960, a joint committee was to be set up in order to settle the concrete problems concerning the Sino-Nepalese border.

There is an interesting aspect of the question which we have to record here. Koirala had just returned to Kathmandu from his Peking visit when he was closely questioned by journalists about the position of Everest, at a press conference he addressed early in April. He categorically stated that China had claimed that Mount Everest belonged to her but Nepal refused to entertain the claim. Chou only confirmed this statement at his press conference as we have seen. The Nepal Prime Minister also said that the question could be discussed during Chou's projected visit which was then scheduled. Koirala also said that the claim to Everest as also other border disputes would be amicably settled through the machinery devised by the two Premiers. So, the Indian correspondent who asked Chou whether the issue would be referred to the Joint Committee was not wrong and Chou's enigmatic reply that there were no loopholes was an exercise in evasion.

The issue could not have been settled during Chou's visit to Kathmandu because Koirala did not change his stand. Before we close this chapter let us recall an exchange between the two Prime Ministers over the name of the mountain. According to Koirala "the Chinese said that Everest is a British name and there is no word for it in Nepali although the Tibetan name has existed since long. I said that the Nepali name for it was Sagarmatha. The Chinese thought it was of recent origin."

In any case, the Chinese did not have a name of their own for the mountain, whether recent or ancient.

## REFERENCES

1. For details see R. K. Jain, *ibid*.
2. There are references based on R. K. Jain, *ibid*.

# 4

# INDIA-CHINA

# 15

# CHINA ON WORLD SCENE

"Let China sleep. When she wakes the world will be sorry." Thus spoke Napoleon who had a better world vision than many present day politicians and diplomats. Jawaharlal Nehru said after the Chinese attack on India in October 1962 "we were stabbed in the back". There is, however, no indication that he had remembered the wise words of Napoleon. Nehru was the foremost world leader who vigorously championed the Chinese cause in the United Nations and outside but when it came to the protection of the Indian borders he was found wanting and, as his words imply, too trustful of the Chinese. No less a person than President Sarvepalli Radhakrishnan, who had also held the post of Indian ambassador to Moscow, said when the Chinese attacked India and he was President : "Our credulity and negligence have caused us some initial setbacks."

India had done everything possible under Nehru, who was the first Prime Minister of India for 17 years and also its External Affairs Minister for all these years, to welcome Communist China in the comity of nations and ensure its rightful place there. India was the second non-Communist nation, after Burma, to recognise the regime within two months of its birth. The United States and its faithful allies took only 23 years to drop the pretence that Taiwan was China and recognise the reds. India fought China's battle in the United Nations during the crucial Korean war during which the United States, taking advantage of a UN resolution, launched a massive attack on North Korea, China's next door neighbour, which inevitably drew Peking into the war. Communists in general, including those at home, did not regard Indian independence as complete and both the Chinese and Russians abused India as a running dog of imperialism.

We have to go a little backwards into history to understand the close ties between India and China. At the height of the second world war, when China was the victim of Japanese aggression, the leader of the Chinese government, General Issimo Chiang Kai-shek and his charming wife visited India. This country was then still under British colonial yoke and Britain and China were allies in the war. Chiang and his wife were showing their solidarity with the Indian freedom movement of which Mahatma Gandhi was the leader and Nehru an outstanding exponent in the international sphere.

**The Kotnis's Mission**

Nehru also organised a medical mission to go China as a token of the Indian people's solidarity with the Chinese people even while they were struggling for their freedom. The Chinese now celebrate year after year the anniversary of the Indian medical mission when they remember Dr. Dwarkanath Kotnis, one of the members of the mission. Kotnis married a Chinese whom he loved and he died while he was actively engaged in bringing succour and relief to the suffering people. The Chinese are careful never to recall the services of Nehru but for whom the mission itself would not have been possible. Kotnis's services were celebrated by the well-known film maker, V. Shantaram, in the feature film, *Doctor Kotnis ki Amar Kahani*. Dwarkanath was wedded to a life of sacrifice and suffering in preference to a comfortable living in Bombay or Poona (now Pune). Like Shantaram, Kotnis was also a Maharashtrian.

Going back into the remote past of Indian history, India and China had close friendly relations for centuries without any war tarnishing the relationship. Buddhism, the religion of many in that country, travelled from India to China via Tibet and several Chinese scholars of repute like Hiuen Tsang came all the way to India to study at that great seat of learning, Nalanda in Bihar state. Many others covered long distances to imbibe the wisdom and learning of the ancient civilizations of each other. There was continuous intercourse in diverse fields like culture, trade, religious and other learning.

For long years before India's independence, the itinerant Chinese trader carrying a huge load of silks and other fabrics on his back for sale was a familiar sight the cities and villages of India. Many Chinese settled in India and Calcutta has its China town, even as Singapore and Hong Kong, both predominantly Chinese in their population, still have theirs. A number of Indians also settled in China and cities like Shanghai had their Indian population, some of them working as humble policemen or petty traders. In far away Sinkiang, there were Indian traders and an Indian consulate was set up after India became independent to serve them and look after their interests.

People thus cut across the barriers put up by administrative systems, barriers of passports and visas and others, and moved to areas of their choice or settled down to make a living, or because they liked the place or out of necessity. The hardening of the travel restrictions and rules governing immigration have created problems in this process and sometimes local administrations have created difficulties. The annual report of the Ministry of External Affairs to Parliament, said in 1948-49, more than a year before the reds assumed power in China: "At the end of the world war we were faced with a major problem in China. Indians in the employment of the Shanghai Municipal Council as guards and menials were thrown out of employment when the Municipal Council was taken over by the Chinese (from the Japanese). Most of them were destitute. At our instance a large number of them were repatriated to India. Their claims on the Shanghai Municipal Council have not yet been met but efforts to reach an early settlement continue."[1]

The report also refers to the sizeable number of Indians settled in the dry region of Sinkiang where an Indian Consultate-General was opened in December 1948: "... there are large colonies of Indian residents in all the cases of southern Sinkiang. Some time ago, lands belonging to the Indian merchants were unjustly confiscated by the Chinese authorities in Sinkiang. We have asked for the restoration of these confiscated lands or for the payment of compensation."

I was living in Hong Kong in 1971 when I met a number of people who had lived in Shanghai and other towns in mainland China but had to move out later because of similar or other problems. Some of them went back to India and some settled down in the British colony at Hong Kong or other South-East Asian nations, sometimes with their milch cattle. The people, on either side, have no preconceived notions and that is one of the reasons why they are important. Indians continue to migrate and I found a few even in the remote and sparsely populated Indonesian region of West Irian in the south pacific. They are there in the deep jungles of Africa and even in Latin America. The story of

Indian immigration in modern times began when the British forcibly took several thousand villagers as indentured labourers in the nineteenth century to work on the sugar fields of Mauritius, West Indies and Fiji, and has continued to this day in spite of the rigid restrictions imposed by the receiving countries. Indians are not an exception; people from other nations have been migrating for similar or different reasons. The British sent away their convicts and inmates of penitentiaries to lands they had captured in the far corners of the world.

Foreign policy makers and analysts fail to take these small facts into account. But they are nevertheless important. Just as history is not merely an account of the conquests of big kings and rulers so also foreign policy is not the sum total of protest notes, notes verbal issues and non-issues, which one foreign office loves to send to another not the joint communiques issued by the VIPs when they tour each other's country, nor the treaties and agreements signed by the countries concerned. The makers of foreign policy have to take into account the views and feelings of others who count and their failure to do so leads to a gap for which the nation has to pay dearly in the years to come because of the miscalculations of the experts.

In a broadcast to the nation when the Interim government was formed in September 1946, as a preliminary step to full freedom in August 1947, and Nehru became the Vice President of the government under the British Viceroy, he said :

> "China that mighty country with a mighty past, our neighbour has been our friend throughout the ages and that friendship will endure and grow. We earnestly hope that her present troubles will end soon and a united and democratic China will emerge playing a great part in the furtherance of world peace and progress. [2]

Little did Nehru realize that where China's troubles ended India's began. The progress of the Chinese Communists in their struggle against the Kuomintang nationalists was keenly watched in India. The Foreign Office, under Nehru, was also scanning the eastern skies while it read carefully the despatches from India's embassy in Peking, the seat of the nationalist government. The question of the recognition of the red regime became a vital issue in the government of free India in Delhi as the communists captured power on October 1, 1949. They soon formally approached New Delhi for establishing diplomatic relations.

**Patel's Letters**

Nehru combined a high degree of international understanding with a somewhat romantic approach to world events. Ignoring the abuses hurled at India and him, in particular, by the Chinese Communist media, he was keen to see that close contacts were built up with the new leaders of China. Consultations were already in progress with other governments, particularly the commonwealth nations, who dominated his thinking for some years, as to the timing of the recognition. At this time he received a letter from Sardar Patel, his equal in the freedom movement but one who agreed to work under him as Deputy Prime Minister in the government of free India. In fact, Patel wrote two letters to Nehru on the same subject of recognition until he received a reply to one of them. In his first tetter of November 3, 1949, Patel told Nehru:

> "There is no evidence yet that the Communist victories in China are influencing the situation in the north of Burma. But such victories will undoubtedly encourage the forces of disorder in the neighbouring countries. Our eyes must, therefore, inevitably rest on our eastern and north-eastern frontiers ... Tibet is likely to be another source of anxiety in the coming months ... With the liquidation of the Nationalists ... it is more than likely that the Communists will turn their eyes towards Tibet and try to establish a regime, either Communistic or in sympathy with the Communists. In either event, the situation cannot but be a matter of serious concern to us."

That China provoked trouble for years by aiding and abetting the armed ethnic groups on Burma's border with China is well known to scholars and laymen alike. Patel had the foresight of seeing all that coming even in 1949 but the Foreign Office, under Nehru, ignored his warnings.

Patel realised the trouble that India would face over Tibet once the new Chinese government consolidated itself and that was to become evident in a year's time. When he received no reply from Nehru on the issue of recognition and the troubles ahead Patel addressed another letter to Nehru on December 6. He told the Prime Minister that the latter was having an intention to recognize China after the UN session ended. While recognising that "recognition must come sooner or later", Patel said this should not be done before the other Commonwealth countries which were going to recognise China had done it. "If you feel that you must recognise China earlier than others, the issue must be placed before the Cabinet. After all, in such an important matter, it is only fair to our Cabinet colleagues that we take them into confidence."

This time Nehru replied to Patel the same day. Often, he would dictate his replies, with or without help from the Secretariat, whether it concerned the Foreign Office or affected his position as Prime Minister. He would do so after dinner at his stately home in what came to be called the Tin Murti House, once the house of the British Commander-in-Chief who ranked next to the Viceroy. The Viceregal House, or Government House, now called Rashtrapati Bhavan, became the home of India's President and Nehru moved into the big house which stands next to the mansion that is Rashtrapati Bhavan. Nehru's reply to Patel bore clear signs of having been dictated by him without any assistance from the Foreign Office which might have put up the relevant file to him long ago. He defended the decision to recognise China ahead of the Commonwealth nations. He said :" Our advisers are of opinion that it would definitely be harmful to recognise them (the Chinese) after the Commonwealth have done so."

What this harm could be Nehru never explained. Patel had a point as he implied that an early Indian action would be wrongly interpreted as a signal of Indian overenthusiasm for the new regime but Nehru paid no heed to it. What is of greater significance here is how Nehru received Patel's suggestion that the matter, which was really important, be placed before the Cabinet. The Prime Minister ridiculed the suggestion because the Cabinet colleagues did not evince sufficient interest. This is a vital point because his entire attitude on the conduct of relations with China in particular and international relations in general was that the subjects were his own preserve and the Cabinet had little to do with it. Only when the border question became really hot and the Chinese began using force did Nehru begin to take his colleagues into confidence. The nation had to pay dearly for his secretive and monopolistic approach.

Here is what he told Patel in reply to the point that the issue be placed before the Cabinet: "If you like I shall put it before the Cabinet. But the date (of recognition) depends on so many factors that it will have to be left open. Most members of the Cabinet have hardly followed these intricate conversations and consultations. But as you are interested I shall, of course, consult you before taking any action."[3]

So Patel was to be consulted, more as a matter of condescension than a matter of duty and Cabinet responsibility. The intricacies of foreign policy could only be grasped by Nehru and one or two others, not by the members of the Cabinet in general which was supposed to be governing the country! This was the state of the Cabinet in the very second or third year of the governance of free India. This was the approach which Nehru followed until the Chinese became unbearable and the world had to know about it. Patel's case was different. He was Nehru's peer and knew how to assert himself. Some others resigned from the Cabinet, John Matthai, Finance Minister, for example, because they felt they were ignored but some others were happy to be there and would have gladly said they did not understand the intricacies of foreign policy, if that was the price they had to pay for staying on.

On December 30, 1949 India granted recognition to China and its Communist regime. A communique from the External Affairs ministry issued on that day said that the "Chinese regime had expressed their desire to enter into diplomatic relations on the basis of the principles of equality, mutual interests and mutual respect for sovereign and territorial rights. Having considered this communication and taken note of subsequent developments, the Government of India have intimated their willingness to the new Government of China to establish diplomatic relations."

India thus accorded recognition within three months of the reds capturing power in China but the world's most powerful state took 23 years. After gaining freedom, India had appointed K. M. Panikkar as its ambassador to the previous Kuomintang regime in Nanking which was its capital. He was a noted scholar, an experienced administrator and even a former editor of a newspaper. Panikkar returned home for some time when the regime was overthrown and went back to his post as India's first ambassador to Communist China after recognition was granted. He presented his credentials to Chairman Mao in a scholarly speech : "The People's Republic of China and the Republic of India representing the oldest communities in the world are now in a position to cooperate effectively for mutual advantage and for the welfare of their people. The two sister republics of Asia, which between them contain over a third of the world's population, can through their cooperation become a great and invincible force." [4]

Panikkar made a few trips to India for consultations and for other reasons. During the visits he would make public speeches and statements to influence public opinion in favour of New China and closer India-China ties. The author was among the enthusiastic listeners of one of these speeches and the question and answer session that followed. During one of these Panikkar was asked: "Did you see beggars and prostitutes in China?" He replied "I did not see any beggars; prostitutes I was in no position to see." The snide remark which some in the audience passed need not be reproduced here. Suffice it to say that Indian diplomats, following the example set by the higher ups, display a great capacity to advocate other nations' causes. From personal knowledge, one could say that they strained every nerve to secure recognition for Bangladesh after the country was liberated by Indian arms. This continued until Dhaka turned hostile to India and a group of fanatics assassinated Mujibur Rahman and his entire family except Sheikh Wajida, his daughter who was then not in the country and who now leads an important opposition party.

How China's cause became India's will be seen in the following chapters. Some scholars would justify it on the ground that diplomacy required it. Some would say that a learned man is different from others because he could justify something which would look odd to ordinary human beings.

## REFERENCES


1. Quoted in *China-South Asia Relations*, vol. I. ed. R. K. Jain, Radinat, Delhi.
2. These and other documents quoted in R. K. Jain, *ibid.*
3. *Ibid.*
4. Quoted in *India's Foreign Policy and Relations, ibid.*

# 16

# INITIAL SUSPICIONS

All the friendliness displayed by India, her great leader Jawaharlal Nehru and the diplomats working under his orders did not prevent China and its media from showering abuses on this country. The Chinese looked upon India as a stooge of the Anglo-Americans and even questioned her independence. In spite of the recognition accorded by India and the strenuous canvassing done by her. The Chinese referred to India's status as a dominion and said this limited her freedom. If it was so, why did the reds ask for recognition by India as soon as they had captured power and offered to establish diplomatic representation? With a British dominion? The Indian Communists were, of course, mocking their own country and its independence. The Chinese magazine, *World Culture*, said in an article in September 1949, hardly three months before India was to grant recognition to Communist China: "The India of Nehru attained dominion status only two years ago and is not even formally independent in the fullest sense of the word. But Nehru, riding behind the imperialists whose stooge he is actually considers himself the leader of the Asian people."[1]

Nehru was the repeated target of the Chinese Communists before and after India's recognition. Obviously, the enthusiasm for the new Chinese regime in India was not reciprocated by the Chinese. Following the line taken by their fellow Communists of India, the Chinese did not realise that the dominion status formula was only a convenient and constitutional device to bridge the gap until India framed her own republican constitution which was already in the making then. Nobody in the Indian government or the system found any difficulty in functioning as an independent country because of the fact that India was still a dominion. It did not hurt the Chinese either as demonstrated by their asking for recognition.

Of course, the Soviet Communists were also behaving no better. Under Stalin, there was the same deeprooted suspicion of India and the USSR dictator never received Nehru's sister, Vijaya Lakshmi Pandit, who was appointed by her brother as India's first ambassador to Moscow. This hostility lasted until Nehru appointed S. Radhakrishnan, who later became India's President at Nehru's instance, to succeed his sister. Radhakrishnan had prepared the ground for a good reception in the Soviet land by making some speeches appreciative of the Soviet system in India. Stalin died in 1953 and gradually this hostility was replaced by active friendship when Nikita Kruschev headed the Communist party of the USSR and he and Marshal Bulganin, President of the USSR, visited India in 1955 following Nehru's visit to their country.

**Torrent of Abuse**

Of course, by that time the relations with China had also improved a great deal and both Nehru and Chou En-lai had visited each other's country. Before all that transformation could take place the torrent of abuse from China was in full flow while India was proclaiming her non-alignment from the house tops and even incurring the wrath of the Anglo-American bloc for that. China was offended in 1950, and for a few years thereafter, because of India's stand on Tibet and the note sent in the end of 1950 as a statement of policy. This being an important matter it has been dealt with in a separate chapter. Mere recognition did not please the Chinese and there were other problems which India had to face. The Chinese takeover of the remote province of Sinkiang described by Nehru's ministry as "peaceful", resulted in seven hundred Indians living in that remote province leaving China and becoming refugees in India. This is what the ministry's annual report to Parliament in March 1950 had to say: "Sinkinag was taken-over peacefully by the Central People's government of China on the 26th September, 1949. This has resulted in an influx of 700 refugees into India. Transit facilities are being afforded to them; and the Indian Red Cross has also given them relief."[2]

Readers would recall that only the year before a Consulate-General was set up by India at Kashgar in Sinkiang to serve these very people.

They were now in good company, joining the refugees from Shanghai after the Communist takeover.

In a Peking Radio broadcast on May 13, 1950 an American conspiracy was alleged to have matured with the collaboration of the "Indian reactionary clique", the Indian government, for making an "imperialist expansion" into Tibet. This was described as a territory under the authority of the Chinese government. Then the script writer remembered to add that this was a province of China, no longer an autonomous region. In a book *How do the US Imperialists Invade South-East Asia*, published officially by the Chinese, the author Tsao Pa-han, again abused Nehru. He said: "The US imperialist bait is sweet; Nehru will sooner or later swallow it up."

This book was released not only after the Indian recognition of China but also after the first Indian attempt in the United Nations to give China its rightful seat had been made. It failed because the General Assembly was too much under the thumb of the State Department in Washington. On September 19, 1950 Benegal Narasimha Rao, one of the illustrious brothers who served India in different capacities, made a brief speech in the Assembly after he had moved a resolution on behalf of India. The Indian motion said categorically, in parts:

> "The General Assembly ... recognising that the Central Government of the People's Republic of China is the only such government functioning in the Republic of China as now constituted... decides that the aforesaid Central government through its Head of State, or its Minister of Foreign Affairs, or its accredited representatives, as the case may be, shall be entitled to represent the Republic of China in the General Assembly."

The resolution failed to win the support of the General Assembly but B.N. Rau made a most cogent and dignified speech in support of the resolution. He spoke of the ancient and historical ties of culture and friendship with China and debunked the US plea that a Communist regime could not be admitted to the UN. "The United Nations was not intended to be a group of nations all thinking one way and excluding everybody else. "He pleaded that for the fulfilment of its obligations the Chinese People's Republic had to be in the UN. Year after year, it was the Indian delegate's bounden duty to bring up the issue and year after year it was the bounden duty of the US delegate to ensure that the General Assembly threw it out until it suited the latter to give the Chinese their due, much, much too later.

That India was taking a principles stand and was going by the merits of the case is beyond doubt. The Americans' gigantic fraud that tiny Taiwan, which had no control over the mainland of China, was itself China was exposed by India until the Chinese turned on India and invaded this land. The Chinese, of course, took note of the Indian action when a spokesman of the Foreign ministry in Peking praised India's first effort. He, however, made a subtle but not quite intelligible distinction between the Indian proposal for seating the Communist regime in the UN and the Soviet motion to the same effect which additionally wanted the "illegal" delegate of the Kuomintang "reactionary remnant group" to be expelled. If red China is seated in its rightful seat the Kuomintang delegate has to go in any case and it passes comprehension why there should be a specific demand for someone's expulsion.

**Whoever is not with us**

The Chinese Communists, like most others of the persuasion, apparently believed that whoever was not with them fully was against them. India, under Nehru, decided not to pay much attention to the abusive language used by the reds and continued to demonstrate its correct stand on issues affecting China. Not only the hardy annual of Chinese admission was brought up but also on other issues involving China. India took a correct and courageous stand, displeasing the Americans. In June 1950 war broke out between Communist North Korea and pro-American South Korea and China was inevitably drawn into the vortex of the war because North Korea was its immediate neighbour and a friendly Communist country. The issue came up before the United Nations which was fully dominated by the United States.

The UN dutifully branded North Korea an aggressor and a so-called UN force, which was virtually the American army using some stooges to give it the colour of a multinational force, launched an attack on North Korea. The Chinese feared that the US armed men were aiming at China, via North Korea, and thus humiliate the Communists using the UN as a safety valve for themselves. China warned the US that if the Americans, operating in the name of the UN, crossed the 38th parallel dividing North from South Korea, it would send its forces into North Korea. China kept its word and thwarted a possible US plan to get a foothold inside China through North Korea, Washington brought a resolution in the General Assembly in February 1951 seeking to brand China an aggressor. The Assembly was so long refusing to take cognisance of the existence of China and day-dreaming that Taiwan was China but now it suddenly woke up at American behest and sought to acknowledge that China existed and should be called an aggressor. The fact that China was only acting in self-defence to prevent the US force, named a UN army, from coming near its border was ignored.

It was India who stood against the mighty Americans to prevent any humiliation of China. In a couple of years Washington took the lead in convening a conference in the beautiful city of San Francisco to end the state of war with Japan and sign a peace treaty for the purpose. Only six years ago, the Americans had launched a nuclear attack on the civilians of Hiroshima and Nagasaki in Japan, the only recorded case of nuclear weapons being used by any country in the civilised world, in which hundreds of thousands of innocent civilians were killed. This was done in spite of the second world war coming soon to a close any way and because the Americans wanted to test the new miracle weapons of mass destruction and also tell the world that they had the bomb. Ironically, US diplomats are never tired of talking of nuclear disarmament and the world media and scholars and analysts endlessly discuss the issue as if they were unaware of who is the real culprit. When the anniversary of the mass destruction arrives in August each year, the media, under American influence, talk of the "dropping" of the bomb, as though it fell from heaven and no human hand was involved.

India refused to attend the conference in San Francisco, not because Indian delegates would not have given their right hand to be in that charming city, but for other reasons. Among them was the fact that China, which had borne the brunt of the Japanese aggression, was not invited to the conference. This ought to have convinced the Chinese Communists that when the time came India could stand up to the US "imperialists" more than anyone else, including the Chinese themselves, more by deeds than words. The country they later favoured at India's cost, Pakistan, was always with the Americans, then and is so even now.

There were several other actions which India took as a matter of a steadfast policy to uphold the principle that China must be given its rightful place in the UN and its rights must be fully respected. India worked closely with the UN in solving the Korean imbroglio. It had two of its best generals, Lt. Gen. K.S. Thimayya , who later became Chief of the Army Staff, and Lt. Gen. S. P. P. Thorat, who failed to reach the coveted post by a whisker. The first was chairman of the Neutral Nations Repatriation Commission, NNRC, and the other as head of a force to handle the prisoners of war. In 1953, India introduced a resolution in the General Assembly on the Korean prisoners of war. This favoured China and Nehru said the resolution was intended to accommodate the Chinese viewpoint relating to the incursions into China's border.

India always took a strong stand on the question of Taiwan and demanded in the UN and elsewhere that this and the other offshore islands of China must be restored to it. In September 1958, just prior to the worsening of the relations between India and China on the border issue, Nehru told a press conference: "No country could tolerate an island twelve miles from its shore being owned as a base for attack on it. India, therefore, felt that the offshore islands immediately and later Formosa (old name of Taiwan) could belong to the People's Republic of China."[3]

These unmotivated actions of India, coupled with the complete acceptance of the Chinese position on Tibet, after some initial conscience-laden protest in defence of the autonomy of Tibet, began to melt the granite-like hardness of the Communist hearts towards India. This led to the *Bhai-Bhai* relationship which lasted three or four years. Nehru's greatness lay in swallowing all the insults hurled at him personally and India as a nation by the Chinese and their media. The Chinese were not alone, among the world communists who believed that India was the running dog of the imperialists when there was clear evidence that India's policy initiatives were not dictated by Washington. They took four long years to disabuse their minds of the myth, much less than the Americans did to forget Taiwan was the real China. It took them 23 years to do it. Whether Nehru was right in his evaluation of Chinese policy towards India, which ultimately brought a heap of indignities on this country, will be examined in a later chapter. The let-down in Tibet is what we turn to now.

## REFERENCES

1. *China-South Asia Relations*, Vol. I, R. K. Jain, *ibid.*
2. R. K. Jain, *Ibid.*
3. Quoted in Appadorai and Rajan, *India's Foreign Policy and Relations*, from the *Asian Recorder, ibid.*

# 17

# TIBET : A LET-DOWN

Tibet is not Chinese even as the Tibetan people are different from the Chinese Han people. It is a land deeply immersed in its religious traditions and practices, rituals and monastery observances. This has been taken advantage of by other peoples more hardy and soldierly in their outlook. There is no doubt that for long periods it has been under Chinese suzerainty but it is equally true that Nepal has looked upon Tibet as a tributary state, as we saw in the second part of the book. Until 1953 an annual tribute was paid by Tibet to Nepal. Both Nepal and India, as a successor state to the British colonialists, had some extra-territorial rights in Tibet.

How is it possible for a state to pay tribute to another country as did Tibet to Nepal, and concede extra-territorial rights, including the posting of military personnel of another country or two countries, Nepal and India, and even give one of the countries facilities to set up post offices and telegraph offices as well as schools, India in this case, if that country, Tibet, was part of yet another country, China in the present case? Did China permit Nepal or the British authorities in India to extract and enjoy these rights in Tibet? Did it even object to this state of affairs until, of course, the Chinese communists came on the scene and forcibly annexed Tibet while India first hesitated and protested, giving the Tibetans hope that the big neighbour would rise to their defence, and finally meekly accepted the Chinese as lords and masters of Tibet and also advised Nepal to do so ?

In 1911 the emperor of the Manchu dynasty was overthrown in China and a republic was proclaimed. The tenuous relationship that existed between Tibet and China also came in for adjustment and the Tibetans felt that they must assert their authority over their own country. The Dalai Lama, religious and temporal head of Tibet, declared himself and Tibet sovereign in 1912 and he assumed full sovereign rights. The Chinese did not, however, officially recognise the independence of Tibet but acquiesced in the situation that prevailed on the ground. Scholars who point out that China did not recognise the sovereign status of Tibet or that the latter had not won international recognition, a *de jure* status, conveniently forget that in the run up to the Simla conference which led to the initialling of the 1914 accord, covering the McMahon line, the Chinese had fully participated in the talks along with Tibet and Britain as the power holding sway over India. Will a country which holds sovereign rights over another ever enter into border and other talks about its subsidiary power with a third country?

Of the long Indian border with China, the eastern and middle sectors, in Arunachal Pradesh, Uttar Pradesh and Himachal Pradesh[1], lie along Tibet and only the border in Ladakh touches Sinkiang province, the Han country. So two-thirds of India's border problem is with Tibet and only a third with China, if we see things in their proper perspective. India also had long-standing cultural and religious ties with Tibet and even now worshippers go every year to Tibet for the *darshan* of Mansarover, with Chinese permission, of course. Trade was another matter of common concern to both countries. The Buddhists in the hilly regions of India and in other parts too revere the Dalai Lama. In the Indian mind, Tibet was of special importance as distinct from the place the Chinese had.

All strong people have a tendency to assert their authority when they are strong. While economic progress and bringing real relief to the ordinary people is a difficult task it is easier to assert one's authority in the matter of territory. This also helps to cover up other failures and is useful in mobilising the support of the masses by appealing to their patriotic feelings. The Chinese communist leaders, well versed in the Marxist ideology, therefore, decided to turn their attention to Tibet and teach its leader a lesson for asserting Tibet's "Independence." At the earliest opportunity, they marched their troops into Tibet and subjugated the nation, much smaller by comparison with the great Chinese nation.

How did India react to this subjugation of small and largely peaceful people by a much stronger nation claiming their territory, the "liberation" of Tibet, as they called it? India sent a note to China on October 21, 1949, very conciliatory in tone and basing itself on reports that "some military action has taken place or is about to take place" in Tibet and this would affect "the peaceful outcome" of the negotiations which the Peking leaders were supposed to be having with the Tibetans. Obviously, the Indian note did not show any concern about the fate of the Chinese army's attack, at this stage in any case. Instead, it pointed out to China that the "timing" of the Chinese military action was inopportune. The note said as much: "The Government of India feel that the time factor is extremely important. In Tibet there is not likely to be any serious opposition..." India was anxious that China's admission to the UN must not be jeopardised by its military action in Tibet, actually an invasion. The Indian note almost suggested that after securing the admission to the UN, China undertake the invasion.

This note[2] was followed up by another on October 28 only a week after the first one, after news reports quoted an official statement in Peking which made no secret of the fact that the "people's army units have been ordered to advance into Tibet." The note quoted some obscure promise made to the Indian ambassador, who was often referred to as China's ambassador to India, that while reiterating the resolve to "liberate" Tibet, China had expressed the desire to do so by peaceful means. It passes one's comprehension that "liberation", which in the Marxist terminology means forcible liberation, was viewed as "peaceful" by the Indian ambassador and even accepted by the External Affairs Ministry and the Minister, Jawaharlal Nehru. The Indian note also said that a Tibetan delegation had been waiting in Delhi for British visas to enter Hong Kong in order to go to Peking from there for negotiations but it was then told not to go to China. The delay was not of its making. The note, however, shed some of Nehru's illusions and called a spade. It referred to "the invasion of Tibet" and deplored the Chinese action. If India was actually convinced that Tibet was part of China, how could there be an invasion of its own territory by China? That India looked upon Tibet as autonomous is clearly established by the use of the word *invasion*, not once but twice in the same note.

**China's Curt Reply**

The Chinese reacted to the two notes by their curt reply of October 30 stressing that "Tibet is an integral part of Chinese territory; the problem of Tibet is entirely a domestic problem of China. The Chinese People's Liberation Army must enter Tibet, liberate the Tibetan people and defend the frontiers of China." The Chinese note exploded two Indian myths. It did not accept that liberation could be peaceful and even more pertinent, it asserted that the army was going into Tibet not merely to liberate the Tibetan people but also to defend the frontiers. Tibet's frontiers were mainly with India (with Nepal also and how this problem was tackled we have already seen). Here there was a clear hint to the Indians that China regarded the frontiers with India as important and they would be "defended" by armed might. May be some official drew Nehru's attention to this implied meaning and equally possibly Nehru paid no heed to it. China also took the position in the reply that its admission to the UN was a separate issue from the problem of Tibet.

Nehru was cut to the quick by the strident Chinese reply. He apparently believed that China could be talked to and persuaded by his diplomatic skill and his world position, a fallacy which he committed throughout the years that followed and for which India paid dearly in its relations with China. Within two days, an Indian reply was despatched to the Chinese note. It said India was amazed by the Chinese assertion that it was affected by foreign influences in sending the earlier notes. Nor was there any foreign influence in the delay in the Tibetan delegation's departure for Peking. The Indian note also did some plain speaking. It told the Chinese that India's repeated suggestion that the Chinese claim of suzerainty over Tibet be reconciled with the Tibetan claim of autonomy was not a matter of interference in China's domestic affairs. Interestingly, the note asserted that the Indian military escort in Tibet and the establishment of the Indian Agent in Lhasa be preserved[3], something which they meekly surrendered by the 1954 "Panchsheel" treaty with China, the only treaty signed by the two countries so far.

The Chinese note, in reply, sent on November 16, was a strong reiteration of its position that Tibet was its domestic problem although it had taken the trouble of keeping India informed of its efforts to settle the Tibetan problem peacefully. In this connection, the note adopted the Indian phrase of "peaceful" liberation. The tone this time was surprisingly a little conciliatory and something which could help in strengthening Nehru's illusions about China's peaceful intentions. But for anyone who cares to read the underlying message of the communication, it was obvious that the Chinese were bent upon ensuring the presence of the Chinese army in Tibet for the important purpose of the defence of the border, which meant, of course, the Indian border.

One reason for the slight modification in China's attitude was that at the UN headquarters India was playing the role of a virtual Chinese spokesman. This successfully prevented an EL Salvador move, instigated by Washington, to take into consideration a Tibetan communication to the UN Secretary General on the difficulties they were facing with the Chinese.

The Tibetans had appealed to the UN for help against the Chinese invaders and the issue could have become a major cause for embarrassment and worse for China but India gallantly rose to her defence. In a speech, the Indian delegate, the Jamsaheb of Navanagar, told the General Assembly on November 24 that the Chinese forces had stopped advancing on Lhasa after the fall of Chamdo, some 480 km from the Tibetan capital. According to him, the Indian government was certain that the Tibetan question could be settled peacefully and Tibet's autonomy would be safeguarded, which "Tibet had enjoyed for several decades while maintaining its historical association with China."[4]

The Jamsaheb, a former princely ruler, was unjustifiably optimistic. His plea was supported by the British and even the Americans and the Soviets, who were then very friendly with the Chinese, and thus India succeeded in shelving the issue. The Jamsaheb even said that in the latest note received by India from China the latter had said that it had not abandoned its intention to settle the problem by peaceful means. The Chinese had not been so peaceful in their note, as we have seen. They had even gone to the extent of saying that the People's army must liberate Tibet. How does an army liberate a territory peacefully, except by the "peaceful" surrender of the people who are "liberated"? The Indian delegate, of course, could say only what he was told to put across. In any case, the note of November 16 was definitely more conciliatory but certainly it did not carry the assurance which the Jamsaheb was giving the UN, unless there were other indications of China's peaceable motives available to the Ministry of External Affairs.

An intense controversy was developing between Nehru and Patel over the line to be followed about Tibet. Patel was justifiably angry that China had not responded properly to India's note on Tibet. As we have seen earlier, he was pressing Nehru to adopt a more vigilant attitude towards China and was particularly keen that Tibet's autonomy be preserved and India should do everything possible for that purpose. In a long communication to Nehru on November 7, 1950, a month and eight days before his death, he told the Prime Minister that the "Chinese government have tried to delude us by professions of peaceful intentions." He also voiced the feeling shared by many knowledgeable people that the Indian ambassador, K. M. Panikkar, was playing into the hands of the Chinese, on instructions or on his own. Patel said, "My own feeling is that at a crucial period they managed to instil into our ambassador a false sense of confidence in their so-called desire to settle Tibetan problem by peaceful means.[5]"

Patel, never the one to hide his feelings, told Nehru that the final action of the Chinese in Tibet "is little short of perfidy." He analysed the issue in the plainest language possible. "The tragedy of it is that the Tibetans put faith in us: they chose to be guided by us and we have been unable to get them out of the meshes of Chinese diplomacy or Chinese malevolence." He referred to the Communist mentality of regarding "whoever is not with them is against them" and said in the strongest terms he had used: "Their (the Chinese's) last telegram to us is an act of gross discourtesy not only in the summary way it disposes of our protest against the entry of Chinese forces into Tibet but also in the wild insinuation that our attitude is determined by foreign influence. It looks as though it is not a friend speaking in that language but a potential enemy.[6]"

These prophetic words were recalled by several specialists and laymen alike when the Chinese Communists attacked India in October 1962. In any case, Nehru has no excuses. He was warned in the frankest manner possible of Chinese real intentions. What is more, Patel told him that Tibet had been betrayed by India. We shall see later that the betrayal story continued all through the years until Nehru could put up no longer with it and agreed to give the Dalai Lama and his entourage asylum in India in 1959.

In his letter Patel analysed the policy for the eastern and north-eastern sectors of India on China border. He drew attention to the military threat from China and the need for a long term policy to meet it. The letter was followed up by a detailed note on the internal security perceptions of the States Military, headed by him, in the light of the Chinese coming closer to India via Tibet. Alarmist at places, the note nevertheless brought out the dangers posed to India which were to be proved true in the years that followed.

**Tibetan Autonomy Dead**

Nehru replied to Patel's letter of November 7 on November 18[7], after the receipt of the Chinese note of November 16. It is a curious mixture of defence of his policy on China and Tibet and of the recognition that Tibetan autonomy was dead. He tried to make out that Pakistan was still the real threat to India. He said that the latest

Chinese note of November 16 was "much the same as their previous notes", but he detected a toning down and an attempt at some kind of a friendly approach. He also admitted that in one of the Indian messages to China the word *sovereignty* was used in referring to Chinese position in Tibet but this was corrected later to "suzerainty" which was the correct usage and position.

Nehru candidly admitted: "I think it may be taken for granted that China will take possession, in a political sense, at least, of the whole of Tibet. There is no likelihood whatever of Tibet being able to resist this or stop it. It is equally unlikely that any foreign power can prevent it. We cannot do so." This was a remarkable acquiescence in a power game by an idealist who fought Anglo-French aggression in Egypt in 1956 and rose to the defence of others under pressure from the all mighty Americans. Obviously, Nehru was playing for higher stakes of establishing long-term friendly relations with China and if in the process a little sacrifice of Tibetan autonomy was made what did it matter. He failed to realise that India had baled China out at the UN when the El Salvador proposal to hear the Tibetan complaint against Chinese aggression was moved. Was it necessary to do so? Here was a real opportunity to uphold Tibetan autonomy and link it to the question of Chinese admission to the UN. As the Indian notes repeatedly points out to China, the two issues were linked, but the latter refused to accept the connection. Diplomacy required that India's national objectives be pursued relentlessly. The foreign policy advisers who were supposed to tell Nehru what was what were also guilty of bending over backwards to please Peking. After all they also wanted governorships after retirement.

Nehru's own assessment was faulty. He told Patel in categorical words: "I think that it is exceedingly unlikely that we may have to face any real military invasion from the Chinese side, whether in peace or war, in the forseeable future." Was 1962 *forseeable* in 1950 or not? And for that matter, long before the actual Chinese invasion there were several border incidents and the Chinese frontier guards freely used their bullets on Indian border guards, whether from the paramilitary forces or the army proper. Apologists of Nehru have tried to find out his utterances[8] where he predicted an uneasy relationship with China but can there be a more telling example of his wrong judgement than this quotation from his letter to Patel? As we have mentioned earlier, scholarship has often become indistinguishable from intellectual subservience to the official point of view. The sacrifice of Tibet was only a step, an important step, in the policy of meekness bordering on surrender towards the Chinese until the real face was unveiled.

Patel was right and Nehru and his foreign policy advisers were wrong. They not only crucified Tibet, but also refused to accept the growing Chinese threat. In particular, they did not read the Chinese notes of 1950 properly. For the Chinese made no secret of the fact that they were entering Tibet in order to guard the Chinese frontiers. Tibet's frontiers are mostly with India and to a limited extent with Nepal.

With such Indian prevarication and unabashed display of pusillanimity, the Tibetans had no option but to conclude an agreement with Peking on May 23, 1951. That an agreement could be signed between a power which claimed complete sovereignty over Tibet and the subject state of Tibet is itself a revelation. China indirectly recognised that Tibet had a peculiar status so that an "agreement" could be signed with it. Indian foreign policy experts would argue: Did not Rajiv Gandhi, as Prime Minister, sign an accord with the Akali leader, Sant Harchand Singh Longowal, and later with the Assam student leaders who later become the Assam Gana Parishad which ruled the state.

Anyway, China agreed, at least in name, that it would not interfere with the religious beliefs and practices of the Tibetan people, or with their political system and maintain the powers and functions of the Dalai Lama. China was given control of Tibet's external affairs, trade and communications and was allowed to keep its army in Tibet. The Chinese agreed to allow the Tibetan officials of "various ranks to hold office as usual."

That even this limited autonomy of Tibet was not to be enjoyed by them in an unfettered manner was to be become evident before long. Incidentally, the agreement recognised that Tibet was not, prior to it, a part of China because it said in the very first article: "The Tibetan people shall return to the big family of the Motherland— the People's Republic of China".

Meanwhile, India was successful in its efforts to improve ties with China. The Chinese were bound to respond positively to the Indian overtures and gestures and relations with the other Communist giant, the Soviet Union, were also getting better. After the let-down in Tibet, the next step was for India to give up the special rights enjoyed by this country in Lhasa and other centres of Tibet. The Nepalis also enjoyed similar rights and, as we have seen, Nepal always considered Tibet their tributary state. The Indian decision to abandon the unequal position it had held came when the two countries entered into a formal treaty on April 29, 1954 in Peking.

Signed by N. Raghavan, Indian ambassador to China, and the

Chinese Vice Foreign Minister, Chang Han-fu, it was called "The India-China Agreement on Trade and Intercourse between Tibet Region of China and India". The treaty was accompanied by an exchange of letters between Raghavan and Chang on the withdrawal of Indian military personnel and facilities. The main agreement is noteworthy for being the first international document in which the five principles of peaceful coexistence are spelt out, something to which the Chinese attached great importance because they inserted the five principles in other documents also and referred to them again and again. Called the *Panchasheel*, or five disciplines after the five principles of nationalism which the Indonesian freedom movement had adopted for itself, the five principles are :

- (i) Mutual respect for each other's territorial integrity and sovereignty;
- (ii) Mutual non-aggression;
- (iii) Mutual non-interference in each other's internal affairs;
- (iv) Equality and mutual benefit; and
- (v) Peaceful coexistence.

After stating that the agreement was being entered into on the basis of the five principles, the two countries agreed to set up trade agencies, at New Delhi, Calcutta and Kalimpong for China, and Yatung, Gyantse and Gartok in Tibet for India. For their personnel and dependents the two countries agreed to provide, without saying in so many words, diplomatic privileges. Yatung, Gyantse and Phari were specified as markets in Tibet where trading could take place and Kalimpong, Siliguri and Calcutta were specified in India as trading centres for customary trade. A number of places in Tibet were named for carrying on trade and India agreed to name a similar number in its territory when trade between the Ari district of Tibet and India had developed to require the centres to be specified.

Buddhist and Hindu pilgrims from India could visit Kailas, called Kang Rimpoche in Tibetan, Manasarovar, also called Mavam Tse, and Buddhist pilgrims from Tibet could visit Banaras, Sarnath (near Banaras, also called Varanasi, where the Buddha preached his first sermon) Gaya (where he received enlightenment) and Sanchi, near Bhopal, in accordance with custom. The five routes by which traders and pilgrims should travel were specified as Shipki La pass (la itself means a pass), Mana pass, Niti pass, Kungri Bangri pass, Darma pass and Lipu Lekh pass. A route along the valley of the Indus, called in Tibetan Shangatsangpu, was also specified for customary travel. For traders and their dependents travel was to be regulated by certificates issued by the local authorities and for petty border trade without any permits. Otherwise, regular travel documents would be needed. Pilgrims need not carry certificates but either government could refuse entry to anyone.

The accompanying letters, signed by the two signatories, provided that the Indian military escorts at Yatung and Gyantse would be withdrawn within six months. The language used was somewhat archaic, "The Government of India will be pleased to withdraw...", Likewise, the Government of India was "pleased to hand over" to the Chinese authorities at a reasonable price, the post offices, telegraph and public telephone facilities which India was operating in Tibet, obviously used by the pilgrims and traders, again at a reasonable price. There were other provisions and arrangements which indicated the depth of the Indian presence in Tibet which was now being handed over to the Chinese. The main agreement was ratified by the two countries on June 3, 1954 but the letters said that they would come into force upon the exchange of the notes.

As we have said in the part dealing with Nepal-China relations, the special rights were a legacy of a period when one country, the stronger one, established some claim on the other by force. They could not be reconciled with the modern outlook of equality between nations to which much outward respect is paid but in reality the stronger nation has an edge over the weaker counterparts. The old colonial concepts had to disappear in any case. But the agreement did much more than that. By the treaty, India recognised Chinese *sovereignty* over Tibet and gave up the earlier position that China had only *suzerainty* there. Not only India abandoned its special rights in Tibet and dealt with only China even when Tibet was concerned but India also advised Nepal to follow suit. Thus Nepal and China also signed an agreement about Tibet, as we have seen.

**China Pleased**

There is little surprise that after such an agreement China would be immensely pleased with India who had developed a kind of amnesia and had forgotten that once it was standing for Tibet's autonomy and even for retaining its special rights in Tibet as we have seen earlier in this chapter. The *Bhai-Bhai* period began and there were many high level visits and intensified contacts.

But behind all that, the undercurrent of discord was also flowing and the disagreement on the border claims was developing into a major crisis in the relations between India and China. Tibet was suffering a great deal and to quote the International Commission of Jurists, "forced labour and compulsory exactions, a systematic persecution of the people, plunder and confiscations of belongings of individuals and monasteries and executions of certain leading men in Tibet, these are the achievements of Chinese rule in Tibet."[9]

The Chinese have shown a pronounced tendency to look at world affairs and relations with neighbours from their own standpoint. This is a common failing of most nations but more so in the case of the Communist rulers of Peking who flouted the Indo-China treaty, based on *Panchsheel*, almost within weeks of the signatures being put on it. Treaties can be sustained by mutual consideration which means equal adherence to its words and spirit, arbitration which the two sides accept, or finally by going to war. The Chinese attacked India in 1962 to enforce their will on the border question and the five principles of peaceful coexistence were thrown out of the window.

Likewise, the agreement between Peking and Tibet of May 1951, also called the seven-point agreement, was violated by the Chinese from the word go. The Dalai Lama, said in a statement[10] he issued from Mussoorie, India, in 1959 after he fled from Tibet.

"It was... clear from the very beginning that the Chinese had no intentions of carrying out the agreement. Although they had solemnly undertaken to maintain my status and power as the Dalai Lama, they did not lose any opportunity to undermine my authority and sow dissension among my people. In fact, they compelled me, situated as I was, to dismiss my Prime Ministers under threat of their execution without trial, because they had in all honesty and sincerity resisted the unjustified usurpations of power by the representatives of the Chinese Government in Tibet."

Even such staunch supporters of Nehru, as Appadorai and Rajan in their book *India's Foreign Policy and Relations*, have noted that a large number of Chinese began to march to Tibet with intent to settle down in the country "inevitably the demand for the scarce supply of goods increased with consequent rise in prices."

The Tibetans, peaceful and immersed in their religious rituals as they were, were bound to revolt. Chou En-lai was plying Nehru with assurances of peaceful intentions towards Tibet and Nehru was relaying them with all his persuasive powers, to the Dalai Lama when he visited the country in 1956, before the revolt and before his flight. The Dalai Lama meekly accepted the Indian-backed assurances but it was clear that the Chinese in Tibet were behaving differently, either with Chou's knowledge or against his wishes. The first of the two alternatives was more likely to be the case. The revolt first began in the eastern part of Tibet where the hardy Khampas live but, as Nehru had to admit, "The great majority of Tibetans sympathised with it." Let us quote Nehru himself from his speech in the Lok Sabha on March 30, 1959, a day before the Dalai Lama arrived in India. "For nearly three years, there has been what is called the Khampa revolt in China... But what has happened in Lhasa does not follow from that, it is a completely new development[11]". There were more details and relevant in a statement by the Foreign Secretary of India to the Chinese ambassador in Delhi on April 26 that year:

"On the 3rd April, the Foreign Secretary informed His Excellency the Ambassador that the Dalai Lama with a small party had entered Indian territory on the 31st March. The Dalai Lama had earlier sent a message to the Government of India asking for political asylum in India. The Government of India had, in accordance with international usage, allowed the Dalai Lama and his party to cross into Indian territory and stay in India..."[12]

The climax of the Tibetan revolt against Chinese atrocities and interference in their affairs was thus reached in March 1959 and there was violence in Lhasa from March 10. There were huge demonstrations in the capital city following rumours that the Chinese wanted to kidnap the Dalai Lama. The Chinese later an alleged that the Dalai was a prisoner of the "reactionary" clique, although the Dalai refuted all such reports himself. Anyway, the trouble was further aggravated by the Chinese garrison in Lhasa firing shells into the Dalai Lama's palace. On that day, March 17, the Tibetans decided that before it was too late the Dalai Lama should flee to India. After a 14-day long hazardous trek across mountains the Dalai Lama reached India on March 31. The entourage with him might be small, but as many as 14,000 Tibetan refugees entered India, following the Dalai's flight and the government made arrangements for their reception and relief.

The world media were in India and the Dalai Lama was besieged but, thanks to Indian official arrangements, he was shielded from them as far as possible. This did not prevent the Chinese from making serious allegations against India of encouraging the flight and of nurturing the revolt, with Kalimpong in West Bengal, always the meeting ground for the hill people of India, Nepal and Bhutan, whose nationals have free access to India, being falsely cited by the Chinese as the centre of the revolt.

What is of considerable significance, Nehru did not seek to challenge the Chinese overlordship of Tibet even after granting asylum to the Dalai Lama. It was not at all clear what policy he was following in respect of Tibet and China. In every major action there is always a long-term objective, hidden or explicitly stated, but Nehru was not challenging Chinese authority in Tibet while paying lip sympathy to Tibetan autonomy which the Chinese had trampled upon. In Nehru's speech on the Tibetan revolt, a day before the Dalai Lama entered India, there is a switch from Chinese "suzerainty" over Tibet to "sovereignty". He said: "All I can say is that we had to recognise Chinese sovereignty over Tibet."[13] That was, of course, a day before the arrival of the Dalai Lama but even after that Nehru never changed his stance. Tibetan autonomy was dead as the dodo and now India was even acknowledging Chinese sovereignty. Nehru himself had once said that there was a slight difference between suzerainty and sovereignty but this slight difference instead of being resuscicated was being killed twice over.

What did the Dalai Lama and his advisers expect when they fled into India? Apart from being at least alive and free in exile, instead of being in some Chinese prison or house arrest in Peking, they had the fresh air of Mussoorie, Kulu, Manali and Dharamshala in Himachal Pradesh, more akin to the cold climate of their country, than in other regions of India. But did they have any hope of going back to Tibet in freedom? They must have entertained such hopes but these were dashed to the ground. Of course, they cannot be allowed to create difficulties for their Indian hosts by indulging in political activity in India but they have no hope of returning to their land in honour. The Tibetan question has figured informally in the talks between India and China in the welcome improvement in their relations over the past decade or so but the Chinese have been as unyielding as before.

The western world has behaved with the duplicity as it has always displayed. President Clinton may have the Dalai for breakfast in the White House in Washington but that does not mean he would take up his case with the Chinese. The United States could have done it in 1972 when Nixon and Kissinger were flying to China and there was great bonhomie between the two nations because finally the United States was seeing its folly that Taiwan was not China. There is no indication, however, that Tibet was made a bargaining point for American recognition of China.

In granting asylum to the Dalai Lama, Nehru was only displaying his annoyance and even his ire to Chou En-lai over the trouble caused by China on the border issue and that conflict was developing into a major crisis. He was also asserting his authority and his status as a world leader which he always did, whether it served India's interests or not. But beyond a demonstration of anger and oneupmanship there was nothing that Nehru did nor his successors could do in the straitened circumstances they were placed after the country was left substantially weakened by the Chinese aggression during Nehru's time. Even when India built up sufficient strength to meet any possible Chinese challenge the thought that Tibet could be restored to its autonomous status never crossed the minds of the foreign policy makers of India.

## REFERENCES

1. The first is called the eastern sector, and the other middle sector. The Ladaka border is the western sector.
2. This and other quotations can be seen in *China-South Asian Relations*, Vol. I, ed. R. K. Jain, *ibid*.
3. This is a highly significant passage and scholars of international relations, for reasons we have noted, have not paid any attention to it. The Indian note of November 1, 1950, as reproduced in R. K. Jain, says *inter alia:* "The Government of India have repeatedly made it clear that they have no political or territorial ambitions in Tibet and they do not seek any novel privileged position for themselves or for their nationals in Tibet. *At the same time, they have pointed out that certain rights have grown out of usage and agreements which are natural between neighbours with close cultural and commercial relations*. These relations have found expression in the presence of an agent of the Government of India in Lhasa, the existence of a trade agencies at Gyantse and Yatung and the maintenance of post and telegraph office on the route up to Gyantse. For protection of this trade route a small military escort has been stationed at Gyantse for over 40 years. *The Government of India are anxious that these establishments which are for the mutual interests of India and Tibet and do not detract in any way from Chinese suzerainty over Tibet, should continue*. The personnel at the Lhasa Mission and agencies at Gyantse and Yatung have accordingly been instructed to stay at their posts. (Italics author's).
4. The quotations are from *China-South Asia Relations*, Vol. I, ed. R. K. Jain, *Ibid*.
5. *Ibid*.
6. *Ibid*.
7. *Ibid*.
8. See page 116 on the China Chapter in *India's Foreign Policy and Relations*, *ibid*.
9. Quoted in *India's Foreign Policy and Relations*, *ibid*.
10. *Ibid*.
11. R. K. Jain, *ibid*.
12. *Ibid*.
13. *Ibid*.

# 18

# BHAI BHAI ERA

In a previous chapter we saw how the Chinese were becoming increasingly friendly towards India and were showing some appreciation of the many good turns India was doing to them. India was sending out one signal after another to tell the Chinese that it meant nothing but well by their country. India had played a highly commendable role in Korea and the Chinese, who fought bravely against the American invaders, knew it at first hand. Some of the notes to the NNRC, headed by Gen. Thimayya of India, were somewhat critical but they knew that India was taking the decisions of its own, not at the bidding of the Americans.

China now began to receive goodwill missions from India and there is no dearth of do-gooders who would like to wangle a free trip to China and do some hectic shopping in Hong Kong on the outward or inward journey, if not both. There were quite a few who were genuinely friendly towards China and were bursting with goodwill. Both were grist to the Chinese propaganda mill. The Tibetan treaty was naturally welcomed in China and that added to the fund of goodwill. India's relations with the most powerful Communist regime, the Soviet Union, had undergone a sea-change and since the Chinese were then greatly dependent on the Soviets this became a favourable factor in the developing India-China ties.

The stage was now set for the *Bhai-Bhai* relationship between the two Asian nations. The Indian people, with their memories strongly influenced by the plight to which their country and many others in Asia, including China, were reduced by the colonialists were happy to see China as their friend. If the official relations were improving fast the people-to-people relations were extremely cordial. In June 1954 the Chinese Prime Minister, Chou En-lai, visited India on the first of his five tours. The pioneering visit was not only greeted with tremendous popular acclaim but also the slogan *Hindi Chini Bhai Bhai*, (Indians and Chinese are brothers), was raised during this visit and became famous later. The doors were opened wide for a long-term relationship of cordiality and friendship. The 2,000-year-old peaceful and friendly relationship was the theme of Chou's speeches and this point about peaceful coexistence was also stressed by the Chinese media. Speaking in the National Committee of the People's Political Consultative Committee in Peking in 1957. Chou said: "The enthusiastic reception given us by the Indian people defies description... wherever we went we heard the hearty cheer *Hindi Chini Bhai Bhai*. What greater affection and cordiality could you show to the people of another country than calling them brothers? The term 'brother' had a special significance to the Chinese leaders who, as good communists, knew that only fellow communists could be called brothers. Indians, as we have said, had long memories of colonial rule under which they were treated as less than human. There is no doubt that while the reception to Chou could have been organised formally by the government, it is the people who raised the slogan and they meant it. And there is no doubt that in responding to it the Chinese were equally sincere while Bhai-Bhaiship lasted.

**Nehru's China Trip**

Nehru paid an extended return visit to China in October 1954 and was greatly honoured by the Chinese. It is not clear why he did not find the time for a second trip at all. It, however, left an indelible mark on his mind and strengthened his anti-imperialist outlook and this further alienated India from the American bloc. The next visit to China by an Indian Prime Minister was to take place after 34 years when Rajiv Gandhi went to China in an ice-breaking operation, although the first effort in that direction was made by Atal Bihari Vijpayee's visit as the Morarji Desai government's External Affairs minister in 1978.

During the period of good relations in 1954-58 goodwill delegations were going and coming. Dr. Sarvepalli Radhakrishnan, then Vice President and in protocol terms one notch higher than even the Prime Minister, visited China. In a return trip Madame Sun Yat-sen, widow of the great revolutionary leader of a previous era, who was much revered by the Communists, cemented the ties still further. She was much in demand in India which had fond memories of the earlier non-communist era. There was a steady flow of cultural, trade and industrial delegations. Nehru was then enamoured of farm cooperatives and tried to introduce some in India, without any success but not without causing a fright among diehard free enterprisemen, sent a team across to study the Chinese experiment in the area.

China extended full support to India's claim on Goa. Situated on the south-west coast of India Goa was a relic of the colonial era and the Portuguese foolishly thought they could hold on to it for ever, a thought in which they were encouraged by professed democrats and republicans in the State Department in the US. There were smaller Portuguese enclaves besides Goa, Dadra and Nagar Haveli, Daman and Div (wrongly written as Diu), all in Gujarat state, and they were all liberated by the Indian army in 1961. The Americans tried to embarrass India in the UN but did not succeed. The people of Goa and the other enclaves are all Indian, the territories are geographically part of India and the residents speak the same language as the people nearby. Embarrassingly for the US and its allies, the relations between India and Portugal became friendly once the dictator Salazar disappeared and now the two countries are on friendly terms. Incidentally, the Chinese have not yet liberated Macao, a tiny Portuguese enclave near Hong Kong.

During this period of Bhaibhaiship, the Chinese took a same line on Kashmir as the Pakistanis had not yet opened their China front when they combined close military relations with the US with similarly close military and other relations with China. This is something which should give food for thought to the mandarins of Delhi's South Block. Going back to the period of cordial ties between India and China, a Chinese delegate once condemned US-Pakistan military alliance. In 1954, the UN Economic Commission for Asia and the Far East, ECAFE, now renamed UN Economic Commission for Asia and the Pacific, met in Ceylon (not yet Sri Lanka) and the Chinese delegation was led by Li Chi Po. He said, "The US government is actively working for a US-Pakistan military alliance which will bring the menace of war to the South and South-East Asian region." [2]

Nehru had gifted an Indian elephant to Chinese children when he visited China in October 1954. Chou was impelled to reciprocate with several gifts of Chinese animals and fish on Nehru's birthday on November 14 that year. In his message to Nehru Chou said: "On the occasion of your 65th birthday please accept these well-known Chinese items—a pair of spotted deer, a pair of red crested cranes, and 100 gold fish of twenty different species which I send through you to the Indian children. I hope that they will like these gifts which symbolise the friendship between our two peoples just as the Chinese children like Asa (should be Asha, the elephant Nehru had presented)"

To cap the treaty on Tibet signed by the two nations in April 1954 a general trade agreement was signed between the two countries in October that year. I was then attached to the Commerce and Industry ministry (as their Information Officer), as it was then constituted and known. I vividly recall the occasion because we went to some trouble to get the agreement printed overnight for distribution to the guests at a party thrown by the Commerce Secretary to mark the occasion. The treaty was signed by that ministry on behalf of India.

Although Nehru never paid a second visit to China he was paying visits to the Soviet Union. India's relations with that country were becoming close to the point when Kruschev said on his second visit to India that "Hindi-Russi" were brothers on the pattern of the "Hindi-Chini Bhai Bhai". His voice rang true because it was well known that while the ties with China were becoming unfriendly those with the USSR were getting closer. There was, however, a setback in 1965 when the Soviet Union compelled India to sign a peace accord with Pakistan after the latter's unsuccessful attack on India. Lal Bahadur Shastri who was India's Prime Minister, having succeeded to the office after Nehru died, was "persuaded" by T.N. Kaul, who was Indian ambassador to the Soviet Union and known to be close to the Soviets to go to Tashkent. Shastri died of a massive heart attack, as announced by the Soviets, in Tashkent after signing the accord which had a hostile reception in India.

What is relevant is that the relations became again friendly after some years and the Indo-Soviet treaty of friendship signed in August 1971 played a crucial role in the war of Bangladesh liberation in December that year. The foundations of this lasting relationship were laid by Nehru who had visited the Soviet Union first in 1927 when he was a middle ranking leader of the freedom movement. He had written approvingly of many things he saw in that country at a time when the term Bolshevik was an expression of abuse in the western media which continue to dominate the world. His visit to the Soviet Union as Prime Minister in 1955 won him laurels at home also and President Rajendra Prasad awarded in July that year the highest honour of 'Bharat Ratna' to him. In a brief speech, the President said he was acting for the first time without the advice of the Prime Minister, as the Constitution required him to do.[1]

Nehru had tried to be friend China in the same manner but the border issue came in the way and China showed utter incapacity to see things except from a narrow point of view and even flexed its muscle. China, however, showed much appreciation of Nehru's visit to the Soviet Union in 1955 as the Soviets had not yet turned "revisionists" for Peking. In fact, China depended a great deal on Moscow for many things and it is not unlikely that the nuclear know-how and missile technology was passed on to it by the USSR. (China, in turn, gave much of it to Pakistan.) The *People's Daily* said that friendly cooperation between India and the Soviet Union was important for the defence of peace irrespective of the different social systems in the two countries. This was when Nehru had made a highly successful trip to Moscow in 1955. The leading Chinese organ stressed the importance of Soviet economic aid to India, including the setting up of a major steel plant in the public sector at Bhilai in Madhya Pradesh state. It said Soviet-Indian friendship was growing daily and Nehru's visit was a very significant event.

Chou En-lai himself commented on the growing friendship between India and the Soviet Union and the exchange of visits by the top leaders of the two countries. Speaking at an Indian embassy reception on India's Republic Day in January 1956 he said: "In 1955 friendly visits were exchanged between Prime Minister Nehru and the national leaders of the Soviet Union. This not only marks a new development in the friendship between India and the Soviet Union but it also has far-reaching international significance.[2]

The shrewd politician that Chou was, he could say things somewhat differently in different places. Visiting Delhi in December 1956 he said that China would support India in defence of its territorial integrity. Later that month he happened to visit Dhaka, then still the capital of East Pakistan, and the newsmen who had to proclaim their Pakistani identity, asked him what he meant by Chinese support to "India's struggle for to defend its territorial integrity," he replied that it was simply an assurance on the part of China that it would "respect the territorial integrity and sovereignty of India as of any other country." All this, he added for good measure, was included in the five principles of peaceful coexistence. There is a proverb in north India which would translate as: "When you go to the Ganga, the holiest of Indian rivers, you call yourself Gangadas, or servant of the Ganga, and when you visit the river Jamuna, another holy river, you call yourself Jamunadas, servant of the river Jamuna."

Since this was an important statement in Delhi—or so the media thought—he was asked by a correspondent when he visited Calcutta after Delhi whether Kashmir was covered by his statement of support for India's territorial integrity. His reply was again an exercise in shrewdness, but this time also an expression of considered policy. He said: "India and Pakistan are sister countries. The people of these countries are of the same race. There can be no dispute between them which cannot be settled." This was at a time when China and Pakistan had begun to cultivate each other and what Chou said then is what China has now come back to after the relations between India and China improved substantially, in the eighties and nineties. China's stand on Kashmir is now almost the same as stated by Chou then. Essentially it is that Kashmir is a bilateral issue, whereas Pakistan would like to internationalise it.

In a report to the Second National Committee of the Chinese People's Political Consultative Conference on March 5, 1957 on his visit to eleven countries of Asia and Europe, including India, Chou paid glowing tributes to the friendship between India and China and to the frank exchange of views with Nehru. He made a detailed reference to the Kashmir question which we may recall here:

> "In the relations between the Asian countries at present, the Kashmir question between India and Pakistan has caused much uneasiness on the part of their neighbours. We have expressed our hope to the leaders of India and Pakistan that they should seek a solution to this problem through peaceful negotiations. In our joint statement of February 5, 1957, Prime Minister Bandaranaike of Ceylon and myself similarly appealed to the two parties to make further efforts for a peaceful settlement of this question for the sake of their own interests as well as for the broader interests of the solidarity of the Asian and African countries. Here we should like to express this hope once again. It is our view that the sister countries of India and Pakistan can reach a friendly settlement themselves through friendly negotiations. *To have this question referred to the United Nations, which in the circumstances of today is in the control of the United States, can only give rise to the danger of foreign interference.*"[3] (Italics ours.)

During the days of *Chini-Pakistani Bhai Bhai* (although no such slogan was known to have been coined) China had gone all out to express solidarity with Pakistan but now it is somewhat back to square one. The US still dominates the UN although China itself is now a full member of the world body and its executive organ, the Security Council where it has the right of veto.

In his report to the Political Consultative Conference, Chou also referred to some differences with Nehru in a friendly sort of way and did it for the first time. After saying that Nehru and he had reached full agreement in our views on many questions, he said: "Naturally China and India do not hold, nor can they hold identical views on all questions. But, just as Prime Minister Nehru said during our visit to India, when we disagree in some matters, it is a friendly disagreement and it does not affect our friendship and cooperation." Whether this disagreement related to the all-important border issue it is difficult to know. More of it in the next chapter.

## REFERENCES

1. *Speeches of President Rajendra Prasad,* Vol. II, Publications Division, Delhi.
2. It is highly significant that the second most important leader of China himself attended the reception and clicked glasses with the Indian ambassador. Normally only a minister, not often the foreign minister, attends such national day receptions in enbassies. Hostility is also displayed by the inviting country sometimes. Thus when the Minister of State for External Affairs, R.L. Bhatia, represented the Government of India at a Pakistan Day reception in Delhi in 1995, he was insulted by not being offered a chair. Some pro-Pakistan newspapers in India defended the Pakistan High Commissioner as though he had a right to insult Bhatia.
3. R. K. Jain, *ibid.*

# 19

# FIFTH LONGEST BORDER

The India-China border is divided into different sectors and the total length is said to extend to around 4000 km which makes it the fifth longest border in the world. The border extends from the trijunction of India, China and Myanmar, in the east to the trijunction of India, China and Afghanistan in the west. The border between the United States and Canada is said to be the longest in the world the second longest is the border between China and the former Soviet Union, now Russia. The Indo-Pakistan border before the separation of Bangladesh from Pakistan was the third longest and the fourth position goes to the border between the Republic of Mongolia and China.[1] Thus India figures in two of the five longest frontiers and China in three of them, including one between China and India.

As we have seen, the eastern and middle sectors of the India-China border touch Tibet, which the Chinese call as the Tibet region of China, and only the western sector in Ladakh, part of India's Jammu and Kashmir state, touches the Chinese or Han part in Sinkiang. For ages this was a peaceful border. Although there was some activity in both the eastern and western parts, during and before the British capture of India, the border on the whole was tranquil. There is no recorded massive troops movements across the border except in modern times.

The two countries entered into a treaty in 1954 on trade and intercourse between the Tibet region of China and India which is the only treaty between the two countries. In a letter to the Chinese Prime Minister, Chou En-lai, on December 14, 1958, the first missive when the behind the scenes border conflict was getting hot, Nehru referred to that treaty and said in some desperation: "No border questions were raised at that time and we were under the impression that there was no border dispute between our respective countries. In fact, we thought that the Sino-Indian agreement which we happily concluded in 1954 had settled all outstanding problems between our two countries."[2]

Within less than three months of the treaty being "happily concluded", the first Chinese note on the border issue had landed in the South Block, the location of the Indian Foreign office, then and now, in Delhi.[3] It alleged that over thirty Indian troops had crossed the Niti Pass in the Tibet region and had entered Wu-Je, known to the Indians as Barahoti, which is part of the Uttar Pradesh state of India. The note asked India to investigate the matter and withdraw the personnel from what it claimed was Chinese territory. The note also said that the action was not in conformity with the five principles of peaceful coexistence of which they quoted non-aggression and peaceful coexistence.

The note was sent by the Counsellor of the Chinese embassy in Delhi who pursued the matter with Chinese doggedness. The Indian reply was sent to him on August 27 of that year and maintained that the allegation by him was entirely incorrect. A party of the BSF, India's frontier guards, had camped in the Hoti plain which was in Indian territory. The Indian note counter charged the Chinese with violation of the Indo-Tibetan treaty in that some of the Tibetan officials had intruded into India without proper documents. There was thus a double violation, one of the provision relating to proper documents being in the possession of the officials and two of the five principles to which the two governments were committed by the treaty, non-aggression and peaceful coexistence in particular. Both sides had referred to the five principles but the Indian note had additionally quoted the treaty of 1954.

### First Exchange of Unpleasant Notes

The period following that first exchange of unpleasant notes was used for strengthening the ties and this and other ugly incidents were not allowed to tarnish the relationship. But now in the end of 1958, when incidents had taken place in which the Chinese had killed some Indians on the western border, Nehru was to admit that he was "under the impression" that with the India-China treaty of 1954 all the border issues had been settled. Chou told him in reply that this was not so. The first Secretary- General of the External Affairs ministry, G. S. Bajpai, now happily ensconced in the Raj Bhavan in Bombay as Governor in his retirement, had written to his old ministry in 1952 when the treaty was being negotiated, that India should take the initiative and raise the issue and of the McMahon Line with the Chinese. Appadorai and Rajan, who quote this piece of information in their book, *India's Foreign Policy and Relations,* were compelled to add, much as they admired Nehru: "It is unfortunate that the advice was not followed."

A golden opportunity of making the Chinese commit themselves to the McMahon Line was thus lost. India was giving away all its rights in Tibet and getting almost nothing in return. Only a study or the relevant files in the ministry could establish who, the officials or Nehru, took the decision not to raise the McMahon Line with the Chinese during the Tibet treaty talks. Officials sometimes could take the view that they knew better than their retired boss but since it was common knowledge that Nehru called the shots in all foreign policy matters it could be safely presumed that he thought the wise Bajpai's suggestion need not be pursued. The special rights in Tibet had to be given up in any case but there was scope for debating the border question since the treaty itself was under negotiations for two years. If the Chinese apparently wanted Indian friendship they could very well have accepted India's proposal for a demarcation of the entire border if one was made.

The exchange of unpleasant notes was resumed in July-August 1958 on the alleged activities of Tibetan refugees in Kalimpong in West Bengal state of India. The Chinese note charged that the American-Chiang Kai-shek clique was instigating the refugees to undertake anti-Chinese activities. The Indian reply, however, denied it and said India did not permit any foreign government to use its territory as a base against such a friendly country as China. This was unrelated to the border question but it showed nevertheless that some people in China could indulge in vituperative language against India even while the leaders and the media were busy at the friendship game.

The issue was, however, hotting up and India had to send two serious notes, on August 21 and October 18 that year. In the first one, India pointed out that a Chinese magazine, *China Pictorial,* of July 1958, carried a map of China in which large areas were shown as Chinese territory. Thus began what is popularly known as "cartographic aggression" which was to be followed by actual aggression by the armed forces of China in another four years. The note said: "The border as depicted in the map includes as Chinese territory (i) four of the five divisions of India's North-East Frontier Agency, NEFA (renamed Arunachal Pradesh in 1972); (ii) some areas in the north of the state of

Uttar Pradesh; and (iii) large areas in eastern Ladakh which form part of the state of Jammu and Kashmir."

The note went on to point out that similar inaccurate maps had been published by China earlier and Nehru had drawn Chou's attention to the matter as early as October 1954 when the former visited China. Chou had then replied that the current maps were based on old maps and the People's Republic had had no time to correct them. Unfortunately Nehru had not obtained any Chinese assurance that the maps when corrected would show the border correctly without any claims on Indian territory and as to when these maps would be corrected. He also remained under the illusion, as he himself admitted, that the 1954 Tibet treaty with China had settled the border problem. India was to pay dearly for the leader's failures and illusions.

The Chinese reply to the Indian note came on November 3 and took the same line that Chou had taken earlier, that is, China had had no time to revise the old maps. But significantly, the Chinese note added it would not make any changes on its own and it had not yet undertaken a survey of the boundary. It said this revision would be done on the basis of the survey and consultation with the countries concerned.

But before this reply could be received a grave situation was created which was conveyed in a note to the Chinese on October 18. This one pointed out that the Chinese had built a motor road across Aksai Chin in eastern Ladakh. This was part of a Chinese road, called the Yehcheng-Gartok road, on the highway linking Tibet with Sinkiang. In order to build a road, linking two parts of China, what did it matter if some part of it lay across Indian territory, specially if the Indians would not be able to find out for some time? This could well be the reasoning of the Chinese who maintained that they were in their country. The Indian note had, however, clearly said that the India-China border was traditionally well-known and follows well marked geographical features.

More importantly, the Indian note asserted, for the second time, that this was a clear violation of the April 1954 treaty. The officials and workers engaged in constructing and maintaining the road and the people using the road were violating article 5 of the treaty which required Chinese officials and nationals to hold passports and visas for travelling across the border. No applications were ever received from the persons for travelling into India. Still following the leader's policy of conciliation, the note referred to this as a "petty frontier dispute."

In this sequence followed the Nehru letter to Chou referred to earlier. Apart from confessing that he assumed that the border issue had been settled with the signing of the Tibet treaty, Nehru asked Chou to recall that in their talks in 1956 Chou had told him that China proposed to recognise the McMahon Line in the eastern sector, as it had already done in the case of Burma. Nehru further recalled Chou telling him that he did not like the British name which Nehru himself did not. On the unreasonable Chinese argument that they had no time to revise the maps Nehru said: "You will appreciate that nine years after the Chinese People's Republic came into power, the continued use of these incorrect maps is embarrassing to us as to others. There is no question of these large parts of India being anything but India and there is no dispute about them."

But the Chinese thought there was a dispute. The maps claimed some 50,000 sq. miles of Indian territory. India had actually taken an inexcusably long time to object to the maps although the fact had been brought to the government's notice long ago. It would not be wrong to say that the government had slept over the issue, obviously again, under Nehru's instructions. Brig. S. S. Mullick, Indian military attache in the embassy in Peking, had sent a report to the government in Delhi as early as November 1955 of China's proposal to build a highway through Aksai Chin. The road was built in 1956-57 and yet the first protest note was sent in October 1958 and even then it was referred to as a "petty frontier dispute." Nehru had a facile defence: the area was inaccessible and remote. That was when he was cornered in Parliament which was now agitated and even furious that he had neglected to maintain Indian borders with China. Some members of his own Congress party had turned hostile to him. Speaking in the Lok Sabha on August 28,1959, he said: "The House will appreciate that these areas are extraordinarily remote almost inaccessible, and even if they can be approached it takes weeks and weeks to march and get there."

**Sounding on Surrender**

Perhaps he was sounding the House to find out how it would react to a surrender of these areas or their exchange for areas claimed by the Chinese in the NEFA sector. That would be somewhat unfair to him but his words were, in fact, troubling many people those days. Nehru was trying to explain that one of the two reconnaissance parties which had been sent out to Aksai Chin in 1958 had met with disaster. The missions were obviously sent out when it became known that the Chinese had built the road across Aksai Chin and one of the two teams was detained by the Chinese and released after a month's detention. In July that year the Chinese intruded into Ladakh and occupied India's Khurnak fort and arrested an Indian party in the Aksai Chin region. They made several other incursions. The climax was reached when a party of border policemen was waylaid in October 1959 near Kongka Pass and nine of them were killed. "Other members of the party were taken into custody and meted out inhuman treatment," said an official publication.[4] Every year policemen in India hold commemorative parades to honour the martyrs of the October 20 incident.

Reference has been made to Barahoti, called Wu-Je by the Chinese, where also they intruded year after year. While the Indians proposed that since this area was claimed by both sides they should refrain from sending armed men there but the Chinese did not agree. There were several incidents in the NEFA area too all of which lead us on to the next chapter. Before we do so, there are some aspects of the border dispute which we have to consider here.

In reply to Nehru's letter of December 14, 1958, referred to earlier, Chou En-lai, in a letter dated January 23 next year, said that the border between the two countries had not been formally delimited. The Chinese leader's statement was true on technicalities only in that there were no markings on the ground but there were treaties between the predecessor governments on either side whose decisions were binding. In addition, the boundary followed the watershed principle recognised universally for determining the frontiers between nations. Usage and custom had sanctioned the boundary in the various sectors and this was also a factor in India's favour. The Chinese objection to the imperialist nature of the old treaties is effectively answered by Appadorai and Rajan:

> "The second issue that China has raised is that the area in question was a legacy of India's "British imperialism" and should, therefore, go back to China as its previous owner.... While the conquest of India as a whole must be correctly desired by the historian as an exercise in imperialism, the British in carrying out the conquest upto the Himalayan watershed were merely completing the consolidation of their hold over the areas once ruled by Indian kings. The key evidence is that the broad belt of Indian frontier territory was once the seat (from west to east) of the kingdoms of Ladakh, Spiri, Bushair, Garhwal, Brahmapura and Kamrupa and the present Indian alignment represents the boundaries of these ancient and medieval Indian kingdoms."[5]

The Chinese are fond of alleging that their territories were seized by the imperialists and Mao Tse-tung, in his famous edict, even claimed Nepal among Chinese possessions but, on political considerations, this and other references to its neighbours were deleted. At the Simla convention of 1914 which resulted in the McMahon Line, the British were keen to recognise Chinese suzerainty over Tibet. The treaty was finally signed by Sir A. Henry McMahon, the British plenipotentiary acting on behalf of India and Lonchen Shatra on behalf of the Dalai Lama of Tibet. In Article II of the treaty it is clearly stated that "the Governments of Great Britain and China recognizing that Tibet is under the suzerainty of China..."

Thus the overlordship of China was recognised although China did not sign it after its plenipotentiary, Ivan Chen was disowned by Peking after he had initialled the treaty. He was disowned not because of any problem with the India-Tibet border, the McMahon Line, but Ivan Chen, was disowned by China after he had put his initials on the treaty, because of the issue of autonomy of Tibet. Under the treaty outer Tibet is granted complete autonomy from China. This is the region touching India. There was no sign of any dispute over the India-Tibet boundary in the eastern sector with which the Simla convention was concerned. If they were really unhappy with the boundary why did they show keenness to resume the negotiations after withdrawing Ivan Chen?[6]

There are similar treaties governing the other sectors of the border. The weakness of the Chinese stand on the eastern sector is revealed by Chou's letter, referred to earlier, which, inter alia, said ".... the Chinese government, on the one hand, finds it necessary to take a more or less realistic attitude towards the McMahon Line."[7]

The exchange of notes between the two Prime Ministers, the governments of India and China and other agencies continued for some more time. When things seemed to be going completely out of hand, Chou himself paid a visit to India, his fifth, to try to persuade the Indian leaders to accept his thesis of an exchange of territories. India recognising Chinese sovereignty Ladakh, the western sector, and China recognising India's sovereignty over NEFA. This deal did not go through and now Nehru, who followed the Indian traditional proverb of drinking buttermilk like hot milk because he had burnt his mouth drinking the latter, or to quote the English saying, once bitten twice shy, exposed Chou to other Indian leaders and did not think his colleagues would not understand the "intricacies" of the border problem. The other Indian leaders did not fail to give Chou a bit of their mind.

Chou arrived in India on April 20 and left on April 25 during which he had intensive discussions with Nehru and his colleagues. He made a proposal for "reciprocal acceptance of present actualities in both sectors (the eastern and western) and constitution of a boundary commission."[8] In more realistic and somewhat sarcastic terms this was known as "China's attempt to barter what it held illegally against what it claimed unjustifiably." In the circumstances of that day Indian public opinion would not have allowed Nehru to enter into a deal of that kind. If it had come some years earlier and accepted by Nehru, public opinion would have swallowed it like the surrender and betrayal of Tibet in 1954 when the *Bhai Bhai* spirit had already started spreading. In the surcharged atmosphere of 1960 the deal amounted to an abject surrender. Nehru himself is reported to have said: "If I give them that I shall no longer be Prime Minister of India—I will not do it."[9]

The joint communique on the talks between the two Prime Ministers, issued on April 25, clearly stated the differences:

> The two Prime Ministers explained fully their respective stands on the problems affecting the border areas. This led to a greater understanding of the views of the two governments but the talks did not result in resolving the differences that had arisen. The two Prime Ministers were of opinion that further examination should take place by officials of the two sides of the factual material in the possession of both the governments."[10]

This examination took place in 1960-61 in which all historical documents, records, accounts, maps and all other material relevant to the boundary question were examined. The labours of the official meetings resulted in two reports, both sides sticking to their respective stands. This process was resumed after Rajiv Gandhi went to China in 1988 and again by the joint working group, as the official meetings were later termed. No agreement has emerged but the tension is now much reduced.

**Morarji's Blunt Talk**

During Chou's trip he met some other senior Ministers also because Nehru did not want to shoulder all the blame which was to come later. A petty controversy is being raised form time to time by some persons who can be described as Nehruphiles, if we take a charitable view, and sycophants if we descend to the realistic level, about the role played then by Morarji Desai. He was then Finance Minister in the Nehru cabinet and later in 1977 he became the first non-Congress Prime Minister of India. It was during his stewardship of the country that the External Affairs Minister, Atal Bihari Vajpayee, went to China in 1978 and broke the ice in the impasse that followed in the wake of the 1962 Chinese attack on India.

What Morarji Desai told Chou En-lai was indeed harsh. But an authentic record of the conversation would not support the interpretation that Desai had insulted Chou or even put him off. This is what he told the visiting Chinese Prime Minister:

> "When nobody supported China, India took your side and put up your case in the United Nations and forged friendship with you. You accepted the principles of *Panchsheela,* India accepted your sovereignty over Tibet, but you had accepted the condition that Tibet's autonomy would be respected and that you would not interfere with it. When that understanding was broken and China began to take possession of Tibet and kept its army there and the Dalai Lama and his followers came to India to save themselves from the oppression of the Chinese army and India gave them refuge, you began to be inimical towards us. We had not raised any dispute about the boundaries before this and we had suggested that we should solve whatever differences there may be about the boundaries by mutual consultation."[11]

What is annoying is that some sycophants even now attack Desai while they ignore the sellout of Tibet and the Indian acquiscence in China grabbing Indian areas during Nehru's rule. Desai may not have spoken in the best diplomatic language of his demeanour may not have been entirely cordial. He only spoke the truth which hurts. Only a Sinophile or a blatant Chinese supporter in those days could have used friendly language. Desai was neither.

There were several moves and countermoves in the days that followed. In a last minute bid to resolve the question India suggested several measures to the Chinese on May 14, 1962. These recalled the suggestions made by Nehru in a letter to Chou in November 1959. He had told the Chinese Prime Minister that to maintain peace on the border Indian troops would be withdrawn in the western sector to the west of the line shown in the Chinese map of 1956 and the Chinese should withdraw to the east of the boundary shown in Indian maps. This would apply to the armed men as well as unarmed civilians and administrative personnel so that the entire area claimed by both sides would bcome a no man's land. This was an interim step and India was showing willingness to let go of its claim on Aksai Chin for the time being.

The Chinese replied on June 2, 1962 that they could not accept the Indian proposal. The reply was not only a negative one but also somewhat undiplomatic in that it accused India of being unfair. The note asked, in reply to India's suggestion that the road the Chinese had built illegally in Indian territory in Aksai Chin could be used for civilian purposes: "Why should China need to ask India's permission for using its own road on its own territory"? Well, all you have to do is to build a road in another's territory and then say why do I need your permission to use my road because your territory is also mine!

Finally, India's offer to refer the dispute to the International Court of Justice at the Hangue and abide by its verdict was also rejected by the Chinese. Remarkably, the Chinese went on to convey their desire to maintain friendly relations with India, almost until the last moment of attack.

Yet another violation of the April 1954 treaty between India and China was the subject of official record. In the External Affairs ministry's annual report to the two houses of Parliament in February 1961 the violation is noted in the following words:

> Difficulties encountered by Indian representatives and traders in Tibet did not materially decrease and the provisions of the 1954 Agreement were not fully observed. Indian traders continued to suffer difficulties because of the lack of facilities to repatriate their legitimate profits after the Indian and Tibetan currencies were declared as illegal tender. Instances of harassment of and discrimination against Indian nationals were also reported. In the early part of the year, the Kashmiri Muslims residing in Lhasa and neighbouring areas were subjected to severe hardship and intimidation but it was gratifying to note that they were eventually permitted to return to India...."[12]

In an earlier chapter we have noted that the Kashmiris were prominent in Tibet as traders many decades ago. It is also noteworthy that that the ministry's report speaks of "continuing difficulties". This means that the Indians in Tibet were subjected to obstructions and other difficulties over a period of time in violation of the treaty.

## REFERENCES

1. *India's China War.* Neville Maxwell, quoted in *India's Foreign Policy and Relations, ibid.*
2. R. K. Jain, *Ibid.*
3. The North and South blocks of the Central Secretariat of the Indian government were built by the British. Now they can accommodate only the Home, External Affairs and Defence ministries and the PM's office, PMO. Over a dozen big buildings have been built in different parts of Delhi to house the other ministries and offices during the years of independence.

4. *India's Foreign Policy and Relations, ibid.*
5. *Ibid.*
6. *The North-East Frontier,* Parshotam Mehra, Oxford University Press, Bombay. "Another aspect of the question needs mention too. And this related to what later came to be known as the McMahon boundary or line. Negotiations concerning it were bilateral as well they might be in a situation where Tibet was completely master of its own house. It is true that Ivan Chen was not directly involved but to suggest that he was completely in the dark would be to fly in the face of known facts. Thus he and his principals in Peking had slept for weeks over the map attached to the convention which showed the McMahon boundary..." *Introduction.*
7. *Ibid.* "There is another aspect of the Simla negotiations which needs to be heavily underlined and it relates to the fact that even though the conference had to be terminated, the Chinese time and again insisted, in the years immediately following at any rate, that the negotiations be resumed 'at the earliest'. *Introduction.*
8. *India's Foreign Policy and Relations, ibid.*
9. R. K. Jain, *ibid.*
10. *Ibid.*
11. *Ibid.*
12. *Ibid.*

# 20

# AGGRESSION AND AFTER

In breaking the 1954 Treaty on Trade and Intercourse between India and the Tibet Region of China between the two Asian nations, Peking had also breached the five principles of peaceful coexistence. India and China were the first in the world to proclaim the principles and incorporate them in a treaty. Now the only treaty signed by free India and free China was not only subject to much strain but almost in disarray. On many occasions Chinese officials and other personnel had traversed the territory of India without any passports and visas as specifically provided in the treaty. India had pointed this out more than once but the Chinese treated the area as their own and they did not feel compelled to take out any travel papers. The treaty was finally torn to shreds as Chinese troops crossed into Indian territory on October 20, 1962 all across the border from Ladakh to Arunachal Pradesh (or NEFA) in naked aggression.

The Chinese had always attached importance to *Panchsheel* but now demonstrated that where they thought their vital interests were involved they could trample on them. Although the climate in India-China relations was not conducive to peace and tranquillity there was no justification for an outright invasion. Following the incidents of violence against the Indian border personnel in the eastern as well as western sectors and the cartographic invasion India had followed a forward policy. A number of posts were set up in the western sector which Nehru had neglected in the past. Comparatively things were better in NEFA but there were no signs of any large-scale military action by India.

**Not Prepared for War**

V. K. Krishna Menon was India's Defence Minister when the Chinese attacked. He was well versed in foreign affairs and was virtually acting as an additional foreign minister of India providing Nehru with significant inputs in his forays in world affairs and globe trotting much of the time in pursuance of these goals. He told a foreign writer in 1964: "I make no secret of the fact that we were not prepared for a war with China." Menon had to resign in the wake of the aggression which served as a safety valve for Nehru himself because the humiliation of the nation was so great it could have asked Nehru to go. Menon had been to the UN in September that year. Nehru himself was paying an extended visit to London and Lagos from the middle of September to October 2. After spending just ten days at home Nehru again made off for Ceylon on October 12 from where he returned on October 15.

Obviously Nehru had not corrected his habit of paying substantial attention to world affairs in general, unconnected with India's security, even when the nation was face to face with a major crisis and Menon was merrily aiding and abetting his master. From the beginning of India's journey as a free nation, which Nehru guided for 17 years, during which he held the portfolio of external affairs, he had shown great interest in Korea, Suez, West Asia, Hungary and other Eastern European nations, Congo, the problems between the two superpowers and Indo-China than in the problems of India's borders while he accused his colleagues of not understanding the intricacies of the problem. There is no doubt that these world issues are also important and the total neglect of them under the rule of P. V. Narasimha Rao was equally inexcusable. But there has to be a balance and the nation's interests have to be supreme. Foreign policy is only an extension of good domestic policy. Unfortunately, Nehru did not grasp the basic truth.

There was an inadequate appreciation of the Chinese threat from the beginning and the romantic in Nehru goaded him to befriend the Chinese at the cost of India's honour. In reply to a letter from Sardar Patel in 1950, referred to earlier, Nehru had underplayed the Chinese threat and, on the contrary, stressed the threat from Pakistan. Both threats are valid as wars have been fought with both but Nehru committed the folly of underplaying one in the hope of establishing cordial relations. These, indeed, became possible for a few years but again Nehru failed to see the threat that could arise and became to emerge on the surface gradually. Menon, who had no base in India and owed his position to Nehru, accepted what his leader said and fed him with material against the Americans which Nehru liked. The Americans were indeed inimically inclined to this country because India defied their authority, on justifiable grounds, but things always have to be put in proper perspective which was not done.

All this is enough to answer the critics who have sought to find fault with this country and place the blame for the war on India and whose writings have been quoted with approval by some intellectuals in this country always ready to accept anti-Indian material. But there is much more by way of almost complete unpreparedness in facing a big threat on the border. Added to this was Nehru's overwhelming romanticism and self-assurance that China would never attack India because he was there. While leaving for Ceylon, he had pompously said, "We have asked the army to throw them out." But what was the state of the army when the Chinese were launching waves of attacks on India?

The army had, in theory, been placed in charge of the border in NEFA, as announced by Nehru in August 1959, but there were no preparations for a major war. Nehru was telling the Chief of the Army Staff, Gen. Thapar, and his deputy, Lt. Gen. Sen as late as October 2, 1962 that he had good reason to believe that the Chinese would not took any strong action against India. This is stated by Nehru's chosen General, Lt. Gen. B. M. Kaul, who was placed by Nehru and Menon in charge of the NEFA border, without much claim to leadership, in his book *The Untold Story*.[1]

Kaul had some kind of special relationship with Nehru. It is not known if they were related, although this is not improbable as Nehru himself was a Kaul. As early as 1947 Nehru had chosen this officer, who belonged to the Service Corps of the army, not usually considered for leadership roles, to be the military attache in the Indian embassy in Washington. The ambassador, M. Asaf Ali, protested to Nehru against the young officer (Kaul was then a Lt. Col.), taking up with the Pentagon the question of the purchase of some bombers and other equipment from the Americans.[2] That Kaul was the chosen man of the two men who mattered in India-China affairs, Nehru and Menon, was well known to the Indian public, the media and the higher echelons of the army. When Kaul arrived for the first time to take command of the NEFA sector, he was received at Tezpur airport by the Eastern Army

Commander, Lt. Gen. L.P. Sen, under whom he was supposed to function. This was considered most unusual but the army officers who were present at the airport did not fail to catch its significance. [3]

Brig. J. P. Dalvi, who was taken prisoner by the Chinese while fighting on the NEFA front in 1962 was a staff officer at army headquarters in Delhi in the preceding years when Kaul was Quarter Master General of the army, "one most intimately concerned with the maintenance of troops." Dalvi gives us a description of an army conference held at the headquarters in February 1961:

> "He arrived a few minutes late and did not even bother to apologise to the chair (Gen. Sen, then Chief of the General Staff who was presiding), merely announced that he had been held up. We were duly impressed with this important and busy man and his immense stature. Without further ado, he announced that whatever our bid for tonnages he could only make available "X" tons and we would have to "make do" with this. He added with supreme confidence that he did not want to hear any "belly-aches" from anyone. He then left the meeting pleading another engagement..... He had not bothered to greet senior officers who had come many miles to attend this conference, which was the normal army custom. He did not bother to discuss the operational situation."[4]

**A Cut Above**

These are only samples to show that Kaul was feeling a cut above everybody else because of his high connections and undue deference was shown to him even by his superiors because Kaul was Nehru's chosen general. Since he held the key post dealing with supplies he could have really influenced higher decisions to step up the supplies to the troops if they were to face a war but did not. This would again show that Nehru and his men did not consider the Chinese threat to blow into an invasion. Noises were made about throwing out the Chinese from the Indian territory but the Indian leaders did not realise that the Chinese would take their talk to mean warlike preparations and provoke them into getting into a fighting mood. There is enough evidence that the Indian army was ill-prepared to face the Chinese then, although it is much better situated now in that regard.

Building forward bases was a good policy, although it was belated. But one has always to be prepared for any eventuality in such situations and the government had not taken any steps to prepare the army for a war. Nor had the higher officers of the army and the Chief of Staff, Gen.

Thapar, briefed the government about the danger. If Nehru told them that the Chinese would not attack they should have disabused his mind of these romantic tales and put him wise about the realities. It is nobody's contention that any other general in Kaul's position would have worked miracles but the same general had not done anything to brief his political bosses who placed so much confidence in him that a full-scale war was a different proposition altogether. The absence of political meddling in the western sector had, however, good results and the army and the officers fought in the best traditional of that great institution. There is no accountability worth mentioning in Indian life and the political bosses and the army brass were allowed to get away with only minor consequences. Nobody was made to face a trial for criminal neglect of national interests.

There was no strategy for throwing out the Chinese. To do that you may have to cross the McMahon Line temporarily because you have to chase the intruders. Where was such a strategy and the preparation in terms of arms and equipment and other cold weather supplies for men fighting in the Thagla ridge and other high altitude places. Today the Indian army is defending Siachen in Ladakh against any Pakistani intruder in icy conditions for years. There have to be preparations if you have to keep the aggressor at bay. All those who talk of India's war against China seem to have caught hold of the wrong end of the stick and the ones who quote them know even less.

When the army is well prepared and has the required support from the political and administrative bosses it can give a proper account of itself as the Indian Army, Navy and Air Force did in the 1971 Bangladesh liberation war against the Pakistan army. The latter had the important backing of the United States and China. Mrs Gandhi as Prime Minister had prepared the nation and the world for the event, Jagjivan Ram as Defence Minister had given the armed forces the necessary support and K. B. Lall as Defence Secretary had given the administrative back-up to them without irritating and annoying the top men. The army had a brilliant head in Gen. (later Field Marshal) Manekshaw and there were able generals in the field. The Americans sent even their Seventh Fleet to the Bay of Bengal but stopped short of intervention. The Chinese gave the Pakistanis much verbal support but carried out none of their threats. Both knew that India was well prepared and now had the backing of the Indo-Soviet Treaty of Friendship. The nation and all the political parties were behind Mrs. Gandhi and this combination of circumstances helped the Indian armed forces notch up a great victory when 90,000 Pakistani troops surrendered to Lt. Gen. Aurora. On the contrary, for years Nehru did not share the secrets of the India-China situation with his colleagues in the cabinet. Only, Patel could challenge him but he was dead by the end of 1950.

Coming back to the Chinese attack of 1962, how did they view the situation on the eve of the war? Indian moves amounted to talk tough but act soft but the Chinese took the talk seriously and prepared for a massive attack on India. They had already pushed forward on the Tibetan plateu, north of the McMahon Line and pushed into Indian territory in September. The Thagla ridge and other areas, south of the McMahon Line, were occupied by them and it was only from these posts that Nehru had told the army to throw them out. But the Chinese were not content with the occupation of a few posts. The Chinese army's order of the day is very clear. "We are crossing the McMahon Line to make the Indians more sober."

Ironically the drunk were claiming that they would make the abstemitious more sober. Even great admirers of Nehru as a foreign policy maker, Appadorai and Rajan, have summed up the situation faced by India:

> "Our credulity and our negligence to which President Radhakrishnan referred, must largely explain why the Chinese occupied our territory: equally important is the fact that we were dealing with a country which professed friendship but which had aggressive intentions. Time and again Chou El En-lai had assured India that the Chinese would never cross the McMohan Line but the Chinese Order of the Day of 8 September 1962 would give a true understanding of the Chinese mind. The order read: 'We are crossing the McMahon Line to make the Indians more sober.'[5]

The Chinese troops occupied large areas south of the McMahon Line and new areas in the western sector, where they were already occupying the whole of Aksai Chin even before the invasion. But on November 21, a month and a day after their massive attack, they announced a unilateral ceasefire and began withdrawal from both sectors. Obviously world opinion which had gone completely against the Chinese after their blatant attack had something to do with the Chinese action, among other things. The people who had gone wild had to be "more sober" now as they realised that naked aggression did not pay. India, in the meantime, had approached the United States and Britain for arms and, according to some sources, for air support and some of this aid was forthcoming. The Anglo-Americans are not the ones to let go an opportunity for a bargain even at such a moment and tried to extract concessions from Nehru on Kashmir in favour of Pakistan. The Chinese perhaps, realising that aid was flowing in from the west, felt that it would not be beneficial from its point of view if India was driven further into the arms of the western powers.

Whatever the Chinese motivations, their withdrawal gave India much needed breathing time, although the five principles were thrown to the winds. Six Asian and African nations—Burma, Cambodia, Ceylon, Egypt, Ghana and Indonesia—all non-aligned and friendly to India but not hostile to China either, got together to forge the basis of peace between the two Asian neighbours. They were called the Colombo powers, after the Ceylonese capital where they met and they put forward proposals for a truce. They said the Chinese should withdraw twenty km in the western sector to form a demilitarised zone, as suggested by Chou to Nehru while the aggression was on while the Indians should keep their existing military positions, in the eastern sector the line of actual control, recognised by both sides, should serve as a ceasefire line.

After the Colombo powers had provided some clarifications, India accepted them but the Chinese did not. After their unilateral military action, they were less amenable to persuasion by powers which were friendly to both sides. In his report to the Third National People's Congress held between December 21, 1964 and January 4, 1965 in Peking, Chou En-lai took a rigid stand: "We will not withdraw from a single one of these posts and at the same time the Indian government has to be reminded (of the) 90,000 km of territory over which China has never relinquished its sovereignty... we can wait." [6]

The relations, under the circumstances, had to remain strained and for several years the ambassadors were withdrawn, although diplomatic ties were never suspended. It was to be expected that relations would remain strained after a major war, although many other nations have made their peace earlier. By 1970, however, India noticed a slight change in the Chinese attitude. This trend could have picked up further but in 1971 came the Bangladesh crisis when China had to take a stand in favour of its friend, Pakistan, even though it was all words and no action. Islamabad had been quick to befriend China after the invasion of India in 1962 and arms and even nuclear information were flowing into Pakistan from China. But for the war between India and Pakistan the India-China ties could have improved even earlier.

I was in Hong Kong in 1971, as ALL INDIA RADIO (AIR) correspondent on South-East Asia, and it took only a small effort on my part to make friends with the pro-Peking elements in that British colony close to China. They were aware that in my despatches and commentaries over AIR I was quite critical of China but they responded to my overtures as a mediaman and invited me to their exclusive Marco Polo club of friends of China and offered other hospitality and accepted mine. The External Affairs ministry was apparently greatly impressed by my interaction and when the *Indian Express* correspondent in Hong Kong sent some despatches on the developments a senior officer of the ministry wrote to me seeking to know the details of the conversations.

The External Affairs ministry was so much interested in my continued stay in Hong Kong that it tried to intervene in my transfer back to Delhi as a result of political-bureaucratic move. The move proved more powerful and I landed in Delhi a day before the Indo-Soviet treaty about which I have written earlier in this book. Soon my assignment in Delhi was to be publicity and public relations concerning the Bangladesh liberation war which was then seen to be approaching fast.

Yet another development which somewhat affected the course of normalization of the relations between India and China was the favourable turn in US-China relations for which India had in the fifties tried hard in the fora of the UN. Both President Nixon and his Secretary of State, Henry Kissinger, visited China and diplomatic relations were established after 23 years of the Communists coming to power in China. This was before Nixon himself was turned out of the White House by the American people for his Watertgate role. The Indians were thrown into a kind of panic by this development for which they had themselves worked assiduously in a previous era. Like all diplomats they took a somewhat narrow view of the sudden improvement in the ties between the two big countries, little realising that the relations between India and China would also take an upswing and the US-China ties would not be without their downswings at times.

In 1971, the Chinese organized a big table tennis tournament as they were trying to emerge on the world sports scene after the setback they had suffered in the Cultural Revolution of the late sixties. They invited the United States to send a team. Although the Americans are a great power in sports—though not as much as they are in politics and diplomacy—they had no creditable performances to boast of in it. India was also invited and accepted. Scholars fail to recognise that this was the beginning of a Chinese entry in world sports where they now hold a big position and have many world records and achievements to their credit. For the ordinary people of the world, unacquainted with and uninterested in politics and diplomacy, sports is always enthralling and China has made a special niche for itself through sports and games.

India's military and, to an extent, diplomatic success in the Bangladesh liberation war in 1971 had its own impact on the Chinese mind as it substantially affected other people and governments on the South Asian region. They came to recognise that India had risen once again and the humiliation of the Chinese invasion was behind her. In military terms the expansion and modernization of the Indian armed forces was helpful to her in facing any threat from both Pakistan and China. There was no jingoism but only a sense of confidence that India could look after its security and defence. Of course, there were other threats like the United States aiding and arming Pakistan and conniving at its proxy war against India and its known interference in Afghanistan's internal affairs. There were other problems too but the defeatism that pervaded the nation in the wake of the Chinese attack of 1962 had dissipated and had been replaced by a new sense of security based on the nation's own effort.

The relations with China, however, could not improve to any notable extent during the latter sixties and even the early seventies. The Chinese have a habit of mounting propaganda attacks on countries with whom they have problems and this resulted in frequent outbursts against India. The Bangladesh war gave it much impetus as the Chinese had to convince their Pakistani friends about their sympathy. But even they had to realise that mere words were no substitute for action when the chips are down. But until this realization dawned upon them, India was subjected to much abuse in the media and in the United Nations where China was now occupying its rightful place for which India had waged a relentless battle for many years.

Wise leaders of China like Deng Hsiao Ping, still going strong at 91, played a notable part in changing the course of Chinese policy towards India as he repeatedly spoke of the good old days, about forgetting the past and building an enduring relationship. More about it in the last chapter.

## REFERENCES


1. *The Untold Story*, B. M. Kaul, Bombay.
2. *M. Asaf Ali Memoirs*, G. N. S. Raghavan, Ajanta, Delhi, p. 395.
3. *Himalayan Blunder*, Brig. Dalvi,Thacker, Bombay, p. 255.
4. *Ibid*, p. 82.
5. *India's Foreign Policy and Relations*, *ibid.*, p.145.
6. R. K. Jain, *ibid*.

# 21

# TOWARDS BETTER RELATIONS

The Tibet treaty of April 1954 has been the only treaty signed by the two countries in modern times. But before the Chinese Communists came on the scene as rulers of modern China, negotiations were in progress between the two countries for a treaty of peace and friendship. India signed treaties of peace and friendship with her several neighbours, Bhutan, Nepal, and Burma in the first years of freedom. In was therefore, natural for the rulers of free India to take up the issue of a friendship treaty with the Kuomintang regime of China whose capital was Nanking. But before the negotiations could be completed there was a change of government in China whose new rulers put all their eggs in the Tibet basket. While India took on itself the task of selling the Communist regime to the world, the rulers in Peking took their own time to seize her hand of friendship. The Tibet treaty had to be entered into because the Communist Chinese attached utmost importance to the assertion of their authority on Tibet and India allowed the autonomy of Tibet to be reduced to nothing. Before the two sides could think of a real friendship treaty the relations began to develop strains.

But as we saw in the first part of the book, relations could be substantially friendly and cordial even without a treaty although a formal treaty has its own uses. The process of improvement and normalization of relations between India and China has to be pursued steadily and patiently and the brick-by-brick approach has to be applied. This process had not yet begun in the sixties and even the seventies when India's relations with the other major Communist power, the Soviet Union, had become extremely close. Since China's relations with that nation were hostile, friction was added to the India-China ties. China, on its part, befriended Pakistan and shared some nuclear information with it, apart from supplying arms, and this became another source of strain. Both nations took their own time to accept the reality and recognise that relations cannot be based on the premise that ties with others must be excluded or one country should not always seek the enemies of the other for friendship.

In the early sixties, after the end of the war, China sent a note to Indian conveying the completion of the "withdrawal" of their troops from most of the areas seized by them during the war. Actually, they had built 26 civil posts six of which were on Indian territory. The setting up of the 26 posts by itself was contrary to the Colombo proposals which required both sides to discuss the issue first. China never did it nor accepted the Colombo proposals. In fact, it was against any kind of international arbitration. During the letters exchanged between the two Prime Ministers in 1963 China rejected this specifically. It also rejected the Indian offer to refer the dispute to the International Court of Justice for arbitration. So convinced was India about the justice of its position and so strong was China in its stand that its rights could not be compromised that there was no meeting ground but comparative peace prevailed.

**China-Pak Protocol**

This peace was disturbed when China signed a protocol with Pakistan under which the latter surrendered about 5,200 sq. km of Indian territory illegally seized by it when its forces occupied parts of Jammu and Kashmir state of India. The free gift of territory enables China to build a road linking parts of its Sinkiang province. Pakistan could not care less about Indian protests because it had gifted that something which was not hers. India pointed out that China and Pakistan had no common frontier. The Indian protest note said in categorical terms: "The signing of the so-called boundary protocol (on March 26, 1965) by the Chinese government is final proof of the fact that motivated solely by their hostility towards India the Chinese government and the government of Pakistan are opportunistically making use of their unlawful seizure of the Indian Union territory of Jammu and Kashmir."

China's ties with Pakistan have been a major source of friction in India-China ties and the source has not been removed even now. In

1965, the protocol caused a further setback in the process of improvement of ties, although each side was watching the other for any signs that could lead to improvement.

The first breakthrough came only after the Janata government of Morarji Desai came to power in India. Although the process was interrupted by fortuitous circumstances the visit was a landmark. The External Affairs Minister, Atal Bihari Vajpayee, arrived in China on February 15, 1978 on a three-day visit. Before that neither foreign minister had travelled to the other's capital and a state of suspended hostility prevailed. The Janata Party had a policy of solving problems with neighbours in a peaceful manner and building bridges with them. This was a major achievement of the regime which lasted from March 1977 to July 1979. It had important gains in the domestic sphere too, like a check on prices, but the intense factionalism fuelled by Charan Singh's overpowering ambition to become Prime Minister led to a loss of people's confidence after the party had won a big majority in the March 1977 elections. Charan Singh ultimately succeeded in becoming Prime Minister after toppling his party's government but could never face the Lok Sabha for lack of a majority.

Vajpayee was in China in pursuance of the policy of restoration of good neighbourly relations with China. The ice was broken and China was now convinced that when India talked of good relations it really meant what it said. Although India was keen that the border issue also be taken up and sorted out, Vajpayee did not mind it first a dialogue was initiated at the political level. But his effort bore no tangible result because while Vajpayee was in the Chinese capital the Chinese launched an attack on Vietnam. India has always had excellent relations with Vietnam and while China was backing a faction in Kampuchea opposed to Vietnam, India was supporting the faction friendly to her. Vajpayee's visit had to be called off.

In the subsequent period, internal squabbles in the Janata Party did not provide a conducive ground for any major moves in foreign policy. When Indira Gandhi bounced back to power in 1980 after three years in the wilderness there was nothing immediately of note to help lift the surrounding darkness. But in the following year, India invited the Chinese Foreign Minister, Huang Hua, to visit Delhi as it was his turn after Vajpayee had visited China. This had a favourable impact. Before that, however, the wise old man of China, Deng Xiao-ping, who had been losing no opportunity to stress the need for better ties, had made package proposals more or less akin to the exchange proposed by Chou En-lai (now spelt Zhou En-lai) in 1960. Huang's visit, the first by a Chinese Minister in 21 years, was crowned with a measure of success. The two nations agreed to take the border issue out of the freeze in which it had gone after the 1962 aggression. While reiterating that they desired friendly relations they modified their rigid stands. China which wanted a settlement so that other matters of importance could be attended to had to agree to re-examine the data on the border issue and India had to give up its stand that China must first vacate the territories illegally seized by it.

At a press conference in Delhi during his visit, Huang said India and China could seek a "fair, reasonable and comprehensive settlement" of the boundary dispute through peaceful negotiations, "taking into account the historical factors, the present situation and the national feelings of the peoples of the two countries."[1]

**Not Threatened**

Deng had meanwhile told an itinerant Indian politician that China had no intention to attack India nor did it feel threatened by her, even if the latter has more troops on the border than China. The Chinese, he said, had to face the problem of oxygen in Tibet. He prescribed that both sides should go on talking on the border issue. His prescription that talking was better than fighting was adopted by both countries now, although some problems did crop up in between. The process of joint talks agreed upon during Hunag's visit, was begun and the first round was held in Beijing in December 1981. Neither at this nor at the second round in Delhi could an agreement be reached. It was futile to hope for it either. The officials could only argue on the basis of the data they had discussed in extenso in the past. Of course, they could sort out minor problems which arose from time to time. The political will to take the bull by the horns was lacking. India, which is a democracy, had to watch the trend of public opinion so vital in a popular set-up, but even China had to pay attention to the various opinions in the party and the administration, from outright hawks to realists and friends of peace, before making a bold offer. This did not fructify then or later.

Visits of goodwill delegations and of experts, including the people who are good at wangling free trips to China with an eye on shopping in Hong Kong on the way to or from China, had now been resumed. There is no doubt that the two countries have much to learn from each other and such visits also help in the process of improving the ties. Premier Zhao Liyang, meeting a friendship delegation, said that the spirit of the 1950s was missed by both sides. He was referring to the *Bhai bhai* era. But while praising Dr. Dwarkanath Kotnis and Dr. Atal, another member of the Indian medical mission sent by Nehru during the second world war, he omitted to mention the role of Nehru which made the mission to China possible.

The official level talks were held with regularity as a hardy annual without any solution being found to the border issue. However, in the Delhi talks in 1983, India agreed to consider the Chinese package approach while the Chinese agreed to discuss the Indian sector-by-sector approach. It was clarified that the Deng proposals envisaged the same kind of solution as Premier Zhou had proposed in 1960. The areas captured by China during the 1962 war were now added to the exchange proposed by Zhou.

More exchanges, in the area of culture and trade, radio and TV, film festivals, exhibitions of arts and handicrafts, and the inevitable exchange of journalists, were agreed upon although the boundary question remained as intractable as ever. Meanwhile important developments were taking place in the wider world affecting both India and China. Mikhael Gorbachev, who advocated a more open society at home and a detente in international relations, had come to power in the Soviet Union. Relations with India which were close were not affected and Gorbachev visited India while Rajiv Gandhi took a trip to the USSR, but a more relaxed relationship with China was foreseen. He agreed to wthdraw Soviet troops from Afghanistan, which unfortunately paved the way for a kind of anarchy with Pakistan openly interfering in Kabul's internal affairs and the US still supplying arms to Pakistan and the regime backed by it.

Finally, the Soviet Union itself dissolved, like several other East European countries, but India and China decided to work towards a better relationship although the border question continued to defy a solution. The assertions of each other's known position from time to time this did not prevent the growth of a spirit of moderate amity which made the Rajiv Gandhi visit of 1988 possible and important. This came off despite some events which were not exactly conducive to the growth of amity. These related to a Chinese intrusion in the Sumdorong Chu valley in Arunachal Pradesh in 1986 and the Chinese outburst at the formation of Arunachal Pradesh as a full-fledged state of the Indian Union.

The intrusion was discussed by the Foreign Ministers of the two countries while they were both attending the session of the United Nations General Assembly in New York. Both maintained that the area was in their territories and the issue was sorted out later without any further incidents and hard feelings. China made some noises over Arunachal becoming a state instead of a union territory which meant it had limited internal autonomy and was ruled more or less directly from Delhi. India was not altering the international character of the region which was formerly known as NEFA and it still fell within the eastern sector of the India-China border. The tribal people of the area were now given a stake in their own destiny and an equal stake in the affairs of the nation along with the more advanced and more populous parts.

India told China that its objection to Arunachal becoming a state was "clear interference in the internal affairs of India. The conferment of statehood was entirely a matter for Parliament to decide." By that time seven rounds of talks had been held between the officials of the two countries and India reminded China of it. The Beijing stand was that Arunachal Pradesh was its territory illegally occupied by India and it had never recognised the McMahon Line. All this happened in December 1986 and nearly a year later the eighth round of talks was held in Delhi. It had become customary for the Foreign Secretary of India to lead the Indian side while the Vice Minister of Foreign Affairs led his country's delegation. Speaking at the National Defence College in Delhi, Prime Minister Rajiv Gandhi cautioned the people not to expect a quick and easy solution of the boundary question, although he was hopeful of a solution being found[2].

That was the view of a sanguine and confident Prime Minister as the ground was being prepared for a visit by Rajiv Gandhi to China, the first by an Indian Prime Minister in 34 years. In May that year, the two countries signed their first cultural agreement to establish, promote and develop close relations in diverse cultural fields. The cultural Secretary in India's Human Resource Development ministry went to Beijing to sign the agreement with China's Vice Minister of Culture. That became a good setting for the major event that came about in December that year, from the 19th to the 23rd. In his first utterance on Chinese soil Prime Minister Rajiv Gandhi spoke of the need to renew India-China friendship but did not omit a reference to the border dispute which, he candidly said, "had soured relations for nearly three decades." He also said that India and China represented nearly a third of humanity and there was much they could do together. Li Peng, China's Prime Minister called for a restoration of the vision of peace and cooperation shared by Nehru and his father Zhou En-lai.[3]

Rajiv Gandhi allayed Chinese fears once more by telling them that India treated Tibet "as an autonomous region of China and will not allow any activity directed against China from Indian soil. "Autonomy had been snuffed out by the Chinese and one wonders if they liked

Rajiv Gandhi's use of the term autonomous. He pleased them with his decla-ration that whatever had happened in Tibet was an internal affair of China. He had meetings not only with Li Peng but also with Deng Xiao Ping and with the Chinese President, Yang Shan Kun, considered close to Deng. Yang said that the fact that the visit had taken place "is an important event."

Three agreements were signed during Rajiv's visit and it was also agreed to raise the official level talks on the border to a joint working group level. There had been eight rounds of talks between the officials of the two countries after contacts were re-established in 1981. The joint working group, which is only a cosmetic elevation of the official meetings, has also met eight times (up to 1995). No solution of the border issue has emerged and the hope expressed during the 1988 visit that the talks would be raised to the political level have not materialised. That can only happen when a political approach is applied instead of the official approach of documents and maps India had once offered to refer the dispute to the International Court but the Chinese have steadfastedly refused to accept it. Apparently, they feel that they have a better chance of settling things the way they would like by discussion and a study of the realities while the Court would only go by documents and maps. The two Prime Ministers witnessed the signing of three agreements, on a cultural programme for three years, a follow-up of the May pact, an air services accord and a science and technology agreement which hurts no one.

**High Point**

The high point of the Rajiv Gandhi visit was definetely his meeting with Deng Xiao Ping. Described as "China's New Renaissance Man" by perceptive journalist and writer on international affairs, D. R. Rajagopal,[4] Deng is certainly the most powerful figure on China after the death of Zhou En-lai. He has always been keen on a revival of India-China friendship and the restoration of the Nehru-Zhou era. While Congress (I) leaders and Indian officials and even some scholars slur over the Janata government's efforts to restore normal relations, Deng had no difficulty in referring to Vajpayee's visit to China and his own meeting with him to put things in perspective. He welcomed Rajiv Gandhi with these words, "Welcome, so welcome, my young friend." He recalled the days of Nehru's visit to China and said he was then a Vice Premier. "Let us forget what happened in between and look forward."[5]

The significance of the Deng-Rajiv meeting lies in the fact that there was a meeting of minds and a definite expression of goodwill which stood both nations in good stead in the years following although the border issue has not been resolved. The joint working group held eight meetings, as many as its predecessor, the official level talks. The change in nomenclature did not result in the two sides moving closer to an agreement. This was despite the fact that subsequently both the Chinese Prime Minister, Li Peng, visited India in 1991 and the Indian Prime Minister, P. V. Narasimha Rao, went to Beijing in 1993.

**The Chinese**

Foreign Minister Qian Qichen visited India in March 1990 when the Janata Dal government was in power. His visit was in the nature of sounding the Indian waters at a time when India was having a non-Congress government for the second time. He found the Janata Dal people as friendly in their approach as their predecessors and equally desirous of close ties between the two Asian neighbours. I. K. Gujral, Minister of External Affairs, told Qian that India desired to settle outstanding issues in a spirit of cooperation and friendship. Contrary to the Congress (I) leaders' habit of ignoring the period when the opposition was in power, Gujral made it a point to recall the work done by Rajiv Gandhi and give him credit for breaking the ice in the India-China relations. He said his government wanted to carry forward the momentum of that trip. Qian said China was ready to work with India in developing friendly relations on the basis of the five principles.

On Kashmir, the Chinese had gone back to the earlier view that the matter was a bilateral one and should be sorted out between India and Pakistan. He stressed mutual consultations by the two sides and said China did not take sides on the issue.[6] The Janata Dal also sent a party delegation to China led by Ramakrishna Hegde, former Chief Minister of Karnataka who was now Deputy Chairman of the Planning Commission, in Delhi. It included S. R. Bommai, also a former Karnataka Chief Minister, and S. Jaipal Reddy, now the party's leader on the Rajya Sabha. Their meeting with the Chinese Communist party General Secretary, Jiang Zemin, was notable for Jiang's assertion that India and China were the initiators of the five principles of peaceful coexistence, *Panchsheel*. He also said that China appreciated the repeated statements of Prime Minister V. P. Singh that India-China relations should be further developed.

The point to be stressed is that the non-Congress government and the ruling party it had brought to power were also committed to a normalization of the relations. This was further emphasized when the Congress (I) came back to power in 1991, first as a minority government and later acquiring the necessary majority through a process of and defections from other parties. Li Peng came to India on a six-day visit on December 11, 1991, just six months after Narasimha Rao had assumed office as Prime Minister. Several agreements were signed it being a standard practice now for a VVIP visit to herald a series of agreements whether they were significant or not. Among the accords, there was one on the resumption of border trade and another on space technology. Both Prime Ministers stressed their desire to find a solution to the border problem, Rao saying that India sought a "fair and reasonable agreement" in consonance with the dignity and self-respect of either party. In conversation with some journalists Li referred to the "very good relations" enjoyed by the two countries in the 1950s which had suffered a setback until Rajiv Gandhi visited China.[7]

Before Narasimha Rao could return the visit President R. Venkataraman visited China in1992 and had the usual round of formal talks. The Chinese knew that under the Indian system the President holds only a constitutional authority and were, therefore, happy that Venkataraman devoted much of his time to indulge in his hobby as an amateur photographer. He avidly took pictures of the scenic spots to which he was taken by his hosts. The Rao's visit in September 1993 was important because of an agreement under which the two countries committed themselves to a resolution of the boundary question through consultation, and not war. It was signed in the presence of the two Prime Ministers by R. L. Bhatia, India's Minister of State for External Affairs, and China's Vice Foreign Minister, Tang Jia Xuan. (A Vice Minister is generally of the rank of the foreign secretary in India.) The agreement also laid down that neither side would use force or threat of force. There was also agreement on respecting the line of actual control, by both countries on taking other confidence building measures and on notifying each other of military exercises which could otherwise raise suspicions.

Rao met all the Politburo members, including the President, Jian Zemin, and invited all of them to visit India. Indian fears that Chinese arms were being supplied to Pakistan were voiced by Foreign Secretary J. N. Dixit who said China had sold missiles to Pakistan and this was a matter of concern to India. The Chinese, however, maintained that there was no transfer of arms which would be used against India. This was not much of an assurance because the United States had given Islamabad plenty of arms in the past and is still doing it and the arms have always been used against India, although they were given to help Pakistan fight the "Communists". For that matter the Chinese are also Communists and yet there is a strong military link between the two countries. Much of this arms supply and even the nuclear information and missile technology that China has made available to Pakistan is based on the technological transfer and arms which the Soviets gave the Chinese when the relations between them were good. China, however, asserted it would not play the Pakistan, card against India.[8]

China's continued anxiety that the Dalai Lama would use his stay in India for political activities against Beijing was conveyed in rather harsh words to an Indian Parliamentary delegation, led by the Lok Sabha Speaker, Shivraj Patil, when it met Li Peng in the Chinese capital. The delegation was in Beijing in 1993 at the invitation of the National People's Congress Chairman, Wan Li. Li Peng told them that India should ensure that no problems were created in regard to the Tibetan issue. Patil, in a correct reply, said that the Indian stand was that the Dalai Lama was a respected religious leader and "we expect that nothing is done by anybody from Tibet in India which will create problems." [9]

One of the reasons which increased China's trust in India's good faith was the stand taken by New Delhi of not interfering in China's internal affairs in the name of human rights as the western nations are still doing. Whether this is a right policy and India should not really live up to her reputation as an upholder of human rights is a different matter. But during all the western media hulabaloo on the Tienanmen square dissent demonstrations and subsequently the Indian government has not done anything to offend the Chinese. This has not gone unnoticed in Beijing which has come to rely on India as a true supporter in difficult situations. Whether the Indian silence on the human rights issue would really result in some dividends remains to be seen.

Vice President K. R. Narayanan, himself a former Indian ambassador to China, visited the country in October 1994. He was given the title of "Old Friend of China." So much was the impact made by a friendly and forthcoming approach by this former diplomat that the Chinese thought it fit to honour him with a title. In the presence of the two Vice Presidents, Narayanan and Rong Li ren, accords were signed in Beijing on banking relations and consular services. [10]

The contacts have thus increased. Although 1995 has been bereft of any major visit on either side, the relations have become closer than before. For India the Chinese commitment to a bilateral solution of the Kashmir problem has been an important gain, although there is no guarantee that if ever Pakistan succeeds in its bid to raise the issue in the United Nations, China, as a permanent member of the Security Council, would use its veto or support the Indian point of view on bilateralism. There has been a conscious attempt on both sides to improve ties and unlike the hostile attitude that is witnessed in Indo-Pakistan relations, now for more than three years, the relations with China have been marked by a strong desire at the highest level and other levels too for normal relations. Care is taken not to allow the border issue to throw a spanner in the works.

Doubts, however, persist. The joint working group meetings have not produced any worthwhile results even as the official level talks earlier did not. There are smaller agreements which have some significance. In the latest eighth round held in Delhi in the second half of 1995 some decisions were taken reportedly on vacating two posts and a retired general, Ashok Mehta, wrote an article in a leading English daily of Delhi, on September 13, 1995 asking "Why are we Quitting our Territory?". He said:

> "For 12 Assam regiment of the (Indian) army the report that India has agreed to abandon the two posts they had constructed to contain the Chinese intrusions in Wangdung (in the eastern sector) in June 1986 will revive bitter memories.... The result of the latest eighth meeting of the India-China Joint Working Group (JWG) is that both sides will withdraw two posts each from the Wangdung area, presumably the two forward checkposts over looking the Chinese posts."[11]

There was no official reaction and no contradiction of the general's article which would mean that he was right about India vacating posts specially built by intrepid soldiers to contain Chinese intrusion in a vital area. The intrusions have apparently not been vacated. An explanation is due from the Indian government.

## REFERENCES


1. *Asian Recorder*, 1982, Vol. XXVIII.
2. *Ibid.*, 1987, Vol. XXXIII.
3. *Ibid.*, 1989, XXXV.
4. *Mainstream*, weekly, Delhi, September 4, 1993.
5. *Asian Recorder*, 1989, Vol. XXXV.
6. *Ibid.*, 1990, Vol. XXXVI.
7. *Ibid.*, 1993, Vol. IXL
8. *Ibid.*, 1993, Vol. IXI.
9. *Ibid.*
10. *Ibid.*, 1994, Vol. XL.
11. *The Hindustan Times*, Delhi.

# APPENDICES

# TREATY[1] OF PEACE AND FRIENDSHIP BETWEEN THE GOVERNMENT OF INDIA AND THE GOVERNMENT OF NEPAL[2]

## Kathmandu, 31 July 1950

The Government of India and the Government of Nepal, recognising the ancient ties which have happily existed between the two countries;

Desiring still further to strengthen and develop these ties and to perpetuate peace between the two countries;

Have resolved therefore to enter into a Treaty of Peace and Friendship with each other, and have, for this purpose, appointed as their plenipotentiaries the following persons, namely,

THE GOVERNMENT OF INDIA:

His Excellency Shri Chandreshwar Prasad Narain Singh, Ambassador of India in Nepal.

THE GOVERNMENT OF NEPAL:

MOHUN SHAMSHER JANG BAHADUR RANA, Maharaja, Prime Minister and Supreme Commander-in-Chief of Nepal,

who having examined each other's credentials and found them good and in due form have agreed as follows :

*Article 1*

There shall be everlasting peace and friendship between the Government of India and the Government of Nepal. The two Governments agree mutually to acknowledge and respect the complete sovereignty, territorial integrity and independence of each other.

*Article 2*

The two Governments hereby undertake to inform each other of any serious friction or misunderstanding with any neighbouring State likely to cause any breach in the friendly relations subsisting between the two Governments.

*Article 3*

In order to establish and maintain the relations referred to in Article 1 the two Governments agree to continue diplomatic relations with each other by means of representatives with such staff as is necessary for the due performance of their functions.

The representatives and such of their staff as may be agreed upon shall enjoy such diplomatic privileges and immunities as are customarily granted by international law on a reciprocal basis: Provided that in no case shall these be less than those granted to persons of a similar status of any other State having diplomatic relations with either Government.

*Article 4*

The two Governments agree to appoint Consuls-General, Consuls, Vice-Consuls and other consular agents, who shall reside in towns, ports and other places in each other's territory as may be agreed to.

Consuls-General, Consuls, Vice-Consuls and consular agents shall be provided with exequaturs or other valid authorization of their appointment. Such exequatur or authorization is liable to be withdrawn by the country which issued it, if considered necessary. The reasons for the withdrawal shall be indicated wherever possible.

The persons mentioned above shall enjoy on a reciprocal basis all the rights, privileges, exemptions and immunities that are accorded to persons of corresponding status of any other State.

*Article 5*

The Government of Nepal shall be free to import, from or through the territory of India, arms, ammunition or warlike material and equipment necessary for the security of Nepal. The procedure for giving effect to this arrangement shall be worked out by the two Governments acting in consultation.

*Article 6*

Each Government undertakes, in token of the neighbourly friendship between India and Nepal, to give to the nationals of the other, in its territory, national treatment with regard to participation in industrial and economic development of such territory and to the grant of concessions and contracts relating to such development.

*Article 7*

The Governments of India and Nepal agree to grant, on a reciprocal basis, to the nationals of one country in the territories of the other the same privileges in the matter of residence, ownership of property, participation in trade and commerce, movement and other privileges of a similar nature.

*Article 8*

So far as matters dealt with herein are concerned, this Treaty cancels all previous Treaties, agreements, and engagements entered into on behalf of India between the British Government and the Government of Nepal.

*Article 9*

This Treaty shall come into force from the date of signature by both Governments.

*Article 10*

This Treaty shall remain in force until it is terminated by either party by giving one year's notice.

Done in duplicate at Kathmandu this 31st day of July 1950.

(*Signed*)
CHANDRESHWAR PRASAD NARAIN SINGH
For the Government of India.

(*Signed*)
MOHUN SHAMSHER JANG BAHADUR RANA
For the Government of Nepal.

**REFERENCES**

1. Came into force on 31 July 1950, as from the date of signature, in accordance with Article 9.
2. *India Bilateral Treaties and Agreements*, Vol. I (1947-52), Ministry of External Affairs, Delhi.

# LETTER EXCHANGED WITH THE TREATY[1]

## (Dated the 31st July 1950, Kathmandu)

EXCELLENCY,

In the course of our discussion of the Treaties of Peace and Friendship and of Trade and Commerce which have been happily concluded between the Government of India and the Government of Nepal, we agreed that certain matters of details be regulated by an exchange of letters. In pursuance of this understanding, it is hereby agreed between the two Governments:

(1) Neither Government shall tolerate any threat to the security of the other by a foreign aggressor. To deal with any such threat, the two Governments shall consult with each other and devise effective countermeasures.

(2) Any arms, ammunition or warlike material and equipment necessary for the security of Nepal that the Government of Nepal may import through the territory of India shall be so imported with the assistance and agreement of the Government of India. The Government of India will take steps for the smooth and expeditious transport of such arms and ammunition through India.

(3) In regard to Article 6 of the Treaty of Peace and Friendship which provides for national treatment, the Government of India recognize that it may be necessary for some time to come to afford the Nepalese nationals in Nepal protection from unrestricted competition. The nature and extent to this protection will be determined as and when required by mutual agreement between the two Governments.

(4) If the Government of Nepal should decide to seek foreign assistance in regard to the development of the natural resources of, or of any industrial project in Nepal, the Government of Nepal shall give first preference to the Government or the nationals of India, as the case may be, provided that the terms offered by the Gov-

ernment of India or Indian nationals, as the case may be, are not less favourable to Nepal than the terms offered by any other Foreign Government or by other foreign nationals.

Nothing in the foregoing provision shall apply to assistance that the Government of Nepal may seek from the United Nations Organization or any of its specialized agencies.

(5) Both Governments agree not to employ any foreigners whose activity may be prejudicial to the security of the other. Either Government may make representations to the other in this behalf, as and when occasion requires.

Please accept Excellency, the assurances of my highest consideration.

(Sd.) MOHUN SHAMSHER JANG BAHADUR RANA
Maharaja, Prime Minister and
Supreme Commander-in-Chief of Nepal

To: His Excellency
Shri Chandreshwar Prasad Narain Singh,
Ambassador Extraordinary and Plenipotentiary of India
at the Court of Nepal, Indian Embassy, Kathmandu.

**REFERENCE**

1. *Nepal-India Border Relations*, Centre for Economic and Technical Studies, Kathmandu.

# TREATY[1] OF TRADE AND COMMERCE BETWEEN THE GOVERNMENTS OF INDIA AND NEPAL[2]
## (Kathmandu, 31 July 1950)

The Government of India and the Government of Nepal being desirous of facilitating and furthering trade and commerce between their respective territories have resolved to conclude a treaty of Trade and Commerce and have, for this purpose, appointed as their plenipotentiaries the following persons, namely,

**The Government of India :**

HIS EXCELLENCY SHRI CHANDRESHWAR PRASAD NARAIN SINGH, Ambassador of India in Nepal ;

**The Government of Nepal :**

MOHUN SHAMSHER JANG BAHADUR RANA, Maharaja, Prime Minister and Supreme Commander-in-Chief of Nepal,

who having examined each other's credentials and found them good and in due form have agreed as follows :

*Article 1*

The Government of India recognise in favour of the Government of Nepal full and unrestricted right of commercial transit of all goods and manufactures through the territory and ports of India as provided in Articles 2, 3 and 4 below.

*Article 2*

Subject to such arrangements as may be agreed upon between the two Governments, the Government of India agree to allow all goods imported at any Indian port and intended for re-export to Nepal to be transmitted to such place or places in Nepal as may be approved by the two Governments, without breaking bulk *en route* and without payment of any duty at any Indian port.

*Article 3*

Subject to such arrangements as may be agreed upon between the two Governments the right of passage without payment of excise or import duties shall similarly extend also to goods of Nepalese origin in transit through Indian territory from one approved place to another within the territories of the Kingdom of Nepal.

*Article 4*

Subject to such arrangements as may be agreed upon between the two Governments, the Government of Nepal shall enjoy full and unrestricted right of commercial transit, from approved place or places in Nepalese territory, through the territories and ports of India, of all goods and manufactures of Nepalese origin for export outside India.

*Article 5*

The Government of Nepal agree to levy at rates not lower than those leviable, for the time being, in India customs duties on imports from and exports to countries outside India. The Government of Nepal also agree to levy on goods produced or manufactured in Nepal, which are exported to India, export duty at rates sufficient to prevent their sale in India at prices more favourable than those of goods produced or manufactured in India which are subject to central excise duty.

*Article 6*

The Government of India and the Government of Nepal agree to assist each other, by making available, to the maximum extent possible, commodities which are essential to the economy of the other.

*Article 7*

The two Governments agree to promote contacts between the trade interests of the two countries and undertake to give every reasonable facility for the import and export of commodities, and in particular to facilitate the use of the routes and methods of transportation which are most economical and convenient.

*Article 8*

Civil aircraft of either State shall be permitted to fly over the territory of the other in accordance with normal international procedure.

*Article 9*

So far as matters dealt with herein are concerned this Treaty cancels all previous treaties, agreements or engagements concluded between the British Government on behalf of India and the Government of Nepal.

*Article 10*

This Treaty shall come into force three months after the date of signature by both parties. It shall remain in force for a period of 10 years, in the first instance, and shall unless terminated by either party by giving notice of not less than one year in writing, continue in force for a further period of 10 years.

Done in duplicate at Kathmandu this 31st day of July 1950.

For the Government of India:

(*Signed*)

CHANDRESHWAR PRASAD NARAIN SINGH

For the Government of Nepal:

(*Signed*)

MOHUN SHAMSHER JANG BAHADUR RANA

**MEMORANDUM**

(*Vide* Articles 2 and 3 of the Treaty of Trade and Commerce between Nepal and India)

PART A

The arrangements contemplated in Article 2 of the Treaty of Trade and Commerce between Nepal and India signed on 31-7-50 shall be as follows :

(1) When goods are imported for re-export to Nepal, the importer or his agent, shall, at the time of entering them at the Customs House—

   (a) declare that the goods are intended for re-export to Nepal and would not be diverted *en route* to any other country;

   (b) furnish, in quadruplicate, an invoice of the goods in a prescribed form, certified by a Nepalese officer appointed for the purpose, specifying therein by which authorised land routes the goods are intended to be transported and also the land customs station through which the goods will be taken out of India;

(c) deposit an amount equal to the duty chargeable under the Indian Customs Tariff, or furnish a bond with the surety of a bank of standing, binding him to pay duty on any portion of the consignment that is not cleared from the custody of the Nepal customs on payment of the (Nepal) customs duty.

(2) On compliance with the above provisions, the goods shall be sealed with the Customs seal and delivered to the owner together with the original copy of the invoice, duly completed and registered. The duplicate and triplicate copy of the invoice shall, at the same time, be forwarded to the land customs officer of the station referred to in paragraph (1) (*b*) above.

(3) The land customs officer to whom the goods are presented shall examine the seals and, if these are intact, certify that the goods have crossed the Indian frontier with the seals intact. The original copy of the invoice shall be returned to the owner with the goods for presentation to the Customs authorities in Nepal. The duplicate copy, duly endorsed, shall be returned to the Customs House whence it was received, and the triplicate copy, duly endorsed, forwarded to the Indian Embassy in Nepal.

(4) In order to secure the refund of the deposit, or cancellation of the bond furnished under paragraph (1) (*c*), the importer or his agent, must present an application to that effect supported by the original invoice, duly certified by the land customs officer referred to in paragraph (3) above to the effect that the goods have crossed the Indian frontier and by the Nepal Customs to the effect that they have reached Nepal with the Indian Customs seal intact, and that the packages corresponding with the details in the invoice have been cleared from their custody on payment of customs duty. The certificate by the Nepal Customs shall be countersigned by an officer or officers designated in this behalf by the Government of Nepal. The original invoice should be received in the Customs House within a period of six months; this period may be raised at the discretion of the Indian Customs authority concerned in any case in which it is proved, to its satisfaction, that the delay is due to circumstances beyond the control of the importer.

(5) Before granting the refund of deposit or cancellation of the bond, the officer concerned in the Customs House shall compare the original copy of the invoice received from the importer with the duplicate copy received from the land Customs officer concerned.

PART B

At present the Government of India do not consider it necessary, for reasons of their administrative convenience, to prescribe any arrangements under Article 3 of the Treaty; but if and when Government of India should decide to do so, the arrangements described in Part A will apply *mutatis mutandis* to the transit of goods under Article 3 of the Treaty.

PART C

The two Governments approve for the purposes of Articles 2 and 3 of the Treaty convenient points, within Nepalese territory contiguous to the following rail heads :

1. Raxaul
2. Jogbani
3. Nepalganj
4. Nautanwa
5. Jayanagar

(*Signed*) CHANDRESHWAR PRASAD NARAIN SINGH
SIGNED at Kathmandu on the 31st July 1950
on behalf of the Government of India.

(*Signed*) MOHUN SHAMSHER JANG BAHADUR RANA
SIGNED at Kathmandu on the 31st July 1950
on behalf of the Government of Nepal.

**MEMORANDUM**

(*Vide* Article 4 of the Treaty of Trade and Commerce between Nepal and India)

PART A

The arrangements contemplated in Article 4 of the Treaty of Trade and Commerce between Nepal and India signed on 31-7-50 shall be as follows :

(1) Goods of Nepalese origin or manufacture imported into India for subsequent re-export to a country outside India, shall enjoy freedom of transit across the territories of India. This shall include

exemption from Indian customs duties, cess or excise duties as well as exemption from compliance with Indian export and import control regulations provided that the exporter or his authorised agent.

(a) makes a declaration in the prescribed form at the Indian land customs station of entry to the effect that the goods are intended for re-export out of India;

(b) furnishes in quadruplicate, an invoice of the goods in a prescribed form, counter signed by a Nepalese officer appointed for the purpose, specifying therein by which authorised land routes the goods are intended to be transported and also the port through which the goods will be taken out of India; and

(c) deposits an amount equal to the duty chargeable under the Indian Customs Tariff, or furnishes a bond with the surety of a bank of standing, binding him to pay duty on any portion of the consignment that is not cleared for export out of India through the Customs House of the port referred to in (b) above.

(2) On compliance with the above provisions, the goods shall be sealed with the seal of the Indian Land Customs station referred to in 1 (a) above and delivered to the exporter or his agent together with the original copy of the invoice, duly completed and registered. The duplicate and triplicate copy of the invoice shall, at the same time, be forwarded to the Customs House of the port of exit referred to in paragraph 1 (b) above.

(3) The Customs Officer at the port of exit shall, before the goods are re-exported, examine the seals and, if these are intact, certify that the goods have been brought for shipment with the seals intact. After the goods have actually been re-exported the original copy of the invoice shall be returned to the owner with a certificate to the foregoing effect for presentation to the Customs authorities, at the land customs station of entry. The duplicate copy, duly endorsed, shall be returned to the land customs station from which it was received, and the triplicate copy, duly endorsed retained in the Customs House for record.

(4) In order to secure the refund of the deposit, or cancellation of the bond furnished under paragraph 1 (*c*), the exporter or his agent must present an application to that effect supported by the original invoice duly certified by the Customs House of the port of exit referred to in paragraph (3) above to the effect that the goods have been re-exported out of India. The original invoice shall be presented at the land customs station of entry within a period of six months or such extended time as the Customs authority at the

port of exit might certify as being due to circumstances beyond the control of the exporter.

(5) Before granting the refund of deposit or cancellation of the bond, the officer concerned in the land customs station shall compare the original copy of the invoice received from the exporter with the duplicate copy received from the Customs House concerned.

## PART B

The two Governments approve for the purpose of Article 4 of the Treaty convenient points, within Nepalese territory contiguous to the following rail heads :

1. Raxaul
2. Jogbani
3. Nepalganj
4. Nautanwa
5. Jayanagar

(*Signed*) CHANDRESHWAR PRASAD NARAIN SINGH
SIGNED at Kathmandu on the 31st July 1950
on behalf of the Government of India.

(*Signed*) MOHUN SHAMSHER JANG BAHADUR RANA
SIGNED at Kathmandu on the 31st July 1950
on behalf of the Government of Nepal.

## REFERENCES

1. Came into force on 1 November 1950, three months after the date of signatur by both parties, in accordance with Article 10.
2. *India Bilateral Treaties and Agreements*, Vol. I (1947-52), Ministry of External Affairs, Delhi.

# TREATY[1] OF PERPETUAL PEACE AND FRIENDSHIP BETWEEN THE GOVERNMENT OF INDIA AND THE GOVERNMENT OF BHUTAN[2]
## Darjeeling, 8 August 1949

The Government of India on the one part, and His Highness The Druk Gyalpo's Government on the other part, equally animated by the desire to regulate in a friendly manner and upon a solid and durable basis the state of affairs caused by the termination of the British Government's authority in India, and to promote and foster the relations of friendship and neighbourliness so necessary for the well-being of their peoples, have resolved to conclude the following treaty, and have, for this purpose named their representatives, that is to say Sri Harishwar Dayal representing the Government of India, who has full powers to agree to the said treaty on behalf of the Government of India, and Deb Zimpon Sonam, Tobgye Dorji, Yang-Lop Sonam, Chho-Zim Thondup, Rin-Zim Tandin and Ha Drung Jigmie Palden Dorji, representing the Government of His Highness the Druk Gyalpo, Maharaja of Bhutan, who have full powers to agree to the same on behalf of the Government of Bhutan.

*Article I*

There shall be perpetual peace and friendship between the Government of India and the Government of Bhutan.

*Article II*

The Government of India undertakes to exercise no interference in the internal administration of Bhutan. On its part the Government of Bhutan agrees to be guided by the advice of the Government of India in regard to its external relations.

*Article III*

In place of the compensation granted to the Government of Bhutan under Article 4 of the Treaty of Sinchula and enhanced by the treaty of the eighth day of January 1910 and the temporary subsidy of Rupees one lakh per annum granted in 1942, the Government of India agrees to make an annual payment of Rupees five lakhs to the Government of Bhutan. And it is further hereby agreed that the said annual payment shall be made on the tenth day of January every year, the first payment being made on the tenth day of January 1950. This payment shall continue so long as this treaty remains in force and its terms are duly observed.

*Article IV*

Further to mark the friendship existing and continuing between the said Governments, the Government of India shall, within one year from the date of signature of this treaty, return to the Government of Bhutan about thirty-two square miles of territory in the area known as Dewangiri. The Government of India shall appoint a competent officer or officers to mark out the area so returned to the Government of Bhutan.

*Article V*

There shall, as heretofore, be free trade and commerce between the territories of the Government of India and of the Government of Bhutan; and the Government of India agrees to grant the Government of Bhutan every facility for the carriage, by land and water, of its produce throughout the territory of the Government of India, including the right to use such forest roads as may be specified by mutual agreement from time to time.

*Article VI*

The Government of India agrees that the Government of Bhutan shall be free to import with the assistance and approval of the Government of India, from or through India into Bhután, whatever arms, ammunition, machinery, warlike material or stores may be required or desired for the strength and welfare of Bhutan, and that this arrangement shall hold good for all time as long as the Government of India is satisfied that the intentions of the Government of Bhutan are friendly and that there is no danger to India from such importations. The Government of Bhutan, on the other hand, agrees that there shall be no export of such arms, ammunition, etc., across the frontier of Bhutan either by the Government of Bhutan or by private individuals.

*Article VII*

The Government of India and the Government of Bhutan agree that Bhutanese subjects residing in Indian territories shall have equal justice with Indian subjects, and that Indian subjects residing in Bhutan shall have equal justice with the subjects of the Government of Bhutan.

*Article VIII*

(1) The Government of India shall, on demand being duly made in writing by the Government of Bhutan, take proceedings in accordance with the provisions of the Indian Extradition Act, 1903 (of which a copy shall be furnished to the Government of Bhutan), for the surrender of all Bhutanese subjects accused of any of the crimes specified in the first schedule of the said Act who may take refuge in Indian territory.

(2) The Government of Bhutan shall, on requisition being duly made by the Government of India, or by any officer authorised by the Government of India in this behalf, surrender any Indian subjects, or subjects of a foreign power, whose extradition may be required in pursuance of any agreement or arrangements made by the Government of India with the said power, accused of any of the crimes, specified in the first schedule of Act XV of 1903, who may take refuge in the territory under the jurisdiction of the Government of Bhutan, and also any Bhutanese subjects who, after committing any of the crimes referred to in Indian territory, shall flee into Bhutan, on such evidence of their guilt being produced as shall satisfy the local court of the district in which the offence may have been committed.

*Article IX*

Any differences and disputes arising in the application or interpretation of this treaty shall in the first instance be settled by negotiation. If within three months of the start of negotiations no settlement is arrived at, then the matter shall be referred to the Arbitration of three arbitrators, who shall be nationals of either India or Bhutan, chosen in the following manner:

(1) One person nominated by the Government of India;
(2) One person nominated by the Government of Bhutan;
(3) A Judge of the Federal Court, or of a High Court in India, to be chosen by the Government of Bhutan, who shall be Chairman.

The judgement of this Tribunal shall be final and executed without delay by either party.

*Article X*

This treaty shall continue in force in perpetuity unless terminated or modified by mutual consent.

DONE in duplicate at Darjeeling this eighth day of August, one thousand nine hundred and forty-nine, corresponding with the Bhutanese date the fifteenth day of the sixth month of the Earth-Bull year.

HARISHWAR DAYAL
*Political Officer in Sikkim.*

DEB ZIMPON SONAM
TOBGYE DORJI
YANG-LOP SONAM
CHHO-ZIM THONDUP
RIN-ZIM TANDIN
HA DRUNG JIGMIE PALDEN DORJI

**Instruments of Ratification**

WHEREAS a Treaty relating to the promotion of, and fostering the relations of friendship and neighbourliness was signed at Darjeeling on the 8th day of August 1949 by representatives of the Government of India and of the Government of His Holiness the Druk Gyalpo, Maharaja of Bhutan, which Treaty is, word for word, as follows :

The Government of India, having considered the treaty aforesaid, hereby confirm and ratify the same and undertake faithfully to perform and carry out all the stipulations therein contained.

IN WITNESS WHEREOF this instrument of ratification is signed and sealed by the Governor-General of India.

DONE at New Delhi, the 22nd day of September, 1949.

C. RAJAGOPALACHARI,
*Governor-General of India.*

WHEREAS a Treaty relating to the promotion of, and fostering, relations of friendship and neighbourliness was signed at Darjeeling on the eighth day of August, 1949 by Representatives of my Government and of the Government of India, which Treaty is, word for word, as follows :

My Government, having considered the treaty aforesaid, hereby confirm and ratify the same and undertake faithfully to perform and carry out all the stipulations therein contained.

IN WITNESS WHEREOF I have signed this instrument of ratification and affixed hereto my seal.

DONE at Tongsa the fifteenth day of September, 1949.

J. WANGCHUK,
*Druk Gyalpo*

*Seal.*

## REFERENCES

1. Ratified by India 22 September and by Bhutan 15 September 1949.
2. *India Bilateral Treaties and Agreements*, Vol. I, Ministry of External Affairs, Delhi.

# TREATY[1] OF FRIENDSHIP BETWEEN INDIA AND THE UNION OF BURMA[2]
## Rangoon, 7 July 1951

The President of India and the President of the Union of Burma being desirous of strengthening and developing the many ties that have bound the two countries for centuries and being urged by mutual recognition of the need for maintaining the peace and friendship that have always existed between the two States, have resolved to conclude this Treaty for the common benefit of their peoples and in furtherance of the objectives of their respective countries, and have, to this end, appointed as their Plenipotentiaries the following persons, namely,

The President of India :

His Excellency Dr. M. A. RAUF,

Ambassador Extraordinary and Plenipotentiary.

The President of the Union of Burma:

The Hon'ble SAO HKUN HKIO, K.S.M.,

Minister for Foreign Affairs.

Who, having examined each other's credentials and found them good and in due form, have agreed to and signed the following Articles:

*Article I*

The two States recognize and respect the independence and rights of each other.

*Article II*

There shall be everlasting peace and unalterable friendship between the two States who shall ever strive to strengthen and develop further the cordial relations existing between the peoples of the two countries.

*Article III*

The two States agree to continue diplomatic and consular relations with each other by means of representatives of either party in the territory of the other and agree that such representatives and their agreed staff shall have, on a reciprocal basis, such privileges and immunities as are customarily granted by recognized international principles.

*Article IV*

The two States agree that their representatives shall meet from time to time and as often as occasion requires to exchange views on matters of common interest and to consider ways and means for mutual co-operation in such matters.

*Article V*

The two States agree to start negotiations for the conclusion of agreements, on a reciprocal basis, relating to trade, customs, cultural relations, communications, extradition of criminals, immigration or repatriation of nationals of each country resident in the other, or of dual nationals of the two countries, and all other matters of common interest to the two countries.

*Article VI*

Any difference or dispute arising out of the interpretation or application of this Treaty or one or more of its Articles shall be settled by negotiations through the ordinary diplomatic channels and if no settlement is reached by that method within a reasonable time, the matter shall be referred to arbitration in such manner as may be mutually determined by a general or special arrangement between the two parties.

*Article VII*

The treaty shall be subject to ratification and shall come into force from the date of exchange of the instruments of ratification, which shall take place as soon as possible at Rangoon.

*Article VIII*

This Treaty shall continue in force for five years from the date of its coming into force and shall thereafter remain in force:

Provided that after the termination of the said period of five years either party may give to the other party a notice of not less than six months intimating its intention to terminate the Treaty and on the expiry of the period of such notice the Treaty shall cease to be in force.

IN FAITH WHEREOF, the said Plenipotentiaries have signed the present Treaty in the Hindi, Burmese and English languages (the English text shall prevail in case of conflict between the three texts) and have affixed hereto their seals.

DONE in duplicate in Rangoon on the seventh day of July 1951.

For the President of the Union of Burma:
(Sd.) S. H. HKIO

In the presence of—
(Sd.) TUN SHEIN

For the President of India:
(Sd.) M. A. RAUF

In the presence of—
(Sd.) K. M. KANNAMPILLY

## REFERENCES

1. Came into force on 31 January 1952 on exchange of ratifications, in accordance with Article VII.
2. *India Bilateral Treaties and Agreements*, Vol. I (1947-52), Ministry of External Affairs, Delhi.

# TREATY[1] OF TRADE AND TRANSIT BETWEEN THE GOVERNMENTS OF INDIA AND HIS MAJESTY'S GOVERNMENT OF NEPAL[2]
## Kathmandu, 11 September 1960

Whereas the Government of India and His Majesty's Government of Nepal (hereinafter referred to as the Contracting Parties).

Being animated by the desire to strengthen economic cooperation between the two countries, and convinced of the benefits likely to accrue from the development of their economies towards the goal of a Common Market,

HAVE RESOLVED to conclude a Treaty of Trade and Transit in order to expand the exchange of goods between their respective territories, encourage collaboration in economic development and facilitate trade with third countries.

They have for this purpose appointed as their plenipotentiaries the following persons, namely,

THE GOVERNMENT OF INDIA :

HIS EXCELLENCY SHRI HARISHWAR DAYAL, AMBASSADOR OF INDIA IN NEPAL

HIS MAJESTY'S GOVERNMENT OF NEPAL :

HIS EXCELLENCY SHRI RAM NARAYAN MISHRA, MINISTER FOR COMMERCE AND INDUSTRIES

who, having exchanged their full powers and found them good and in due form, have agreed as follows:

## TRADE

### *Article I*

The Contracting Parties shall promote the expansion of mutual trade in goods originating in the two countries and shall to this end endeavour to make available to each other commodities which one country needs from the other. The Contracting Parties shall further take care to avoid to the maximum extent practicable diversion of commercial traffic or deflection of trade.

### *Article II*

Subject to such exceptions as may be mutually agreed upon, goods originating in either country and intended for consumption in the territory of the other shall be exempt from customs duties and other equivalent charges as well as from quantitative restrictions.

### *Article III*

Notwithstanding the foregoing provisions, either Contracting Party may maintain or introduce such restrictions as are necessary for the purpose of

(a) protecting public morals,
(b) protecting human, animal and plant life,
(c) safeguarding national treasures,
(d) safeguarding the implementation of laws relating to the import and export of gold and silver bullion,
(e) safeguarding such other interests as may be mutually agreed upon.

### *Article IV*

Payment for goods and services between the two countries will continue to be made as heretofore.

### *Article V*

The trade of the Contracting Parties with third countries shall be regulated in accordance with their respective laws, rules and regulations relating to imports and exports.

### *Article VI*

Payment for transactions with third countries will be made in accordance with the respective foreign exchange laws, rules and regulations of the two countries. The Contracting Parties agree to take effective steps, in cooperation with each other, to prevent infringement and circumvention of the laws, rules and regulations of either country in regard to matters relating to foreign exchange.

## TRANSIT

### *Article VII*

Goods intended for import into or export from the territories of either Contracting Party from or to a third country shall be accorded freedom of transit through the territories of the other party. No distinction shall be made which is based on the flag of vessels, the place of origin, departure, entry, exit, destination or ownership of goods.

### *Article VIII*

Goods (including baggage) shall be deemed to be in transit across the territory of a Contracting Party when the passage across such territory, with or without transhipment, warehousing, breaking bulk or change in the mode of transport, is only a portion of a complete journey beginning and terminating beyond the frontier of the Contracting Party across whose territory the traffic passes. Traffic of this nature is termed "traffic in transit."

### *Article IX*

Traffic in transit shall be exempt from customs duty and from all transit duties or other charges imposed in respect of transit, except reasonable charges for transportation and such other charges as are commensurate with the costs of services rendered for the supervision of such transit.

### *Article X*

The procedure to be followed for traffic in transit to or from third countries is laid down in the Protocol hereto annexed. Except in case of failure to comply with the procedure prescribed, such traffic in transit shall not be subjected to unnecessary delays or restrictions.

### *Article XI*

Traffic in transit through the territories of one Contracting Party from one place to another in the territories of the other Party shall be subject to such arrangements as may be mutually agreed upon.

## GENERAL

### *Article XII*

Nothing in this Treaty shall affect any measure which either of the

Contracting Parties may be called upon to take in pursuance of general international conventions to which it is a party or which may be concluded hereafter relating to the transit, export or import of particular kinds of articles such as opium or other dangerous drugs or in pursuance of general conventions intended to prevent infringement of industrial, literary or artistic property or relating to false marks, false indications of origin or other methods of unfair competition.

*Article XIII*

The Contracting Parties shall take appropriate measures to ensure that the provisions of this Treaty are effectively and harmoniously implemented and to consult with each other periodically so that such difficulties as may arise in its implementation are resolved satisfactorily and speedily.

*Article XIV*

This Treaty, which replaces the Treaty of Trade and Commerce between the two countries of 31st July, 1950, shall come into force on 1st November, 1960. It shall remain in force for a period of five years. It shall continue in force for a further period of five years thereafter, subject to such modification as may be agreed upon, unless terminated by either party by giving notice of not less than one year in writing.

DONE in duplicate in English, Hindi and Nepali, all the texts being equally authentic, at Kathmandu on September 11, 1960, corresponding to the twenty seventh day of Bhadra, Bikram Sambat two thousand and seventeen. In case of doubt, the English text will prevail.

(Signed) HARISHWAR DAYAL
For the Government of India.

(Signed)
RAM NARAYAN MISHRA
For His Majesty's
Government of Nepal.

**REFERENCES**

1. Came into force from 1 November, 1960.
2. *India Bilateral Treaties and Agreements*, Vol. III (1958-60), Ministry of External Affairs, Delhi.

# PROTOCOL

*(Vide Article X)*

1. All Traffic in Transit shall
   (i) be duly entered at the proper Customs Houses at the points of entry and exit,
   (ii) pass via routes prescribed for such traffic,
   (iii) comply with the following procedure :
      (a) The import/export licence authorising importation/exportation of the goods to or from the territory of one Contracting Party shall be produced before the Customs Officer at the point of entry of the goods in the territory of the other Contracting Party (hereinafter referred to as "Country of Transit").
      (b) Except in the case of goods imported or exported by Their Majesties, other privileged members of the Royal Family of Nepal, and by His Majesty's Government of Nepal (including those received by its foreign aid), a bond with suitable guarantee shall be executed by the importer/exporter or by his authorised agent guaranteeing and undertaking that the goods shall not be diverted *en route*.
      (c) An importer/exporter or his authorised agent shall produce within a specified period satisfactory evidence to the appropriate Customs Officer of the country of transit to the effect that the goods have duly passed into the territory of the other.
      (d) Any other detailed regulations which may be prescribed in mutual consultation by the Contracting Parties shall also be compiled with.
2. Wherever it becomes necessary to break bulk in respect of a consignment in transit, such breaking shall be done only under the supervision of the appropriate Customs Officer of the Party in whose territory such break of bulk takes place.
3. Warehousing of all consignments shall be subject to the relevant laws and regulations of the Party in whose territory such warehousing occurs.
4. To facilitate the movement in transit of goods through India to

and from Nepal, the Government of India agree to arrange with the Commissioners of the Port of Calcutta to assign a separate shed in the Calcutta Port area wherein all goods in transit (other than hazardous goods) may be stored pending onward transmission to or from Nepal in compliance with the procedures prescribed.

5. The Government of India taking note of the desire on the part of His Majesty's Government of Nepal to appoint Customs Liaison Officers at the port of Calcutta and Barauni railway station with a view to facilitating in collaboration with the appropriate Indian authorities, the smooth working of the procedures prescribed for the regulation of Traffic in Transit agree to accord to these officers all appropriate countries and reasonable facilities for the due discharge of these functions including access to examination centres, transit sheds, or transhipment points in Calcutta or Barauni railway station, in which goods in transit to and from Nepal are stored, opened for examination or transhipped. Customs examination of goods in transit at Calcutta and Barauni will normally be carried out in the presence of the Nepalese Liaison Officers.
6. The Government of India will similarly appoint, where necessary, Customs Liasion Officers in Nepal for discharging similar functions particularly in respect of goods carried to Nepal from a customs port in India in transit by air. His Majesty's Government of Nepal shall extend similar courtesies and accord similar facilities to such officers.

| Sd./HARISHWAR DAYAL | Sd./ RAM NARAYAN MISHRA |
|---|---|
| For the Government of India | For His Majesty's Government of Nepal |

HIS MAJESTY'S GOVERNMENT OF NEPAL

EXCELLENCY:

**In the course of the discussions which resulted in the conclusion of the Treaty of Trade and transit between the Government of India and His Majesty's Government of Nepal signed today, the measures necessary to achieve the objectives of the Treaty have been discussed and the following understanding was reached:**

1. With reference to Articles I & V, while the Contracting Parties may follow independent policies on trade with third countries, it is understood that if Nepal pursues a policy divergent from that of India, there will be mutual consultations so as to ensure that there is no flow into India of goods imported from third countries.
2. In regard to Article II it is agreed that :
   (a) His Majesty's Government of Nepal, having regard to their requirements of raising resources for the economic development of Nepal, may continue to levy existing import and export duties on goods imported from or exported to India. The rates of such duties shall not, however, exceed those applicable to imports from the exports to third countries. It is understood that there will be no such duties on Government to Government transactions.
   (b) The existing arrangements between the Contracting Parties for the refund to His Majesty's Government of Nepal of central excise duties on goods exported from India to Nepal are not affected.
   (c) In order to assist Nepal's industrial development the Government of India agree that His Majesty's Government may impose protective duties or quantitative restrictions on such goods as may be produced by newly established industries in the country.
3. In regard to clause (e) of Article III, it is understood that either Party may, in agreement with the other, take measures, if that becomes necessary, to secure a balance in mutual payments, to prevent the smuggling of their currencies from or to third countries, to prevent the re-entry into its territory of goods passed in transit or to prevent the re-export of goods exported to the territory of the other.
4. Imports from third countries will normally be permitted by either country only against its own foreign exchange resources except for capital goods, spares and industrial raw materials which may be imported against foreign investment. Neither party will, however, issue any import licence on the basis that the foreign exchange required for it will be arranged by nationals of the other party.
5. With reference to Article XIII of the Treaty, it has been agreed that inter-governmental consultations shall for the time being be carried out through normal diplomatic channels on the request of either Party at a place and time to be mutually agreed upon, the meetings being held within 30 days of the request.

I shall be grateful if you would kindly confirm that the above correctly sets out the understanding reached between us.

Accept, Excellency, the assurances of my highest consideration.

Sd./-RAM NARAYAN MISHRA
Minister for Commerce and Industry,
His Majesty's Government of Nepal
September 11, 1960

His Excellency Shri HARISHWAR DAYAL
Ambassador Extraordinary and
Plenipotentiary at the Court of Nepal
Indian Embassy
Kathmandu.

AMBASSADOR OF INDIA
Kathmandu, September 11, 1960
Bhadra 20, 1882 (Saka)

EXCELLENCY :

I write to acknowledge receipt of your letter of today's date which reads as follows :

*(Not reproduced)*

I confirm that the foregoing correctly sets out the understanding reached between us.

Accept, Excellency, the assurances of my highest consideration.

Sd./ HARISHWAR DAYAL
Ambassador of India.

His Excellency Shri RAM NARAYAN MISHRA,
Minister for Commerce and Industries,
His Majesty's Government of Nepal,
Kathmandu.

**MEMORANDUM**

1. In pursuance of the provisions of sub-clause (d) of clause (iii) of Para 1 of the Protocol to the Treaty of Trade and Transit, His Majesty's Government of Nepal and the Government of India agree that the following detailed procedures shall apply to goods in Transit :

## IMPORT PROCEDURE

1. When the goods are imported for Nepal in transit through India the importer or his agent shall be required to observe the following procedure at the Indian Port of importation :

   (i) Transit of the goods meant for Nepal shall be allowed against Nepal Government licences permitting goods to be carried into Nepal.

   Note: His Majesty's Government of Nepal will arrange to supply, through the Indian Embassy at Kathmandu, to the Collectors of Customs concerned, the specimen signature of officer/officers who sign Nepal Government import/export licences. It will also arrange to have one copy each of all licences issued by it, sent direct to the Collectors of Customs concerned for his information.

   (ii) The importer or his agent shall make the following declaration on the relative Bill of Entry at Indian Custom House:

   "I/We declare that the goods entered herein are the goods in respect of which the Nepal Import licence No. ...................... dated .................. has been issued and I/We further declare that the goods are intended for import into Nepal within the prescribed time-limit-*vide* Rule 6—and shall not be diverted *en-route* to any other country."

   (iii) He shall furnish a bond to the Custom House in the form prescribed by the Collector of Customs with the surety of a bank of standing binding him to say the duty and penalty for contravening Import Trade Control restrictions on any portion of the consignment that is not proved to have duly entered Nepal.

   Note : Where an importer or his agent deals or expects to deal with a series of consignments over a period of time, a continuing general bond may be taken to cover all such consignments instead of an individual bond for every such consignment.

   (iv) On compliance with the above provisions he shall prepare an invoice in quadruplicate, in the prescribed form, specifying therein the number of Nepal import licence, the particulars of the goods, namely the marks, numbers, weight of the packages, description and value of the goods, etc., the route and also the border custom post (established by agreement between His Majesty's Government of Nepal and the

Government of India) through which the goods will be taken out of India to Nepal.

(v) Thereafter he shall present all the four copies of the invoice and the Nepal import licence at the Custom House together with a copy of the Bill of Entry. The Collector of Customs shall compare the copy of the licence produced by the importer with that received by him from His Majesty's Government of Nepal.

(vi) The four copies of the invoice shall be examined by the Custom House to ensure that the particulars stated in the invoice correspond in all material respects to the particulars on the Nepal import licence. In order to ensure that the goods conform to the description thereof in the invoices the Indian Customs authorities will where necessary, open for examination certain percentage of the packages. There shall, however, be no opening for examination of packages imported by Their Majesties, other privileged members of the Royal Family, by His Majesty's Government of Nepal (including goods received by it as foreign aid), by United Nations' and Diplomatic personnel and Missions accredited to His Majesty's Government of Nepal.

(vii) The goods shall then be sealed with the Customs seal.

(viii) The goods will be loaded under Customs supervision. Where Railway wagons are exclusively provided for transit goods, the wagons will be sealed by the Railways and/or the Customs.

Note 1 In the case of open wagons loading heavy articles, such as cars, trucks, machinery, iron and steel etc., sealing may be dispensed with.

Note 2 In the matter of priorities for the booking of wagons, the Railways would give the same consideration to the transit goods to Nepal as to other goods transported on behalf of Indian citizens.

Note 3 The transhipment of goods at Barauni station from broad to meter gauge wagons will be done under customs supervision and where Railway wagons are exclusively provided for transit goods, the wagons will be sealed by the Railways and/or the Customs.

2. The original copy of the invoice duly completed and registered by the Custom House will be handed over to the importer or his agent along with the Nepal import licence, suitably endorsed by the Custom House. The duplicate and triplicate copies of the invoice

shall be forwarded simultaneously by the Indian Custom House to the authorised officer of the Land Customs and Central Excise in charge of the border Customs post mentioned in the invoice. The quadruplicate copy shall be retained in the Indian Custom House.

3. On arrival of the goods at the border Customs post the goods shall be presented by the importer or his agent to the authorised officer of Land Customs and Central Excise along with the original copy of the invoice.
4. The authorised officer of Land Customs and Central Excise shall:
   (i) compare the original copy of the invoice with the duplicate and the triplicate copies received by him from the Indian Custom House;
   (ii) examine the seals on the packages, and identify the packages with the particulars shown on the invoice;
   (iii) if the particulars on the original copy of the invoice agree with the particulars on the duplicate and triplicate copies and the seals are intact, and the packages are satisfactorily identified, allow the goods to proceed and certify accordingly on each of the three copies of the invoice;

   Note: In case the seals are not found intact, he may reseal the packages with his own seal, after satisfying himself as to the identity of the packages and the goods from the particulars shown on the invoice, and if necessary by opening and examining the goods themselves. It should not, however, be necessary to detain the entire consignment if seals on some packages are found broken. After ascertaining the shortages and indicating these on the relevant Nepal invoices, goods should be allowed to go forward without delay;

   (iv) deliver the original copy duly endorsed to the importer or his agent alongwith the goods for presentation to the Nepalese Officer at the corresponding Nepalese border customs post and send the duplicate duly endorsed to the Collector of Customs at the port through which the goods were imported.

   Note: The duplicate copy should be despatched to the Collector of Customs by the authorised officer of Land Customs and Central Excise within 24 hours of the passing of the goods through the Indian Border Customs post;

   (v) send the triplicate copy duly endorsed to the Nepalese

customs officer at the corresponding Nepalese border customs post through the Nepalese representative deputed for the purpose, for advance information, and shall retain that copy after it has been returned duly endorsed by him.

5. The Nepalese Customs Officer shall:
   (i) deal with the goods in such manner as may be directed by His Majesty's Government of Nepal;
   (ii) endorse a certificate over his signature and authenticate it under customs stamp on the original copy of the Nepal import licence and invoice that the goods have reached Nepal with the Indian Customs seals intact and that the packages correspond in all respects with the particulars shown in the invoice and in all material respects with the Nepal import licence and that the goods have been cleared from Nepalese customs custody for entry into Nepal;
   (iii) return the original copy of the invoice and the original copy of the Nepal import licence to the importer or his agent;
   (iv) return the triplicate copy duly endorsed to the authorised officer of Land Customs and Central Excise after the goods have crossed the Nepalese border customs post.
6. In order to secure the cancellation of the bond furnished under rule 1 (iii) the importer or his agent must present an application to that effect to the Collector of Customs, supported by the original copy of the invoice duly certified by the authorised officer of Land Customs and Central Excise and the Nepalese Customs Officer to the effect that the goods have been cleared from Nepalese Customs custody for entry into Nepal with the Indian Customs seals intact. The original invoice should reach the Collector of Customs concerned, *not later than six months* after the date on which the invoices were completed at the Indian port of importation, or such extended time as the Collector of Customs might certify as being due to circumstances beyond the control of the importer.
7. Before allowing the cancellation of the bond, the Collector of Customs shall compare the original copy of the invoice received from the importer with the duplicate copy received from the authorised officer of Land Customs and Central Excise.
8. The procedure outlined above will apply *mutatis mutandis* to goods imported into India from abroad by sea or by air and meant for being sent in transit therefrom to Nepal by air.

## EXPORT PROCEDURE

1. When goods of Nepalese origin, despatched from the border customs posts (established by agreement between His Majesty's Government of Nepal and Government of India) are cleared from Nepalese customs custody and are exported for re-export to foreign countries in transit through India, the exporter or his agent shall be required to observe the following procedure at the corresponding Indian border customs post:
   (i) He shall prepare an invoice in quadruplicate in the prescribed form, specifying therein the particulars of the goods namely the marks, numbers and weight of the packages, description and value of the goods etc., the number of the Nepal export licence and also the route through which the goods will pass from the point of entry to the port of exit. The invoice shall have been verified and certified accordingly by the Nepal Customs Officer. The exporter or his agent shall make the following declaration thereon:
   "I/We declare that the goods entered herein are of Nepalese origin, exported from Nepal by virtue of Nepal export licence No. ............... dated ................ and are intended for export to .............. (name of foreign country) within the prescribed time limit—*vide* Rule 6-and shall not be diverted *en-route* to any other country."
   (ii) He shall present all four copies of the invoice duly certified over his signature by the Nepal Customs Officer and authenticate it by customs stamp to the authorised officer of Land Customs and Central Excise at the border Customs post along with the goods.
   (iii) With regard to goods, the import of which into India is prohibited, restricted or subject to excise duty, he will furnish the authorised officer of the Land Customs and Central Excise at the Indian border customs post with a bond in the form prescribed by the Collector of Land Customs with a surety of a Bank of standing, undertaking to produce a certificate from the Custom House at the port of exit that the goods have been duly shipped.
   NOTE : 1. Such bonds shall not be required in respect of other commodities.
   2. Where an exporter or his agent deals or expects to deal with a series of consignments over a period of time, a continuing general bond may

be taken to cover all such consignments instead of an individual bond for every such consignment.

2. After the packages containing the goods have been examined and the correctness of the contents and description certified by the authorised officer of the Land Customs and Central Excise at the border Customs post, the goods shall be sealed by him and released for onward transmission to the port of exit *via* the route declared.
3. The original copy of the invoice shall be handed over to the exporter; the duplicate and triplicate copies of invoice shall be forwarded simultaneously to the Collector of Customs at the port of exit. The quadruplicate copy shall be retained by the authorised officer of Land Customs and Central Excise.
4. On arrival of the goods at the port of exit the exporter or his agent shall produce the original copy of the invoice to the Collector of Customs or an Officer appointed by him for the purpose. The goods will remain under customs control until they are duly exported after filing an export Shipping Bill.
5. The Collector of Customs or the Officer appointed by him shall:
   (i) compare the original copy of the invoice with the duplicate and triplicate copies received by him from the authorised officer of Land Customs and Central Excise;
   (ii) examine the seals on the packages and identify the packages with the particulars shown on the invoice;
   (iii) if the particulars on the original copy of the invoice agree with the particulars on the duplicate and triplicate copies and the seals are intact and the packages are satisfactorily identified, allow the goods to be shipped and certify accordingly on each of the three copies of the invoice;

   NOTE: In case the seals are not found intact, he may re-seal the packages with his own seal after satisfying himself as to the identity of the packages, and the goods from the particulars shown on the invoice, and if necessary by opening and examining the goods themselves. It should not, however, be necessary to detain the entire consignment if the seals on some packages are found broken. After ascertaining the shortages and indicating these on the relevant Nepal invoices, goods should be allowed to go forward without delay.

   (iv) retain the triplicate copy and return the original duly endorsed to the exporter or his agent and send the duplicate to the authorised officer of Land Customs and Central Excise at the border.

6. In order to secure the cancellation of any bond furnished under rule 1(iii) the exporter or his agent must present an application to that effect to the authorised officer of Land Customs and Central Excise, supported by the original invoice duly certified by the Collector of Customs at the port of exit to the effect that the goods have been shipped with the Indian Customs seals intact and that the packages correspond with the details in the invoice. The original invoice should be received at the Indian border Customs post *not later than six months* from the date of completion of the invoice by the authorised officer of Land Customs and Central Excise or such extended time as the Collector of Land Customs and Central Excise might certify as being due to circumstances beyond the control of the exporter.
7. The authorised officer of Land Customs and Central Excise at the Indian border Customs post shall compare the original copy of the invoice produced by the exporter with the duplicate copy received from the customs house, before cancelling any bond furnished by the exporter. He shall report promptly to the Collector of Land Customs and Central Excise concerned, the detail of all cases where the cancellation of the bonds has not been secured within the prescribed period.

II. As regards opening for customs examination of such goods in transit, the Government of India agree that it should be reduced to the minimum (ordinarily not exceeding 3 per cent) consistent with the necessity of the Customs Officer satisfying himself that the goods imported or about to be exported are fully in accordance in respect of quantity, description and value with those described in the respective Nepal invoice and that they also otherwise conform with import/export licence issued by His Majesty's Government of Nepal to cover their importation or exportation as the case may be.

III. In respect of goods imported by Their Majesties other privileged members of the Royal family, by His Majesty's Government of Nepal (including goods received by it as foreign aid), and by the United Nations' and Diplomatic personnel and Missions accredited to His Majesty's Government of Nepal, special priorities will be afforded in the matter of compliance with the requisite formalities. As regards unaccompanied baggage of passengers who have already passed in through transit to Nepal, priority of treatment will be similarly accorded provided the Customs Officer is satisfied that the articles imported as such baggage are intended for the *bonafide* personal use in Nepal of that passenger.

IV. His Majesty's Government of Nepal may wish to employ a special agent for the purpose of observance of these formalities and for handling and transmission of goods in transit at the port of Calcutta. It is agreed that facilities for the due discharge of these functions will be made available to such an agent by the Customs authorities at Calcutta in terms of Sections 4 and 203 of the Indian Sea Customs Act, 1878.

V. With regard to Article XI of the Treaty of Trade and Transit the procedure agreed upon between the representatives of the Governments of India and Nepal on the 18th May, 1954, to regulate the transmission of goods of Nepalese origin from the one part of Nepal to another part through Indian territory shall apply *mutatis mutandis* in respect of all articles subject to import, export or excise duty and or prohibitions or restrictions on their import into or export from India.

For the Government of India.

Sd./-B. N. BANERJI
Joint Secretary to the
Government of India,
Ministry of Finance.

For His Majesty's
Government of Nepal.
Sd./- R.P. JOSHI
Secretary to His Majesty's
Government of Nepal,
Ministry of Finance,
11-9-1960

# TREATY OF EXTRADITION BETWEEN THE GOVERNMENT OF INDIA AND THE GOVERNMENT OF NEPAL[1]
## Kathmandu, 2 October 1953

The Government of India and the Government of Nepal, being desirous of regulating extradition of criminals as between the two countries, have resolved to enter into a new Treaty of Extradition with each other, and have for this purpose, appointed as their plenipotentiaries the following persons, namely,

THE GOVERNMENT OF INDIA:

HIS EXCELLENCY SHRI BHALCHANDRA KRISHNA GOKHALE, Ambassador of India in Nepal,

THE GOVERNMENT OF NEPAL :

THE HON'BLE SHRI MATRIKA PRASAD KOIRALA, Prime Minister of Nepal,

Who having examined each other's credentials and found them good and in due form have agreed as follows:

*Article I*

The two Governments hereby engage on a basis of strict reciprocity to deliver up to each other those persons, who, being accused, or convicted, of a crime committed in the territory of one Government, shall be found within the territory of the other Government, under the circumstances and conditions stated in the present Treaty.

*Article II*

Neither Government shall be bound in any case to surrender any person who is not a national of the country by the Government of which the requisition has been made, except where such person is accused of having committed the offence specified in clause (10) of Article 3.

*Article III*

The offences for which extradition is to be granted in accordance with this Treaty are the following, namely:

(1) Murder or attempt or conspiracy to murder.
(2) Culpable homicide not amounting to murder.
(3) Grievous hurt.
(4) Rape.
(5) Dacoity.
(6) Highway robbery.
(7) Robbery with violence.
(8) Burglary or house-breaking.
(9) Arson.
(10) Desertion from Armed Forces.
(11) Offences against the laws prohibiting the export and import of goods.
(12) Embezzlement by public officers.
(13) Serious theft, that is to say cases of theft where violence has been used or where the value of the property stolen exceeds Rs. 500 and cattle stealing.
(14) Abduction or kidnapping.
(15) Forgery and the use of what is known to be forged, counterfeiting or altering money; uttering or bringing into circulation counterfeited or altered money.
(16) Receiving of illegal gratification by a public servant.
(17) Escaping from custody while undergoing punishment after conviction for any of the offences specified in clauses (1) to (16).

*Article IV*

In no case shall either Government be bound to surrender any person accused of an offence except upon a requisition duly made by or under the authority of the Government in whose territories the offence is alleged to have been committed and also upon such evidence of criminality as according to the laws of the country in which the accused person shall be found, would justify the apprehension and sustain the charge if the offence had been committed there.

*Article V*

Neither Government shall be bound to surrender any person if the offence in respect of which the surrender is demanded be of a political character, or if he proves that the requisition for his surrender has in fact been made with a view to trying or punishing him for an offence of a political character.

### Article VI

Extradition shall not take place if the person whose extradition is claimed by one of the Governments has already been tried and discharged or punished or is still under trial in the territory of the other Government for the crime for which extradition is demanded.

### Article VII

If the person whose extradition is claimed by one Government is under trial for any crime in the territory of the other, his extradition may be deferred until the conclusion of the trial.

### Article VIII

A person surrendered shall in no case be detained or tried in the territory of the Government to which the surrender has been made for any other crime or on account of any matter other than those for which extradition has taken place until he has been resorted, or had an opportunity of returning, to the territory of the Government from which he was surrendered.

### Article IX

If evidence sufficient to justify the extradition is not produced within two months from the date of apprehension of the fugitive or within such further period as may be allowed by the Government to which the requisition for extradition has been made or by the Court before which the evidence is to be produced, the fugitive shall be set at liberty.

### Article X

The expenses of any apprehension, detention or surrender made in pursuance of this Treaty shall be borne and defrayed by the Government making the requisition.

### Article XI

This Treaty supersedes and cancels all previous Treaties, Agreements and Engagements on the subject.

### Article XII

This Treaty shall come into force without ratification, one month after the date of signature by both parties and may be terminated by either party by giving one year's notice.

DONE in duplicate at Kathmandu, this 2nd day of October, 1953.

BHALCHANDRA KRISHNA GOKHALE,
For the Government of India.

MATRIKA PRASAD KOIRALA,
For the Government of Nepal.

## REFERENCE

1. *India Bilateral Treaties and Agreements*, Vol. II (1953-57), Ministry of External Affairs, Delhi.

# AGREEMENT BETWEEN THE REPUBLIC OF INDIA AND THE PEOPLE'S REPUBLIC OF CHINA ON TRADE AND INTERCOURSE BETWEEN TIBET REGION OF CHINA AND INDIA[1]

## Peking, 29 April 1954

The Government of the Republic of India and

The Central People's Government of the People's Republic of China,

Being desirous of promoting trade and cultural intercourse between Tibet Region of China and India and of facilitating pilgrimage and travel by the peoples of China and India,

Have resolved to enter into the present Agreement based on the following principles:

(1) mutual respect for each other's territorial integrity and sovereignty,
(2) mutual non-aggression,
(3) mutual non-interference in each other's internal affairs,
(4) equality and mutual benefit, and
(5) peaceful co-existence.

And for this purpose have appointed as their respective Plenipotentiaries:

The Government of the Republic of India, H.E. Nedyam Raghavan, Ambassador Extraordinary and Plenipotentiary of India accredited to the People's Republic of China; the Central People's Government of the People's Republic of China, H. E. Chang Han-fu, Vice-Minister of Foreign Affairs of the Central People's Government, who, having examined each other's credentials and finding them in good and due form, have agreed upon the following:

*Article I*

The High Contracting Parties mutually agree to establish Trade Agencies:

(1) The Government of India agrees that the Government of China may establish Trade Agencies at New Delhi, Calcutta and Kalimpong.

(2) The Government of China agrees that the Government of India may establish Trade Agencies at Yatung, Gyantse and Gartok.

The Trade Agencies of both Parties shall be accorded the same status and same treatment. The Trade Agents of both Parties shall enjoy freedom from arrest while exercising their functions, and shall enjoy in respect of themselves, their wives and children who are dependent on them for livelihood, freedom from search.

The Trade Agencies of both Parties shall enjoy the privileges and immunities for couriers, mail-bags and communications in code.

*Article II*

The High Contracting Parties agree that traders of both countries known to be customarily and specifically engaged in trade between Tibet Region of China and India may trade at the following places :

(1) The Government of China agrees to specify (1) Yatung, (2) Gyantse and (3) Phari as markets for trade. The Government of India agrees that trade may be carried on in India, including places like (1) Kalimpong, (2) Siliguri and (3) Calcutta, according to customary practice.

(2) The Government of China agrees to specify (1) Gartok, (2) Pulanchung (Taklakot), (3) Gyanima-Khargo, (4) Gyanima-Chakra, (5) Ramura, (6) Dongbra, (7) Pulang-Sumdo, (8) Nabra, (9) Shangtse and (10) Tashigong as markets for trade; the Government of India agrees that in future, when in accordance with the development and need of trade between the Ari District of Tibet Region of China and India, it has become necessary to specify markets for trade in the corresponding district in India adjacent to the Ari District of Tibet Region of China, it will be prepared to consider on the basis of equality and reciprocity to do so.

*Article III*

The High Contracting Parties agree that pilgrimage by religious believers of the two countries shall be carried on in accordance with the following provisions :

(1) Pilgrims from India of Lamaist, Hindu and Buddhist faiths may

visit Kang Rimpoche (Kailas) and Mavem Tso (Manasarovar) in Tibet Region of China in accordance with custom.

(2) Pilgrims from Tibet Region of China of Lamaist and Buddhist faiths may visit Banaras, Sarnath, Gaya and Sanchi in India in accordance with custom.

(3) Pilgrims customarily visiting Lhasa may continue to do so in accordance with custom.

*Article IV*

Traders and pilgrims of both countries may travel by the following passes and route :

(1) Shipki La pass, (2) Mana pass, (3) Niti pass, (4) Kungri Bingri pass, (5) Darma pass and (6) Lipu Lekh pass.

Also, the customary route leading to Tashigong along the valley of the Shangatsangpu (Indus) River may continue to be traversed in accordance with custom.

*Article V*

For travelling across the border, the High Contracting Parties agree that diplomatic personnel, officials and nationals of the two countries shall hold passports issued by their own respective countries and visas by the other Party except as provided in Paragraphs 1, 2, 3 and 4 of this Article.

(1) Traders of both countries known to be customarily and specifically engaged in trade between Tibet Region of China and India, their wives and children who are dependent on them for livelihood and their attendants will be allowed entry for purposes of trade into India or Tibet Region of China, as the case may be, in accordance with custom on the production of certificates duly issued by the local government of their own country or by its duly authorised agents and examined by the border check-posts of the other Party.

(2) Inhabitants of the border districts of the two countries who cross the border to carry on petty trade or to visit friends and relatives may proceed to the border districts of the other Party as they have customarily done heretofore and need not be restricted to the passes and route specified in Article IV above and shall not be required to hold passport, visas or permits.

(3) Porters and mule team drivers of the two countries who cross the border to perform necessary transportation services need not hold passports issued by their own country, but shall only hold certificates good for a definite period of time (three months, half a

year or one year) duly issued by the local government of their own country or by its duly authorised agents and produce them for registration at the border checkposts of the other Party.

(4) Pilgrims of both countries need not carry documents of certification but shall register at the border checkposts of the other party and receive a permit for pilgrimage.

(5) Notwithstanding the provisions of the foregoing paragraphs of this Article, either Government may refuse entry to any particular person.

(6) Persons who enter the territory of the other Party in accordance with the foregoing paragraphs of this Article may stay within its territory only after complying with the procedures specified by the other Party.

*Article VI*

The present Agreement shall come into effect upon ratification[2] by both Governments and shall remain in force for eight (8) years. Extension of the present Agreement may be negotiated by the two Parties if either Party requests for it six (6) months prior to the expiry of the Agreement and the request is agreed to by the other Party.

DONE in duplicate in Peking on the *twentyninth day* of April, 1954 in Hindi, Chinese and English languages, all texts being equally valid.

(Sd.) NEDYAM RAGHAVAN,
Plenipotentiary of the
Government of the
Republic of India.

(Sd.) CHANG HAN-FU.
Plenipotentiary of the
Central People's
Government, People's
Republic of China.

**REFERENCES**

1. *India Bilateral Treaties and Agreements*, Vol. II (1953-57), Ministry of External Affairs, Delhi.
2. Ratified by Government of India and China on 3rd June 1954.

# NOTES EXCHANGED[1]

*Peking, April 29, 1954*

NOTE

Your Excellency Mr. Vice-Foreign Minister,

In the course of our discussions regarding the Agreement on Trade and Intercourse between Tibet Region of China and India, which has been happily concluded today, the Delegation of the Government of the Republic of India and the Delegation of the Government of the People's Republic of China agreed that certain matters be regulated by an exchange of notes. In pursuance of this understanding, it is hereby agreed between the two Governments as follows :

(1) The Government of India will be pleased to withdraw completely within six (6) months from date of exchange of the present notes the military escorts now stationed at Yatung and Gyantse in Tibet Region of China. The Government of China will render facilities and assistance in such withdrawal.

(2) The Government of India will be pleased to hand over to the Government of China at a reasonable price the postal, telegraph and public telephone services together with their equipment operated by the Government of India in Tibet Region of China. The concrete measures in this regard will be decided upon through further negotiations between the Indian Embassy in China and the Foreign Ministry of China, which shall start immediately after the exchange of the present notes.

(3) The Government of India will be pleased to hand over to the Government of China at a reasonable price the twelve (12) rest houses of the Government of India in Tibet Region of China. The concrete measures in this regard will be decided upon through further negotiations between the Indian Embassy in China and the Foreign Ministry of China, which shall start immediately after the exchange of the present notes. The Government of China agrees that they shall continue as rest houses.

(4) The Government of China agrees that all buildings within the compound walls of the Trade Agencies of the Government of India at Yatung and Gyantse in Tibet Region of China may be retained by the Government of India. The Government of India may continue to lease the land within its Agency compound walls from the Chinese side. And the Government of India agrees that the Trade Agencies of the Government of China at Kalimpong and Calcutta may lease lands from the Indian side for the use of the Agencies and construct buildings thereon. The Government of China will render every possible assistance for housing the Indian Trade Agency at Gartok. The Government of India will also render every possible assistance for housing the Chinese Trade Agency at New Delhi.

(5) The Government of India will be pleased to return to the Government of China all lands used or occupied by the Government of India other than the lands within its Trade Agency compound walls at Yatung.

If there are godowns and buildings of the Government of India on the above mentioned lands used or occupied and to be returned by the Government of India and if Indian traders have stores, godowns or buildings on the above-mentioned lands so that there is a need to continue leasing lands, the Government of China agrees to sign contracts with the Government of India or Indian traders, as the case may be, for leasing to them those parts of the land occupied by the said godowns, buildings or stores and pertaining thereto.

(6) The Trade Agents of both Parties may, in accordance with the laws and regulations of the local governments, have access to their nationals involved in civil or criminal cases.

(7) The Trade Agents and traders of both countries may hire employees in the locality.

(8) The hospitals of the Indian Trade Agencies at Gyantse and Yatung will continue to serve personnel of the Indian Trade Agencies.

(9) Each Government shall protect the person and property of the traders and pilgrims of the other country.

(10) The Government of China agrees, so far as possible, to construct rest houses for the use of pilgrims along the route from Pulanchung (Taklakot) to Kang Rimpoche (Kailas) and Mavam Tso (Manasarover); and the Government of India agrees to place all possible facilities in India at the disposal of pilgrims.

(11) Traders and pilgrims of both countries shall have the facility of hiring means of transportation at normal and reasonable rates.

(12) The three Trade Agencies of each party may function throughout the year.

(13) Traders of each country may rent buildings and godowns in accordance with local regulations in places under the jurisdiction of the other Party.

(14) Traders of both countries may carry on normal trade in accordance with local regulations at places as provided in Article II of the Agreement.

(15) Disputes between traders of both countries over debts and claims shall be handled in accordance with local laws and regulations.

On behalf of the Government of the Republic of India I hereby agree that the present Note along with Your Excellency's reply shall become an agreement between our two Governments which shall come into force upon the exchange of the present Notes.

I avail myself of this opportunity to express to Your Excellency Mr. Vice-Foreign Minister, the assurances of my highest consideration.

(Sd.) N. RAGHAVAN,
Ambassador Extraordinary and
Plenipotentiary of the
Republic of India.

His Excellency Mr. CHANG HAN-FU,
Vice-Minister of Foreign Affairs,
Central People's Government,
People's Republic of China.

NOTE

*Peking, April 29, 1954*

Your Excellency Mr. AMBASSADOR :

I have the honour to receive your note dated April 29, 1954 which reads :

[*Not reprinted*]

On behalf of the Central People's Government of the People's Republic of China, I hereby agree to Your Excellency's note, and your note along with the present note in reply shall become an agreement between our two Governments, which shall come into force upon the exchange of the present notes.

I avail myself of this opportunity to express to Your Excellency, Mr. Ambassador, the assurances of my highest consideration.

(Sd.) CHANG HAN-FU.
Vice Minister,
Ministry of Foreign Affairs,
People's Republic of China.

H. E. NEDYAM RAGHAVAN,
Ambassador Extraordinary and Plenipotentiary,
Republic of India.

(Original in English)

## NOTES REGARDING RATIFICATION

*Peking, the 17th August, 1954*

EXCELLENCY,

I have the honour to state that :

WHEREAS an agreement between the Government of the Republic of India and the Central People's Government of the People's Republic of China on trade and intercourse between Tibet region of China and India was signed at Peking on the 29th Day of April, 1954, by the respective plenipotentiaries of the two Governments, namely,

For the Government of the Republic of India.

His Excellency Nedyam Raghavan, Ambassador Extraordinary and Plenipotentiary of India,

For the Central People's Government of the People's Republic of China,

His Excellency Chang Han-fu,

Which Agreement is reproduced, word for word, in the Annexure[2] hereto.

## REFERENCES

1. *India Bilateral Treaties and Agreements*, Vol. II.
2. Not printed.

# AGREEMENT ON BILATERAL RELATIONS BETWEEN THE GOVERNMENTS OF INDIA AND PAKISTAN, SIGNED AT SIMLA 2 July 1972[1]

1. The Government of India and the Government of Pakistan are resolved that the two countries put an end to the conflict and confrontation that have hitherto marred the relations and work for the promotion of a friendly and harmonious relationship and the establishment of durable peace in the sub-continent, so that both countries may henceforth devote their resources and energies to the pressing task of advancing the welfare of their peoples.

In order to achieve this objective, the Government of India and the Government of Pakistan have agreed as follows:

(i) That the principles and purposes of the Charter of the United Nations shall govern the relations between the two countries.

(ii) That the two countries are resolved to settle their differences by peaceful means through bilateral negotiations or by any other peaceful means mutually agreed upon between them. Pending the final settlement of any of the problems between the two countries, neither side shall unilaterally alter the situation and both shall prevent the organisation, assistance or encouragement of any acts detrimental to the maintenance of peaceful and harmonious relations.

(iii) That the pre-requisite for reconciliation, good neighbourliness and durable peace between them is a commitment by both the countries to peaceful coexistence, respect for each other's territorial integrity and sovereignty and non-interference in each other's internal affairs, on the basis of equality and mutual benefit.

(iv) That the basic issues and causes of conflict which have bedevilled the relations between the two countries for the last

25 years shall be resolved by peaceful means.

(v) That they shall always respect each other's national unity, territorial integrity, political independence and sovereign equality.

(vi) That in accordance with the Charter of the United Nations, they will refrain from the threat or use of force against the territorial integrity or political independence of each other.

2. Both Governments will take all steps within their power to prevent hostile propaganda directed against each other. Both countries will encourage the dissemination of such information as would promote the development of friendly relations between them.

3. In order progressively to restore and normalise relations between the two countries step by step, it was agreed that :

(i) Steps shall be taken to resume communications—postal, telegraphic, sea, land including border posts and air links including over-flights.

(ii) Appropriate steps shall be taken to promote travel facilities for the nationals of the other country.

(iii) Trade and cooperation in economic and agreed fields will be resumed as far as possible.

(iv) Exchange in the fields of science and culture will be promoted. In this connection, delegations from the two countries will meet from time to time to work out the necessary details.

4. In order to initiate the process of the establishment of durable peace, both the Governments agreed that :

(i) Indian and Pakistani forces shall be withdrawn to their side of the international border.

(ii) In Jammu and Kashmir the line of control resulting from the ceasefire of December 17, 1971 shall be respected by both sides without prejudice to the recognised position of either side. Neither side shall seek to alter it unilaterally irrespective of mutual differences and legal interpretations. Both sides further undertake to refrain from the threat or the use of force in violation of this line.

(iii) The withdrawals shall commence upon entry into force of this Agreement and shall be completed within a period of 30 days thereafter.

5. This Agreement will be subject to ratification by both countries in accordance with their respective constitutional procedures and will come into force with effect from the date on which the Instruments of Ratification are exchanged.

6. Both Governments agree that their respective Heads will meet

again at a mutually convenient time in the future and that, in the meanwhile, the representatives of the two sides will meet to discuss further the modalities and arrangements for the establishment of durable peace and normalisation of relations, including the questions of repatriation of prisoners of war and civilian internees, a final settlement of Jammu and Kashmir and the resumption of diplomatic relations.

| (INDIRA GANDHI) | (ZULFIQAR ALI BHUTTO) |
|---|---|
| *Prime Minister* | *President,* |
| *Republic of India* | *Islamic Republic of Pakistan* |

**REFERENCE**

1. *Foreign Affairs Record*, July 1972.

# INDO-BANGLADESH TREATY OF FRIENDSHIP AND PEACE SIGNED BY THE PRIME MINISTERS OF INDIA AND BANGLADESH IN DACCA, 19 March 1972[1]

Inspired by common ideals of peace, secularism, democracy, socialism and nationalism,

Having struggled together for the realisation of these ideals and cemented ties of friendship through blood and sacrifices which led to the triumphant emergence of a free, sovereign and independent Bangladesh,

Determined to maintain fraternal and good-neighbourly relations and transform their border into a border of eternal peace and friendship,

Adhering firmly to the basic tenets of non-alignment, peaceful co-existence, mutual cooperation, non-interference in internal affairs and respect for territorial integrity and sovereignty,

Determined to safeguard peace, stability and security and to promote progress of their respective countries through all possible avenues of mutual cooperation,

Determined further to expand and strengthen the existing relations of friendship between them, convinced that the further development of friendship and cooperation meets the national interests of both States as well as the interests of lasting peace in Asia and the world,

Resolved to contribute to strengthening world peace and security and to make efforts to bring about a relaxation of international tension and the final elimination of vestiges of colonialism, racialism and imperialism,

Convinced that in the present-day world international problems can be solved only through cooperation and not through conflict or confrontation,

Reaffirming their determination to follow the aims and principles of the United Nations Charter, the Republic of India, on the one hand,

and the People's Republic of Bangladesh, on the other, have decided to conclude the present Treaty.

*Article 1*

The high contracting parties, inspired by the ideals for which their respective peoples struggled and made sacrifices together, solemnly declare that there shall be lasting peace and friendship between their two countries and their people's, each side shall respect the independence, sovereignty and territorial integrity of the other and refrain from interfering in the internal affairs of the other side.

The high contracting parties shall further develop and strengthen the relations of friendship, good-neighbourliness and all-round cooperation existing between them, on the basis of the above-mentioned principles as well as the principles of equality and mutual benefit.

*Article 2*

Being guided by their devotion to the principles of equality of all peoples and states, irrespective of race or creed, the high contracting parties condemn colonialism and racialism in all forms and manifestations and are determined to strive for their final and complete elimination.

The high contracting parties shall co-operate with other states in achieving these aims and support the just aspirations of peoples in their struggle against colonialism and racial discrimination and for their national liberation.

*Article 3*

The high contracting parties reaffirm their faith in the policy of non-alignment and peaceful co-existence as important factors for easing tension in the world, maintaining international peace and security, and strengthening national sovereignty and independence.

*Article 4*

The high contracting parties shall maintain regular contacts with each other on major international problems affecting the interests of both States, through meetings and exchanges of views at all levels.

*Article 5*

The high contracting parties shall continue to strengthen and widen their mutually advantageous and all-round cooperation in the economic, scientific and technical fields. The two countries shall develop mutual co-operation in the fields of trade, transport and communications between them on the basis of the principles of equality, mutual benefit and the most-favoured nation principle.

*Article 6*

The high contracting parties further agree to make joint studies and take joint action in the fields of flood control, river basin development and the development of hydro-electric power and irrigation.

*Article 7*

The high contracting parties shall promote relations in the fields of art, literature, education, culture, sports and health.

*Article 8*

In accordance with the ties of friendship existing between the two countries each of the high contracting parties solemnly declares that it shall not enter into or participate in any military alliance directed against the other party.

Each of the high contracting parties shall refrain from any aggression against the other party and shall not allow the use of its territory for committing any act that may cause military damage to or constitute a threat to the security of the other high contracting party.

*Article 9*

Each of the high contracting parties shall refrain from giving any assistance to any third party taking part in an armed conflict against the other party. In case either party is attacked or threatened with attack, the high contracting parties shall immediately enter into mutual consultations in order to take appropriate effective measures to eliminate the threat and thus ensure the peace and security of their countries.

*Article 10*

Each of the high contracting parties solemnly declares that it shall not undertake any commitment, secret or open, toward one or more States which may be incompatible with the present Treaty.

*Article 11*

The present Treaty is signed for a term of twenty-five years and shall be subject to renewal by mutual agreement of the high contracting parties.

The Treaty shall come into force with immediate effect from the date of its signature.

*Article 12*

Any differences in interpreting any article or articles of the present Treaty that may arise between the high contracting parties shall be settled on a bilateral basis by peaceful means in a spirit in mutual respect and understanding.

*DONE IN DACCA ON THE NINETEENTH DAY OF MARCH NINETEEN HUNDRED AND SEVENTYTWO*

Sd/-
(Smt.) Indira Gandhi
Prime Minister
For the Republic of India

Sd/-
Sheikh Mujibur Rahman
Prime Minister
For the People's
Republic of Bangladesh

**REFERENCE**

1. *Foreign Affairs Record*, March 1972.

# TIBETO-NEPALESE TREATY OF 1792[1]

1. That China should henceforth be considered as father to both Nepal and Tibet, who should regard each other as brothers;
2. That after due investigation by the Chinese Government, the full value of the articles plundered at Lhasa would be paid to the Nepalese sufferers by the Tibetan authorities;
3. That all Nepalese subjects; with the exception of armed soldiers would be permitted to travel, to establish factories and to carry on trade within the jurisdiction of Tibet and China.
4. That if either of the two brotherly States should commence an unprovoked dispute with the intention of possessing the territories of the other, the representatives of the two Governments would report all particulars to the court of Peking which would finally decide the dispute;
5. That if Nepal be ever invaded by a foreign power, China would not fail to help her;
6. That the two brotherly States would send to China some produce of their country every five years in token of their filial love;
7. That the Chinese Government would in return send to Nepal a friendly present, and would make every necessary arrangement for the comfort of the mission to and from Peking.

## REFERENCE

1. *China-South Asian Relations*, Vol. 2, ed. R. K. Jain, Radiant Publishers, Delhi.

# TREATY OF PEACE BETWEEN NEPAL AND TIBET, 24 March 1856[1]

We, the undermentioned Nobles, Bharadars, and Lamas representing the Gorkha Government and the Tibetan Government have mutually settled a Treaty of the following ten Articles, and with Supreme Being as witness we have affixed our seals unto it of our own free will and choice. The Emperor of China shall continue to be regarded with respect[3] as heretofore. So long as the two Governments continue to abide by the terms set forth herein, they shall live in amity like two brothers. May the Supreme Being not allow that side to prosper which may make war upon the other; and may the side be exempt from all sin in making war upon the other side which violates the terms contained in this agreement (Treaty).

[Here follow the names and seals of the signatories]

*Article 1*

Tibet shall pay a sum of rupees ten thousand annually to the Gorkha Government.[2]

*Article 2*

Gorkha and Tibet have both been regarding the Emperor of China with respect[3]. Tibet being merely a country of Monasteries of Lamas and a place for recitation of prayers and practice of religious austerities, should troops of any other Raja invade Tibet in future, Gorkha will afford such assistance and protection as it can.

*Article 3*

Tibet shall not levy any taxes (on routes), duties (on merchandise), and rates (of any other kind) leviable by Tibet on the merchants and subjects of the country of Gorkha.

*Article 4*

Tibet shall return to the Gorkha Government all Sikh soldiers held as prisoners and also all officers, soldiers, women, and guns of Gorkha that were captured and taken during the war; and the Gorkha Government shall return to Tibet all the soldiers of Tibet captured in the war, as also the arms, the yaks whatever there may be belonging to the Rayats of Kirong, Kuti, Jhunga, Taklakhar, and Chhewar-Gumbha, and on the completion of this Treaty all the Gorkha troops that are in Taklakhar, Chhewar-Gumbha, Kirong, Jhunga, Kuti, Dhyaklang, and upto Bhairab Lanbur range shall be withdrawn and the places evacuated.

*Article 5*

Hencefourth not a Naikya (Headman) but a Bharadar shall be posted by the Gorkha Government at Lhasa.

*Article 6*

The Gorkha Government will establish its own trade factory at Lhasa which will be allowed to trade freely in all kinds of merchandise from gems and ornaments to articles of clothing and food.

*Article 7*

The Gorkha Bharadar at Lhasa shall not try and determine suits and cases amongst Gorkha subjects, merchants, the Kasmeries of Nepal, residing within the jurisdiction of Lhasa. In the event of dispute between the subjects and merchants of Gorkha and those of Tibet, the Bharadars of both Gorkha and Tibet shall sit together and jointly adjudicate the cases. All incomes (fines, etc.) from such adjudications realized from the Gorkha subjects and merchants and Kasmeries shall be taken by Gorkha.

*Article 8*

A Gorkha subject who goes to the country of Tibet after committing murder of any person of Gorkha shall be surrendered by Tibet to Gorkha; and a Tibetan subject who goes to the country of Gorkha after committing murder of any person of Tibet shall be surrendered by Gorkha to Tibet.

*Article 9*

If the property of Gorkha subjects and merchants be plundered by any person of Tibet, the Bharadars of Tibet shall compel the restoration of such property to Gorkha subjects and merchants; should the property be not forthcoming from the plunderer, Tibet shall compel him to enter into arrangement for restitution (of such property). If the property of Tibetan subjects and merchants be plundered by any person of Gorkha, Gorkha shall compel the restoration of such property to the Tibetan subjects and merchants. Should the property be not forthcoming from the plunderer Gorkha shall compel him to enter into an agreement for the restitution (of such property).

*Article 10*

After the completion of the Treaty neither side shall act vindictively against the person or property of the subjects of Tibet who may have joined the Gorkha Durbar during the war, or of the subjects of Gorkha who may have so joined the Tibetan Durbar.

This the third day of Light fortnight of Chaitra in the year of Sumbat 1912.

N.B. Bharadars are the high civil or military officers under the Government of Nepal or of Tibet.

## REFERENCES

1. *Ibid.*, R. K. Jain.
2. The Tibetan text inserts the words "in cash." Aitchison adds the words as "tribute" and Sir Charles Bell "as a present".
3. Aitchison translates the relevant word as "borne allegiance".

# MAO TSE-TUNG'S BROCHURE, THE CHINESE REVOLUTION AND THE CHINESE COMMUNIST PARTY, December 1939 (EXTRACT)[1]

In defeating China in war, the imperialist States have taken away many Chinese dependent States and a part of her territories. Japan took away Korea, Taiwan and Ryuku islands, the Pescadores, Port Arthur; England seized Burma, Bhutan, Nepal and Hong Kong; France occupied Annam and even an insignificant country like Portugal took Macao.

## REFERENCE


1. *Ibid.*, R. K. Jain.

# CHINA-NEPAL AGREEMENT TO MAINTAIN FRIENDLY RELATIONS AND ON TRADE AND INTERCOURSE, 20 September 1956 (Effective From 17 January 1958)[1]

The Government of the People's Republic of China and the Government of the Kingdom of Nepal,

Being desirous of further developing the friendly relations between the two countries as good neighbours on the basis of the long-standing friendship between the two peoples,

Reaffirm that the five principles (*Panch shila*) of —

1. Mutual respect for each other's territorial integrity and sovereignty,
2. Non-aggression,
3. Non-interference in each other's internal affairs for any reasons of an economic, political or ideological character,
4. Equality and mutual benefit, and
5. Peaceful co-existence,

Should be the fundamental principles guiding the relations between the two countries.

The two Parties have resolved to conclude the present agreement in accordance with the above-mentioned principles and have for this purpose appointed as their respective plenipotentiaries... who, having examined each other's credentials and finding them in good and due form, have agreed upon the following :

*Article I*

The High Contracting Parties declare that peace and friendship shall be maintained between the People's Republic of China and the Kingdom of Nepal.

*Article II*

The High Contracting Parties hereby reaffirm their decision to mutually exchange diplomatic representatives on ambassadorial level.

*Article III*

All treaties and documents which existed in the past between China and Nepal including those between the Tibet Region of China and Nepal are hereby abrogated.

*Article IV*

In order to maintain and develop the traditional contacts between the peoples of the Tibet Region of China and Nepal the High Contracting Parties agree that the nationals of both Parties may trade, travel and make pilgrimage in those places in each other's territory as agreed upon by both Parties, and the two Parties agree to safeguard the proper interests of the nationals of the other Party in its territory in accordance with the laws of the country of residence, and for this purpose the High Contracting Parties agree to do as follows:

Paragraph I. The High Contracting Parties mutually agree to establish Trade Agencies:

1. The Chinese Government agrees that the Government of Nepal may establish Trade Agencies at Shigatse, Kyerong and Nyalam;
2. The Government of Nepal agrees that the Chinese Government may establish an equal number of Trade Agencies in Nepal, the specific locations of which will be discussed and determined at a later date by both Parties;
3. The Trade Agencies of both Parties shall be accorded the same status and same treatment. The Trade Agents of both Parties shall enjoy freedom from arrest while exercising their functions, and shall enjoy in respect of themselves, their wives and their children who are dependent on them for livelihood freedom from search. The Trade Agencies of both Parties shall enjoy the privileges and immunities for couriers, mail-bags and communications in code.

Paragraph II. The High Contracting Parties agree that traders of both countries may trade at the following places:

1. The Chinese Government agrees to specify (1) Lhasa, (2) Shigatse, (3) Gyantse and (4) Yatung as markets for trade;
2. The Government of Nepal agrees that when with the

development of Chinese trade in Nepal, it has become necessary to specify markets for trade in Nepal, the Government of Nepal will specify an equal number of markets for trade in Nepal;

3. Traders of both countries known to be customarily and specifically engaged in border trade between the Tibet Region of China and Nepal may continue trade at the traditional markets for such trade.

Paragraph III. The High Contracting Parties agree that pilgrimage by religious believers of either country to the other may continue according to religious custom. Personal baggages and articles used for pilgrimage carried by the pilgrims of either Party shall be exempted from taxation by the other Party.

Paragraph IV. For travelling across the border between the Tibet Region of China and Nepal, the High Contracting Parties agree that the nationals of both countries shall use the customary routes.

Paragraph V. For travelling across the border by the nationals of the two countries, the High Contracting Parties agree to adopt the following provisions:

1. Diplomatic personnel and officials of the two countries and nationals of the two countries except those provided by Sub-paragraphs 2, 3 and 4, who travel across the border between the Tibet Region of China and Nepal, shall hold passports issued by their respective countries and visaed by the other Party. Nationals of the two countries who enter the Tibet Region of China or Nepal through a third country shall also hold passports issued by their respective countries and visaed by the other Party.
2. Traders of the two countries known to be customarily and specifically engaged in trade between the Tibet Region of China and Nepal, their wives and children dependent on them for livelihood and their attendants, not covered by Sub-paragraph 3 of this Paragraph, who enter into the Tibet Region of China or Nepal as the case may be for the purposes of trade, shall hold passports issued by their respective countries and visaed by the other Party, or certificates issued by their respective Governments or by organs authorized by their respective Governments.
3 Inhabitants of the border districts of the two countries who cross the border to carry on petty trade, to visit friends or relatives, or for seasonal changes of residence, may do so as they have customarily done heretofore and need not hold

passports, visas or other documents of certification.

4. Pilgrims of either party who travel across the border between the Tibet Region of China and Nepal for the purpose of pilgrimage need not hold passports, visas or other documents of certifications but shall register at the border checkposts or the first authorized government office of the other Party, and obtain permits for pilgrimage therefrom.
5. Notwithstanding the provisions of the foregoing Sub-paragraphs of this Paragraph, either Government may refuse entry to any particular person.
6. Nationals of either country who enter the territory of the other Party in accordance with the foregoing Sub-paragraphs of this Paragraph may stay within the territory only after complying with the procedures specified by the other party.

*Article V*

This Agreement shall be ratified. It shall come into effect after mutual notice of ratifications, and remain in force for eight (8) years. Extension of the present Agreement may be negotiated by the two Parties if either party requests for it six (6) months prior to the expiry of the Agreement and the request is agreed to by the other Party.

Done in Kathmandu on the 20th day of September 1956, in duplicate in the Chinese, Nepalese and English languages, all texts being equally authentic.

## REFERENCE

1. *Ibid.* R. K. Jain

# EXCHANGE OF NOTES BETWEEN CHINESE AMBASSADOR PAN TZU-LI AND NEPALESE FOREIGN MINISTER C. P. SHARMA ON CERTAIN MATTERS CONCERNING RELATIONS BETWEEN CHINA AND NEPAL, 20 September 1956

**(a) Chinese Ambassador Pan Tzu-li's Note:**

In the course of our discussions regarding the Agreement to Maintain the Friendly Relations between the People's Republic of China and the Kingdom of Nepal and on Trade and Intercourse between the Tibet Region of China and Nepal, the Delegation of the Government of the People's Republic of China and the Delegation of the Government of the Kingdom of Nepal agreed that certain related matters be regulated by an exchange of notes. In pursuance of this understanding, it is hereby agreed between the two Governments as follows:

1. The two Parties mutually agree to establish Consulates-General:

The Chinese Government agrees that the Government of Nepal may establish a Consulate-General at Lhasa of the Tibet Region of China.

The Government of Nepal agrees that the Chinese Government may establish a Consulate-General at Kathmandu of Nepal, the date for the establishment of which will be discussed and determined at a later date.

2. The Government of Nepal will be pleased to withdraw completely within six (6) months after this exchange of notes its military escorts now in Lhasa and other places in the Tibet Region of China, together with all their arms and ammunition. The Chinese Government will render facilities and assistance in such withdrawal.

3. Nepalese nationals in the Tibet Region of China and Chinese nationals in Nepal shall be subjected to the jurisdiction of the Government of the country of residence, observe the laws and regulations of the country of residence, pay taxes to that Government and respect the local customs. All civil and criminal cases or disputes in which nationals of one Party in the territory of the other may be involved, shall be dealt with by the Government of the country of residence.
4. The Government of either Party will protect and safeguard the person, property and legitimate interests of the nationals of the other Party in its territory.
5. (A) The Governments of the two Parties agree that the nationals of either Party in the territory of the other Party, under the condition that they pay rents according to market prices and sign contracts for lease with the house owners on a mutually voluntary basis, may have the facility to rent houses.
   (B) Nationals of either Party who have already rented houses in the territory of the other Party, under the condition that they pay rents according to market prices and that contracts for lease are or have been concluded with the house owners on a mutually voluntary basis, may continue to rent the houses.
6. Both Parties agree to adopt necessary measures to promote and expand the trade relations between the two countries, and to levy customs duties on the import and export commodities of the two Parties in accordance with the favoured tax-rates of each Government.
7. The range of business engaged in by the traders of either Party in the territory of the other shall comply with the relevant laws and regulations of the Government of the country of residence.
8. The Nepalese primary school in Lhasa of the Tibet Region of China shall be changed into a primary school for children of Nepalese nationals and shall complete registration procedures in accordance with the relevant regulations of the Chinese Government.
9. The two Parties agree to establish direct wireless telegraphic service between Lhasa and Kathmandu, the specific arrangements of which will be discussed and decided upon at a later date by the departments concerned of both Parties.
10. The Government of either Party will assist the Consulate-General and the Trade Agencies of the other in its territory in renting houses.
11. The Trade Agents of both Parties may, in accordance with the laws and regulations of the country of residence, have access to

their nationals involved in civil or criminal cases.

12. The Trade Agents and traders of both countries may hire employees in the locality.
13. Traders and pilgrims of both countries shall have the facility of hiring means of transportation at normal and reasonable rates.
14. The two Parties agree that any person residing in the Tibet Region of China born of parents holding respectively the nationality of the People's Republic of China and the nationality of the Kingdom of Nepal and of eighteen years of age or above, may, according to their own will, choose the nationality of the People's Republic of China for themselves and their children who are under the age of 18, by completing relevant procedures at the Chinese Government. After the completion of the above mentioned procedures, they and their children under the age of 18 shall be considered to have lost automatically the nationality of Nepal.

If the Government of the Kingdom of Nepal agrees to the present note, the present note along with Your Excellency's reply shall become an agreement between our two Governments which shall come into force upon the exchange of the present note and Your Excellency's reply.

**(b) C. P. Sharma's Note.**

I have the honour to acknowledge receipt of Your Excellency's note of September 20, 1956, which reads as follows .....

[as above ....] On behalf of the Government of the Kingdom of Nepal, I hereby agree to Your Excellency's note. Your Excellency's note along with this reply shall become an agreement between our two governments which shall come into force upon the exchange of the present notes.

# CHINA-NEPAL BOUNDARY AGREEMENT, 21 March 1960[1]

The Government of the People's Republic of China and His Majesty's Government of Nepal have noted with satisfaction that the two countries have always respected the existing traditional customary boundary line and lived in amity. With a view to bringing about the formal settlement of some existing discrepancies in the boundary line between the two countries and the scientific delineation and formal demarcation of the whole boundary line, and to consolidating and further developing friendly relations between the two countries, the two Governments have decided to conclude the present Agreement under the guidance of the Five Principles of Peaceful Co-existence and have agreed upon the following:

*Article I*

The Contracting Parties have agreed that the entire boundary between the two countries shall be scientifically delineated and formally demarcated through friendly consultations, on the basis of the existing traditional customary line.

*Article II*

In order to determine the specific alignment of the boundary line and to enable the fixing of the boundary between the two countries in legal form, the Contracting Parties have decided to set up a joint committee composed of an equal number of delegates from each side and enjoin the committee, in accordance with the provisions of Article III of the present Agreement, to discuss and solve the concrete problems concerning the Sino-Nepalese boundary, conduct survey of the boundary, erect boundary markers, and draft a Sino-Nepalese boundary treaty. The joint committee will hold its meetings in the capitals or other places of China and Nepal.

*Article III*

Having studied the delineation of the boundary line between the two countries as shown on the maps mutually exchanged (for the map submitted by the Chinese side, see attached map 1; for the map submitted by the Nepalese side, see attached map2)[2] and the information furnished by each side about its actual jurisdiction over the area bordering on the other country, the Contracting Parties deem that, except for discrepancies in certain sections, their understanding of the traditional customary line is basically the same. The Contracting Parties have decided to determine concretely the boundary between the two countries in the following ways in accordance with three different cases:

1. Sections where the delineation of the boundary line between the two countries on the maps of the two sides is identical.

In these sections the boundary line shall be fixed according to the identical delineation on the maps of the two sides. The joint committee will send out joint survey teams composed of an equal number of persons from each side to conduct survey on the spot and erect boundary markers.

After the boundary line in these sections is fixed in accordance with the provisions of the above paragraph, the territory north of the line will conclusively belong to China, while the territory south of the line will conclusively belong to Nepal, and neither Contracting Party will any longer lay claim to certain areas within the territory of the other Party.

2. Sections where the delineation of the boundary line between the two countries on the maps of the two sides is not identical, whereas the state of actual jurisdiction by each side is undisputed.

The joint committee will send out joint survey teams composed of an equal number of persons from each side to conduct survey on the spot, determine the boundary line and erect boundary markers in these sections in accordane with concrete terrain features (watersheds, valleys, passes, etc.) and the actual jurisdiction by each side.

3. Sections where the delineation of the boundary line between the two countries on the maps of the two sides is not identical and the two sides differ in their understanding of the state of actual jurisdiction.

The joint committee will send out joint teams composed of an equal number of persons from each side to ascertain on the spot the state of actual jurisdiction in these sections, make adjustments in accordance with the principles of equality, mutual benefit, friendship and mutual accommodation, determine the boundary line and erect boundary markers in these sections.

*Article IV*

The Contracting Parties have decided that, in order to ensure tranquillity and friendliness on the border, each side will no longer dispatch armed personnel to patrol the area on its side within twenty kilometres of the border, but only maintain its administrative personnel and civil police there.

*Article V*

The present Agreement is subject to ratification and the instruments of ratification shall be exchanged in Kathmandu as soon as possible.

The present Agreement will come into force immediately on the exchange of the instruments of ratification and will automatically cease to be in force when the Sino-Nepalese boundary treaty to be signed by the two Governments comes into force.

Done in duplicate in Peking on the twenty-first day of March, 1960, in the Chinese, Nepalese and English languages, all texts being equally authentic.

| Signed | Signed |
|---|---|
| CHOU EN-LAI | B. P. KOIRALA |

**REFERENCES**

1. *Ibid.*, R. K. Jain.
2. The maps are not included in this book.

# CHINA-NEPAL TREATY OF PEACE AND FRIENDSHIP, 28 April 1960[1]

The Chairman of the People's Republic of China and His Majesty the King of Nepal, desiring to maintain and further develop peace and friendship between the People's Republic of China and the Kingdom of Nepal,

Convinced that the strengthening of good-neighbourly relations and friendly cooperation between the People's Republic of China and the Kingdom of Nepal is in accordance with the fundamental interests of the peoples of the two countries and conducive to the consolidation of peace in Asia and the world,

Have decided for this purpose to conclude the present Treaty in accordance with the Five Principles of peaceful co-existence jointly affirmed by the two countries, and have appointed as their respective Plenipotentiaries:

The Chairman of the People's Republic of China: Premier Chou En-lai of the State Council,

His Majesty the King of Nepal: Prime Minister Bishweshwar Prasad Koirala.

The above-mentioned Plenipotentiaries, having examined each other's credentials and found them in good and due form, have agreed upon the following:

*Article I*

The Contracting Parties recognize and respect the independence, sovereignty and territorial integrity of each other.

*Article II*

The Contracting Parties will maintain and develop peaceful and friendly relations between the People's Republic of China and the

Kingdom of Nepal. They undertake to settle all disputes between them by means of peaceful negotiation.

*Article III*

The Contracting Parties agree to develop and further strengthen the economic and cultural ties between the two Countries in a spirit of friendship and cooperation, in accordance with the principles of equality and mutual benefit and of non-interference in each other's internal affairs.

*Article IV*

Any difference or dispute arising out of the interpretation or application of the present Treaty shall be settled by negotiation through normal diplomatic channels.

*Article V*

This present Treaty is subject to ratification and the instruments of ratification will be exchanged in Peking as soon as possible.

The present Treaty will come into force immediately on the exchange of the instruments of ratification and will remain in force for a period of ten years.

Unless either of the Contracting Parties gives to the other notice in writing to terminate the Treaty at least one year before the expiration of this period, it will remain in force without any specified time limit, subject to the right of either of the Contracting Parties to terminate it by giving to the other in writing a year's notice of its intention to do so.

Done in duplicate in Kathmandu on the twenty-eighth day of April 1960, in the Chinese, Nepali and English languages, all texts being equally authentic.

## REFERENCE

1. *Ibid.*, R. K. Jain.

# CHINA-NEPAL BOUNDARY TREATY, 5 October 1961[1]

The Chairman of the People's Republic of China and His Majesty the King of Nepal,

Being of the agreed opinion that a formal settlement of the question of the boundary between China and Nepal is of fundamental interest to the peoples of the two countries;

Noting with satisfaction that the friendly relations of long standing between the two countries have undergone further development since the establishment of diplomatic relations between the two countries and that the two parties have, in accordance with the Five Principles of Peaceful Co-existence and in a spirit of fairness, reasonableness, mutual understanding and mutual accommodation, smoothly achieved an overall settlement of the boundary question between the two countries through friendly consultations;

Firmly believing that the formal delimitation of the entire boundary between the two countries and its consolidation as a boundary of peace and friendship not only constitute a milestone in the further development of the friendly relations between China and Nepal, but also are a contribution towards strengthening peace in Asia and the world;

Have resolved for this purpose to conclude the present treaty on the basis of the Agreement between the Government of the People's Republic of China and His Majesty's Government of Nepal on the Question of the Boundary between the two countries of March 21, 1960 and have agreed upon the following:

*Article I*

The Contracting Parties, basing themselves on the traditional customary boundary line and having jointly conducted necessary on the spot investigations and surveys and made certain adjustments in accordance with the principles of equality, mutual benefit, friendship and mutual accommodation, hereby agree on the following alignment of the entire boundary line from west to east, Chinese territory being north of the line and Nepalese territory south thereof:

(1) The Chinese-Nepalese boundary line starts from the point where the watershed between the Kali River and the Tinkar River meets the watershed between the tributaries of the Mapchu (Karnali) River on the one hand and the Tinkar River on the other hand, thence it runs southeastwards along the watershed between the tributaries of the Mapchu (Karnali) River on the one hand and the Tinkar River and the Seti River on the other hand, passing through Niumachisa (Lipudhura) snowy mountain ridge and Tinkarlipu (Lipudhura) pass to Pehlin (Urai) pass.

(2) From Pehlin (Urai) pass, the boundary line runs along the mountain ridge southeastwards for about 500 metres, then northeastwards to height 5655 metres, thence continues to run along the mountain ridge northwestwards to Tojang (Tharodhunga Tuppa), then northeastwards passing through height 5580.6 metres to Chimala pass, thence it runs generally northwestwards, passing through Chimala to Lungmochiehkuo (Numoche Tuppa); thence the boundary line runs generally eastwards, passing through Paimowotunkuo (Kitko Tuppa) and then runs along Chokartung (Kitko) mountain spur down to the Chilungpa (Yadangre) stream, then it follows the Chilungpa (Yadangre) stream northwards to its junction with the Mapchu (Karnali) River, then it follows the Mapchu (Karnali) River generally eastwards to Yusa (Hilsa). At Yusa (Hilsa), the boundary line departs from the Mapchu (Karnali) River and runs northeastwards along the mountain spur up to Chialosa (Takule), then along the mountain ridge, passing through Kumalatse (Kumalapche), Kangpaochekuo (Ghanbochheko) and Mainipaimikuo (Manepamango) to Kangkuona (Kangarje), then northwards passing through Kangchupeng (Kandumbu) and height 6550 metres to Nalakankar.

(3) From Nalakankar, the boundary line runs generally northeastwards along the watershed between the tributaries flowing into the Manasarowar Lake and the tributaries of the Humla Karnali River passing through Nalakankar pass to Latsela (Lapche) pass; thence it runs generally southeastwards along the watershed between the tributaries flowing into the Manasarowar Lake and the tributaries of the Machuan River on the one hand and the tributaries of the Humla Karnali River, the Mugu Karnali River and the Panjang Khola on the other hand, passing through Changla Mountain, Namja Pass, Khung (Thau) Pass and Marem

Pass to Pindu Pass, then it continues to run southeastwards along the watershed between the tributaries of the Machuan River on the one hand and the tributaries of the Barbung River and the Kali Gandaki River on the other hand gradually turning northeastwards to height 6214.1 metres.

(4) From height 6214.1 metres, the boundary line runs northeastwards along the mountain spur, passing through height 5025 metres and crossing the Angarchubo (Angarchhu) stream to height 5029 metres; thence it runs generally eastwards along Tuchu (Thukchu) mountain spur, passing through height 4730 metres and Bungla (Panglham) to the foot of Tingli Bhodho spur at its northwestern end, then turns northeastwards and runs along the southern bank of the Roumachushui (Rhamarchhushu) seasonal stream to the foot of Tingli Bhodho spur at its northeastern end; thence turns southeastwards, crosses the junction of two seasonal streams flowing northwards, and runs to the junction of three seasonal streams flowing northwards, and then up the eastern stream of the above three seasonal streams to height 4697.9 metres, then turns southwestwards crossing a seasonal stream to height 4605.8 metres; thence it runs generally southeastwards passing through Pengpengla (Phumphula) and then along Chukomaburi (Chhukomapoj) mountain ridge, passing through height 4676.6 metres and height 4754.9 metres to height 4798.6 metres, thence along the mountain ridge northeastwards passing through Hsiabala, then generally eastwards passing through height 5044.1 metres to Chaulo.

(5) From Chaklo, the boundary line runs generally southwards along the watershed between the tributaries of the Yalu Tsangpo River and the tributaries of the Kali Gandaki River, passing through height 6724 metres to Lugula Pass, thence it runs generally eastwards along Lugula snowy mountain and the watershed between the tributaries of the Yalu Tsangpo River and the tributaries of the Marshiyangdi River to Gya (Gyala) Pass.

(6) From Gya (Gyala) Pass, the boundary line runs along the mountain ridge eastwards to height 5782 metres, then southeastwards to Lajing Pass, then it runs along Lajing mountain ridge, passing through height 5442 metres and Lachong (Lajung) Pass to height 5236 metres, then turns southwestwards to Sangmudo snowy mountain; thence generally southeastwards and continues to run along Lajing mountain ridge, passing through height 6139 metres to height 5494 metres, and then in a straight line crosses the Dougar (Tom) River to height 5724 metres; thence the boundary line runs

generally northeastwards along the snowy mountain ridge, passing through height 6010 metres, height 5360 metres and height 5672 metres to Thaple Pass.

(7) From Thaple Pass, the boundary line runs generally northeastwards along the snowy mountain ridge, passing through Tsariyangkang snowy mountain to Khojan; thence it continues to run generally southwards along the snowy mountain ridge, passing through Mailatsaching Pass, Pashuo snowy mountain and Langpo snowy mountain to Yangrenkangri (Yangra) snowy mountain.

(8) From Yangrenkangri (Yangra) snowy mountain, the boundary line runs along the mountain ridge southwards to Tsalasungkuo and then generally eastwards and then northeastwards along a day stream bed and passes through Jirapo (Kerabas) to reach the Sangching (Sanjen) River, then follows that river southeastwards, passes through its junction with the Changchieh (Bhryange) River and continues to follow the Sangching (Sanjen) River to a point where a small mountain spur south of Genjungma (Pangshung) pasture ground and north of Chhaharey pasture ground meets with the Sangching (Sanjen) River; then it runs along the above small mountain spur eastwards and then southeastwards to height 4656.4 metres, then runs eastwards to the black top; thence it runs along a mountain spur to the junction of the Bhurlung River and the Tanghsiaka (Khesadhang) Stream, then runs eastwards along the Bhurlung River to its junction with the Kyerong River; thence follows the Kyerong River southwards and then eastwards to its junction with the Tungling Tsangpo (Lende) River; then runs northeastwards up the Tungling Tsangpo (Lende) River, passing through Rasua Bridge to the junction of the Tungling Tsangpo (Lende) River and the Guobashiachu (Jambu) Stream; thence turns eastwards up the Guobashiachu (Jambu) Stream, passing through the junction of the Chusumdo Tsangpo River and the Phuriphu Tsangpo River, both the tributaries of the upper Guobashiachu (Jambu) Stream, to reach the boundary marker point at Chusumdo.

(9) From the boundary marker point at Chusumdo, the boundary line runs generally southeastwards along the ridge of Tsogakangri (Seto Pokhari) snowy mountain, Langtang snowy mountain, Dorley mountain and Gulinchin (Phurbo Chyachu) Mountain to Chakesumu (Kharaney) Mountain; thence runs down to reach the Changnibachu (Kharaney) River and then follows that river southwards to its junction with the Bhochu (Bhote Kosi) River; then follows the Bhochu (Bhote Kosi) River southwards, passing

through Dalaima (Bhaise) Bridge to the junction of the Bhochu (Bhote Kosi) River and the Junchu (Jum) River; thence eastwards up the Junchu (Jum) River to its source at Tsaje Mountain (Jum Khola Ko Sir Ko Tuppa); thence the boundary line runs generally northwards along the mountain ridge to Chomo Pamari (height 6208.8 metres).

(10) From Chomo Pamari (height 6208.8 metres), the boundary line runs generally northwards along the mountain ridge to height 5914.8 metres, then generally northeastwards along Shondemo Kangri (Sudemo) snowy mountain passing through height 5148 metres, and then crosses two tributaries of the Shondemo Chu (Shongdemo) Stream, passing through Shondemo (Sudemo) which lies between the above two tributaries to Gyanbayan, then in runs along Gyanbayan mountain spur downwards, crosses the Pinbhu Tsangpo River (the western tributary of the Lapche River), and then along the mountain spur up to height 5370.5 metres at Sebobori (Korlang Pari Ko Tippa); thence the boundary line turns southeastwards along the mountain spur downwards, crosses the Lapche Khung Tsangpo River (the eastern tributary of the Lapche River), then it runs along Bidin Kangri (Piding) snowy mountain to height 5397.2 metres; thence the boundary line turns westwards along the mountain ridge to height 5444.2 metres at Kabobori (Raling), then generally southwards along Rasumkungpo (Rishinggumbo) mountain ridge to Niehlu (Niule) Bridge.

(11) From Niehlu (Niule) Bridge, the boundary line runs generally eastwards to Chejenma (Gauri Shankar), and then eastwards along the mountain ridge and then northwards along the watershed between the Rongshar River and the Rongbuk River on the one hand and the tributaries of the Dudhkosi River on the other hand to Nangpa Pass, and then runs generally southeastwards along the mountain ridge, passing through Cho Oyu Mountain, Pumoli Mountain (Gnire Langur), Mount Jolmo Lungma (Sagar Matha) and Lhotse, to Makalu Mountain runs southeastwards and then eastwards along the mountain ridge to Popti Pass.

(12) From Popti Pass, the boundary line runs along the mountain ridge eastwards passing through Tsagala (Kepu Dada) to Kharala (Khade Dada), and then generally northeastwards passing through Lanapo (Lhanakpu) and Chebum (Chhipung) to the source of the Sunchunchu (Shumjung) River; then it follows the Sunchunchu (Shumjung) River to its junction with the track leading from Kimathangka to Chentang, then it runs along the track to the bridge on the Karma Tsangpo (Kama) River; thence it runs

generally southeastwards along the Karma Tsangpo (Kama) River passing through its junction with the Pengchu (Arun) River, and then along the Pengchu (Arun) River to its junction with the Nadang River, then continues to follow the Pengchu (Arun) River westwards to its junction with the Tsokangchingpo (Chhokang) River; thence the boundary line departs from the Pengchu (Arun) River and runs generally eastwards along a mountain spur passing through Angde and Dalai (Tale) Pass to Dalaila (Tale), and then runs along the mountain ridge passing through Jungkan (Dukan), Kaijungkan (Khachunkha), Renlangbu (Relinbu) and Sulula to reach Ragla (Rakha) Pass.

(13) From Ragla (Rakha) Pass, the boundary line runs generally eastwards along the watershed between the tributaries of the Nadang River and the tributaries of the Yaru River on the one hand and the tributaries of the Tamur River on the other hand, passing through Ombola (Ombak) Pass, Theputala (Tiptala) Pass, Yangmakhangla (Kangla) Pass and Chabukla to the terminal point where the watershed between the Khar River and the Chabuk River meets the watershed between the Khar River and the Lhonak River.

The entire boundary line between the two countries as described in the present article is shown on the 1:500,000 maps of the entire boundary attached to the present treaty; the location of the temporary boundary markers erected by both sides and the detailed alignment of certain sections of the boundary are shown on the 1:50,000 maps of those sections attached to the present treaty.

*Article II*

The Contracting Parties have agreed that wherever the boundary follows a river, the midstream line shall be the boundary. In case a boundary river changes its course, the original line of the boundary shall remain unchanged in the absence of other agreements between the two parties.

*Article III*

After the signing of the present treaty, the Chinese-Nepalese Joint Boundary Committee constituted in pursuance of the agreement of March 21, 1960 between the two parties on the question of the boundary between the two countries shall set up permanent boundary markers as necessary on the boundary line between the two countries, and then draft a protocol setting forth in detail the alignment of the entire boundary line and the location of the permanent boundary markers, with detailed maps attached thereto showing the boundary line and the location of the permanent boundary markers. The above-mentioned protocol, upon being signed by the governments of the two countries, shall become an annex to the present treaty and the detailed maps shall replace the maps now attached to the present treaty.

Upon the signing of the above-mentioned protocol, the tasks of the Chinese-Nepalese Joint Boundary Committee shall be terminated, and the agreement of March 21, 1960 between the two parties on the question of the boundary between the two countries shall cease to be in force.

*Article IV*

The Contracting Parties have agreed that any dispute concerning the boundary which may arise after the formal delimitation of the boundary between the two countries shall be settled by the two parties through friendly consultations.

*Article V*

The present treaty shall come into force on the day of the signing of the treaty.

Done in duplicate in Peking on October 5, 1961, in the Chinese, Nepalese and English languages, all three texts being equally authentic.

| | |
|---|---|
| (Signed)<br>Liu Shao-Chi<br>Chairman of the<br>People's Republic<br>of China | (Signed)<br>Mahendra Bir Bikram<br>Shah Deva<br>His Majesty the<br>King of Nepal |

## REFERENCE

1. *Ibid.*, R. K. Jain.

# AGREEMENT ON TRADE, INTERCOURSE AND RELATED QUESTIONS BETWEEN TIBET AUTONOMOUS REGION OF CHINA AND NEPAL, PEKING, 2 May 1966[1]

The Government of the People's Republic of China and His Majesty's Government of Nepal,

Being desirous of further developing the friendly and good-neighbourly relations between the two countries, reaffirming the five principles, i.e.

1. Mutual respect for each other's territorial integrity and sovereignty,
2. Mutual non-aggression,
3. Non-interference in each other's internal affairs for any reasons of an economic, political or ideological character,
4. Equality and mutual benefit, and
5. Peaceful co-existence

as the fundamental principles guiding the relations between the two countries,

Desiring to develop on the basis of these principles the traditional friendly relations between the peoples of the two countries and particularly between the inhabitants of the Tibet Autonomous Region of China and the people of Nepal.

Have agreed to conclude the present Agreement on the basis of the "Agreement to Maintain the Friendly Relations between the People's Republic of China and the Kingdom of Nepal and on Trade and Intercourse between the Tibet Region of China and Nepal" signed by the two Governments on September 20, 1956.

After friendly consultations, the two Governments have agreed upon the following:

*Article 1*

The two Governments agree that the movement of persons between the Tibet Autonomous Region of China and Nepal shall be governed by the following provisions:

1. Diplomatic personnel, civil servants and other nationals (except those covered by paragraphs 2, 3, 4, and 5 of this Article) of either country shall hold passports issued by their own country and visaed by the other country. Nationals of either country entering the Tibet Autonomous Region of China or Nepal via a third country shall also hold passports issued by their own country and visaed by the other country.
2. Traders of either country known to be customarily and specially engaged in trade between the Tibet Autonomous Region of China and Nepal (not being those persons covered by paragraph 3 of this Article), their wives and children dependent upon them for livelihood and their attendants shall hold passports issued by their own country and visaed by the other country or other certificates issued by their own Government or its duly authorised agency.
3. Inhabitants of the border districts of either country who proceed to the border districts of the other country to carry on petty trade, to visit friends or relatives, or for seasonal change of residence, need not have passports, visas or other certificates, but shall register at the border checkpost or the first encountered duly authorised government agency of the other country.
4. Religious believers of either country who travel for the purpose of pilgrimage need not have passports, visas or other certificates, but shall register at the border checkpost or the first encountered duly authorised government agency of the other country and obtain permits for pilgrimage.
5. Porters and muleteers of either country shall only hold certificates valid for a period of not more than one year issued by the local government of their own country or by its duly authorized agency and register at the border checkpost of the other country and need not have passports or visas.
6. Border inhabitants of both countries while travelling across the border shall use the customary routes.
7. Government officials, pilgrims and traders of both countries shall have the facility of engaging the means of transport at normal

and reasonable rates.

8. Notwithstanding the provisions of the foregoing paragraphs of this Article, either Government may refuse entry in its territory to any particular person, should it deem this necessary.
9. Nationals of either country who enter the territory of the other country in accordance with the foregoing paragraphs of this Article may stay within the territory of the other country only after complying with the procedures specified by the other country.

*Article II*

The two Governments agree that pilgrimage between the Tibet Autonomous Region of China and Nepal shall be maintained, and for this purpose have agreed on the following provisions:

1. The local authorities concerned of either country shall suitably facilitate the entry into or departure from its territory of pilgrims from the other country.
2. Pilgrims of either country entering or leaving the territory of the other country shall comply with procedures specified in Article 1 paragraph 4 of the present Agreement.
3. The personal luggage and articles used for pilgrimage carried by pilgrims shall be exempted from duties by both Governments.

*Article III*

Subject to the procedures to be mutually agreed upon, the two Governments agree to make full use on a reciprocal basis of the Lhasa-Kodari and Kathmandu-Kodari Highways to develop friendly intercourse between the two countries in respect of official and trade purposes.

*Article IV*

In order to ensure the peaceful living and normal pursuits of either country's nationals in the territory of the other and promote the development of friendship between the two countries, the two Governments have agreed on the following:

1. The respective Governments shall protect the life, property and legitimate interests of the nationals of the other country in its territory.
2. Nationals of one country in the territory of the other shall be subject to the jurisdiction of the Government of the host country and abide by its laws and regulations, pay taxes and respect the local customs.
3. All civil and criminal cases or disputes in the territory of either country involving nationals of the other country shall be handled by the Government of the host country.

*Article V*

The two Governments shall encourage and support the development of trade relations between the Tibet Autonomous Region of China and Nepal. The authorities concerned of either country shall protect the legitimate interests of the traders of the other country in its territory and facilitate their business activities. The traders of either country in the territory of the other must abide by the relevant laws and regulations and shall be subject to the jurisdiction of the host country.

The two Governments should promote traditional petty trade across the border between the Tibet Autonomous Region of China and Nepal. The local authorities concerned should give facility and protection to the border inhabitants of the other country engaged in such normal petty trade based on barter.

*Article VI*

The Government of the People's Republic of China agrees to the establishment of a consulate-general in Lhasa by His Majesty's Government of Nepal.

His Majesty's Government of Nepal agrees to the establishment of a consulate-general in Kathmandu by the Government of the People's Republic of China.

*Article VII*

In order to strengthen the friendship between the local officials of the two Governments and settle in time problems arising in the intercourse between the border inhabitants of the two countries, the local officials of the border districts of the two Governments may hold meetings as and when necessary.

The rank, time, place and other matters concerning each meeting shall be decided through consultation between the local officials concerned of the two Governments themselves.

*Article VIII*

The present Agreement abrogates the "Agreement to Maintain the Friendly Relations between the People's Republic of China and the Kingdom of Nepal and on Trade and Intercourse between the Tibet Region of China and Nepal" of September 20, 1956 and also the letters exchanged on the same date in relation to the same Agreement.

The present Agreement shall come into force on the date of its signing and shall remain in force for a period of ten years. Amendment or extension of the present agreement may be negotiated by the two Governments six months before its expiration, if either Government proposes to amend or extend the present Agreement and obtains the consent of the other Government.

Done in duplicate in Peking on the 2nd day of May, 1966, in the Chinese, Nepali and English languages, all texts being equally authentic.

## REFERENCE

1. *Ibid.*, R. K. Jain.

# CONVENTION AMONG GREAT BRITAIN, CHINA AND TIBET (1914)[1]

His Majesty the King of the United Kingdom of Great Britain and Ireland and of the British Dominions beyond the Seas, Emperor of India, His Excellency the President of the Republic of China, and His Holiness the Dalai Lama of Tibet, being sincerely desirous to settle by mutual agreement various questions concerning the interests of their several states on the Continent of Asia, and further to regulate the relations of their several Governments, have resolved to conclude a Convention on this subject and have nominated for this purpose their respective Plenipotentiaries, that is to say:

His Majesty the King of the United Kingdom of Great Britain and Ireland and of the British Dominions beyond the Seas, Emperor of India, Sir Arthur Henry McMahon, Knight Grand Cross of the Royal Victorian Order, Knight Commander of the Most Eminent Order of the Indian Empire, Companion of the Most Exalted Order of the Star of India, Secretary to the Government of India, Foreign and Political Department;

His Excellency the President of the Republic of China, Monsieur Ivan Chen, Officer of the Order of the Chia Ho;

His Holiness the Dalai Lama of Tibet, Lonchen Ga-den Shatra Paljor Dorje; who having communicated to each other their respective full powers and finding them to be in good and due form have agreed upon and concluded the following Convention in eleven Articles:

*Article I*

The Conventions specified in the Schedule to the Present

Convention shall, except in so far as they may have been modified by, or may be inconsistent with or repugnant to, any of the provisions of the present Convention, continue to be binding upon the High Contracting Parties.

*Article II*

The Governments of Great Britain and China recognizing that Tibet is under the suzerainty of China, and recognizing also the autonomy of Outer Tibet, engage to respect the territorial integrity of the country, and to abstain from interference in the administration of Outer Tibet (including the selection and installation of the Dalai Lama), which shall remain in the hands of the Tibetan Government at Lhasa.

The Government of China engages not to convert Tibet into a Chinese province. The Government of Great Britain engages not to annex Tibet or any portion of it.

*Article III*

Recognizing the special interest of Great Britain, in virtue of the geographical position of Tibet, in the existence of an effective Tibetan Government, and in the maintenance of peace and order in the neighbourhood of the frontiers of India and adjoining States, the Government of China engages, except as provided in Article 4 of this Convention, not to send troops into Outer Tibet, nor to station civil or military officers, nor to establish Chinese colonies in the country. Should any such troops or officials remain in Outer Tibet at the date of the signature of this Convention, they shall be withdrawn within a period not exceeding three months.

The Government of Great Britain engages not to station military or civil officers in Tibet (except as provided in the Convention of September 7, 1904, between Great Britain and Tibet) nor troops (except the Agents' escorts), nor to establish colonies in that country.

*Article IV*

The foregoing Article shall not be held to preclude the continuance of the arrangement by which, in the past, a Chinese high official with suitable escort has been maintained at Lhasa, but it is hereby provided that the said escort shall in no circumstances exceed 300 men.

*Article V*

The Governments of China and Tibet engage that they will not enter into any negotiations or agreements regarding Tibet with one another, or with any other Power, excepting such negotiations and agreements between Great Britain and Tibet as are provided for by the Convention of September 7, 1904, between Great Britain and Tibet and the Convention of April 27, 1906, between Great Britain and China.

*Article VI*

Article 3 of the Convention of April 27, 1906, between Great Britain and China is hereby cancelled, and it is understood that in Article 9 (d) of the Convention of September 7, 1904, between Great Britain and Tibet the term 'Foreign Power' does not include China. Not less favourable treatment shall be accorded to British commerce than to the commerce of China or of the most favoured nation.

*Article VII*

The Tibet Trade Regulations of 1893 are hereby cancelled. (b) The Tibetan Government engages to negotiate with the British Government new Trade Regulations for Outer Tibet to give effect to Articles 2, 4 and 5 of the Convention of September 7, 1904, between Great Britain and Tibet without delay; provided always that such Regulations shall in no way modify the present Convention except with the consent of the Chinese Government.[2]

*Article VIII*

The British Agent who resides at Gyantse may visit Lhasa with his escort whenever it is necessary to consult with the Tibetan Government regarding matters arising out of the Convention of September 7, 1904, between Great Britain and Tibet, which it has been found impossible to settle at Gyantse by correspondence or otherwise.

*Article IX*

For the purpose of the present Convention the borders of Tibet, and the boundary between Outer and Inner Tibet, shall be shown as in red and blue respectively on the map attached hereto.[3]

Nothing in the present Convention shall be held to prejudice the existing rights of the Tibetan Government in Inner Tibet, which include the power to select and appoint the high priests of monasteries and to retain full control in all matters affecting religious institutions.[4]

*Article X*

The English, Chinese and Tibetan texts of the present Convention have been carefully examined and found to correspond, but in the event of there being any difference of meaning between them the English text shall be authoritative. [5]

*Article XI*

The present Convention will take effect from the date of signature. In token whereof the respective Plenipotentiaries have signed and sealed this Convention, three copies in English, three in Chinese and three in Tibetan.

Done at Simla this third day of July, A.D., one thousand nine hundred and fourteen, corresponding with the Chinese date, the third day of the seventh month of the third year of the Republic, and the Tibetan date, the tenth day of the fifth month of the Wood-Tiger year.

| | |
|---|---|
| Initial* of the Lonchen Shatra. | (Initialled) A. H. M. |
| Seal of the | Seal of the |
| Lonchen Shatra | British Plenipotentiary |

*Schedule*

(1) Convention between Great Britain and China relating to Sikkim and Tibet, signed at Calcutta the 17th March, 1890.

(2) Convention between Great Britain and Tibet, signed at Lhasa the 7the September 1904.

(3) Convention between Great Britain and China respecting Tibet, signed at Peking the 27th April 190[illegible].

The notes exchanged are to the following effect:

(1) It is understood by the High Contracting Parties that Tibet forms part of Chinese territory.

(2) After the selection and installation of the Dalai Lama by the Tibetan Government, the latter will notify installation to the Chinese Government, whose representative at Lhasa will then formally communicate to His Holiness the titles consistent with his dignity, which have been conferred by the Chinese Government.

(3) It is also understood that the selection and appointment of all officers in Outer Tibet will rest with the Tibetan Government.

(4) Outer Tibet shall not be represented in the Chinese Parliament or in any other similar body.

It is understood that the escorts attached to the British Trade Agencies in Tibet shall not exceed seventy-five per centum of the escort of the Chinese Representative at Lhasa.

Owing to it not being possible to write initials in Tibetan the mark of the Lonchen at this place is his signature.

(5) The Government of China is hereby released from its engagements under Article 3 of the Convention of March 17, 1890, between Great Britain and China to prevent acts of aggression from the Tibetan side of the Tibet-Sikkim frontier.

* Owing to it not being possible to write initials in Tibetan the mark of the Lonchen at this place is his signature.

(6) The Chinese high official referred to in Article 4 will be free to enter Tibet as soon as the terms of Article 3 have been fulfilled to the satisfaction of representatives of the three signatories to this Convention, who will investigate and report without delay.

Initial of the Lonchen Shatra.
Seal of the
Lonchen Sharat

(Initialled) A. H. M.
Seal of the
British Plenipotentiary

## REFERENCES

1. *The North-Eastern Frontier*, Vol. I, Parshotam Mehra, Oxford University Press.
2. The earlier, February 17, 1914 draft of the Convention had this additional clause :
   The Government of China is hereby released from its engagements under Article III of the Convention of 1890 between Great Britain and China to prevent acts of aggression from the Tibetan side of the Tibet-Sikkim frontier.
3. For the map see *An Atlas of the Northern Frontier of India* (New Delhi, 1960), Map 24.
   For the map referred to in Article 9 of the Convention initialled by the Chinese delegate (in addition to the British and the Tibetan) on April 27, see Map 23 in *Ibid*. The map was signed, *not* initialled, by Ivan Chen.
4. In the February 17 draft of the Convention, Article 9 concluded as follows: religious institutions, *to issue appointment orders to chiefs and local officers, and to collect all customary rents and taxes.*
5. In the February 17 draft of the Convention, this article read as follows : The Government of China hereby agrees to pay compensation amounting to Rs. 4,28,840 due for losses incurred by Nepalese and Ladakhis in Tibet in consequence of acts done by Chinese soldiers and officials in that country.
   In the April 27 draft, it read :
   In case of differences between the Governments of China and Tibet in regard to questions arising out of this Convention the aforesaid Governments engage to refer them to the British Government for equitable adjustment.

# DECLARATION APPENDED TO THE SIMLA CONVENTION, 3 July, 1914[1]

We, the Plenipotentiaries of Great Britain and Tibet, hereby record the following declaration to the effect that we acknowledge the annexed Convention as initialled to be binding on the Governments of Great Britain and Tibet, and we agree that so long as the Government of China withholds signature to the aforesaid Convention, she will be debarred from the enjoyment of all privileges accruing therefrom.

In token whereof we have signed and sealed this declaration, two copies in English and two in Tibetan.

Done at Simla this third day of July, A.D. one thousand nine hundred and fourteen, corresponding with the Tibetan date, the tenth day of the fifth month of the Wood-Tiger year.

Seal of the
Dalai Lama

(Signed) A. Henry McMahon
British Plenipotentiary

Signature and seal
of the Lonchen Shatra

Seal of the British
Plenipotentiary

| Seal of the Drepung Monastery | Seal of the Sera Monastery | Seal of the Gaden Monastery | Seal of the National Assembly |
|---|---|---|---|

## REFERENCE

1. P. Mehra, *ibid*.

# SAARC CHARTER[1]

"We, the Heads of State or Government of Bangladesh, Bhutan, India, Maldives, Nepal, Pakistan and Sri Lanka:

"Desirous of promoting peace, stability, amity and progress in the region through strict adherence to the principles of the United Nations Charter and Non-alignment, particularly respect for the principles of sovereign equality, territorial integrity, national independence, non-use of force and non-interference in the internal affairs of other States and peaceful settlement of all disputes;

"Conscious that in an interdependent world, the objectives of peace, freedom, social justice and economic prosperity are best achieved in the South Asian region by fostering mutual understanding, good neighbourly relations and meaningful co-operation among the member States which are bound by ties of history and culture;

"Aware of the common problems, interests and aspirations of the people of South Asia and the need for joint action and enhanced co-operation within their respective political and economic systems and cultural traditions;

"Convinced that regional co-operation among the countries of South Asia is mutually beneficial, desirable and necessary for promoting the welfare and improving the quality of life of the peoples of the region;

"Convinced further that economic, social and technical co-operation among the countries of South Asia would contribute significantly to national and collective self-reliance;

"Recognizing that increased co-operation, contacts and exchanges among the countries of the region will contribute to the promotion of friendship and understanding among their peoples;

"Recalling the Declaration signed by their Foreign Ministers in New Delhi on August 2, 1983 and noting the progress achieved in regional co-operation;

"Re-affirming their determination to promote such co-operation within an institutional framework;

"Do hereby agree to establish an organization to be known as the South Asian Association for Regional Co-operation, hereinafter referred to as the Association, with the following objectives, principles, institutional and financial arrangement;

*Article I*

"**Objective**: The objectives of the Association shall be:

"(a) To promote the welfare of the peoples of South Asia and to improve their quality of life;

"(b) To accelerate economic growth, social progress and cultural development in the region and to provide all individuals the opportunity to live in dignity and to realise their potentials ;

"(c) To promote and strengthen collective self-reliance among the countries of South Asia;

"(d) To contribute to mutual trust, understanding and appreciation of one another's problems;

"(e) To promote active collaboration and mutual assistance in the economic, social, cultural, technical and scientific fields;

"(f) To strengthen co-operation with other developing countries;

"(g) To strengthen co-operation among themselves in international forums on matters of common interests; and

"(h) To co-operate with international and regional organizations with similar aims and purposes.

*Article II*

**"Principles:**

"(1) Co-operation within the framework of the Association shall be based on respect for the principles of sovereign equality, territorial integrity, political independence, non-interference in the internal affairs of other States and mutual benefit.

"(2) Such co-operation shall not be a substitute for bilateral and multilateral co-operation but shall complement them.

"(3) Such co-operation shall not be inconsistent with bilateral and multilateral obligations.

*Article III*

"Meetings of the Heads of State or Government:

"(1) The Heads of State or Government shall meet once a year or more often as and when considered necessary by the member-States.

*Article IV*

"**Council of Ministers:** A Council of Ministers consisting of the Foreign Ministers of the members-States shall be established with the following functions: formulation of the policies of the Association; review of the progress of co-operation under the Association; decision on new areas of co-operation; establishment of additional mechanism under the Association as deemed necessary; decision on other matters of general interest to the Association.

"The Council of Ministers shall meet twice a year. Extraordinary sessions of the Council may be held by agreement among the member-States.

*Article V*

"**Standing Committee**: The Standing Committee comprising the ForeignSecretaries shall have the following functions; overall monitoring and co-cordination of programme of co-operation; approval of projects and programmes, and the modalities of their financing; determination of inter-sectoral priorities; mobilization of regional and external resources; identification of new areas of co-operation based on appropriate studies;

"The Standing Committee shall meet as offen as deemed necessary;

"The Standing Committee shall submit periodic reports to the Council of Ministers and make reference to it as and when necessary for decisions on policy matters.

*Article VI*

"**Technical Committees**: Technical Committees comprising representatives of member-States shall be responsible for the implementation, coordination and monitoring of the programmes in their respective areas of co-operation.

"They shall have the following terms of reference: determination of the potential and the scope of regional cooperation in agreed areas; formulation of programmes and preparation of projects; determination of financial implications of sectoral programmes; formulation of recommendations regarding apportionment of costs; implementation and co-ordination of sectoral programmes; monitoring of progress in implementation.

"The Technical Committees shall submit periodic reports to the Standing Committee.

"The Chairmanship of the Technical Committees shall normally rotate among member-States in alphabetical order every two years.

The Technical Committees may, *inter-alia*, use the following mechanisms and modalities, if and when considered necessary: meetings of heads of national technical agencies; meetings of experts in specific fields; contact amongst recognized centres of excellence in the region.

*Article VII*

"**Action Committees:** The Standing Committee may set up Action Committees comprising member-States concerned with implementation of projects involving more than two but not all member-States.

*Article VIII*

"**Secretariat:** There shall be a Secretariat of the Association.

*Article IX*

"**Financial Arrangements:**

"The contribution of each member-State towards financing of the activities of the Association shall be voluntary.

"Each Technical Committee shall make recommendations for the apportionment of costs of implementing the programmes proposed by it.

"In case sufficient financial resources cannot be mobilized within the region for funding activities of the Association, external financing from appropriate sources may be mobilized with the approval of or by the Standing Committee.

*Article X*

"**General provisions:**

"Decisions at all levels shall be taken on the basis of unanimity.

"Bilateral and contentious issues shall be excluded from the deliberations.

"In faith whereof we have set our hands and seals hereunto.

"Done in Dhaka, Bangladesh, on this the eighth day of December of the year one thousand nine hundred eighty five.

"Hussain Muhammad Ershad, President of the People's Republic of Bangladesh.

"Jigme Singye Wangchuk, King of Bhutan.

"Rajiv Gandhi, Prime Minister of the Republic of India.

"Maumoon Abdul Gayoom, President of the Republic of Maldives.

"Birendra Bir Bikram Shah Dev, King of Nepal.

"Muhammad Zia-ul Haq, President of the Islamic Republic of Pakistan.

"Junius Richard Jayewardene, President of Democratic Socialist Republic of Sri Lanka. Dhaka, December 8, 1985."

## REFERENCE

1. *Asian Recorder*, 1986.

# INDEX